INSPIRING
ACCOUNTABILITY
IN THE WORKPLACE

Unlocking the

brain's secrets to

employee engagement,

accountability,

and results

ELAINA NOELL

ISBN (print): 978-0-9967766-1-5
ISBN (ebook): 978-0-9967766-4-6

Published by
Elaina Noell
Petaluma, CA
www.inspiringaccountability.com

Cover design by Jesh Art Studio, LaBruzzi Media Craft
Interior design and production by Domini Dragoone
Cover photo © Elaina Noell
Author photo © Jeff Singer

ACKNOWLEDGMENTS

Thank you to the dream team who kept me fueled and inspired to persevere: Tanner, Dawn, Beth, Ken, Rose, Sarita, Tony, Sarah, Nicole, and Tawny.

Thank you to NLP Marin, Carl, Michelle, and Carla, the TA's, and my many cohorts. Our work together empowered me to bring this work into the light. Your support has been, and continues to be, invaluable.

Thank you to my family for helping me become who I am today.

Thank you to my editors at Black Dot Writing–Kate, Justin, and Matt–and my bonus helpers, Anna, Ron, and Jasmine.

Thank you to all the managers I've had before who provided mentorship, development opportunities, and valuable learned lessons.

Thank you to my clients, with whom I continue to grow and expand this content. I celebrate your commitment to your people.

And thank you to *you*, the reader, for reaching for new ways to contribute to making the workplace and world a better place.

CONTENTS

Managers who motivate create moments.
Leaders who inspire create momentum.
—ELAINA NOELL

PART I

INTRODUCING ACCOUNTABILITY

The End of Traditional Accountability

"Toto, I've a feeling we're not in Kansas anymore."

—DOROTHY, *THE WIZARD OF OZ*, 1939

In today's hyper-competitive business environment, the desperate demand for better "results" has pressurized corporate cultures and put leaders in a difficult position. Most leaders want to inspire optimal performance from their teams but lack the time and skills to devote to crafting a new approach while their own deadlines creep, email boxes fill, and corporate boards hold them accountable for profits.

The privilege of having a job used to be enough to instill accountability among employees. But, as Dorothy points out, we are in a new place now. Leaders are no longer able to rely on traditional accountability, the kind inherently built into receiving a paycheck.

As leaders demand more from their employees, employees are now expecting more in return. In a 2017 survey conducted by Hays, a worldwide recruiting firm, almost half (43%) of the 2,000 participants said they are looking for a new job and that "corporate culture was the main reason." Additionally, The Bureau of Labor Statistics has reported that, starting in 2010, the number of employees quitting has increased for nine consecutive years.

Today, most employees just want to be *happier* at work. Employees seek workplaces and leaders that value the human experience, where they can be recognized for their contribution, competence, and importance, and statistics indicate that employees are no longer afraid to leave jobs that aren't delivering.

Let's look quickly at the economics of attrition. According to Payscale's report on *The Cost of Losing Employees*, the Society for Human Resources Management cites the cost of replacing an employee between 90% and 200% of their annual salary. Researchers at Columbia University suggest it's 150%, depending on the position. With that ballooning cost in mind, companies are finally accepting that to get better results from employees and remain competitive in their sector, they must prioritize making the employee experience more enjoyable.

Therefore, companies are scrambling to compete at providing the best employee experience to retain and attract top talent. Leaders at all levels are trying to bridge the demand for results with the demand for work-life balance, requiring a seemingly unmanageable combination of company values, time, and resources.

As employees set aside company loyalty in favor of seeking greater personal happiness and fulfillment, companies equally can't rely on the outdated traditional motivation of employees being grateful for "having a job" to ensure accountability and performance.

We are now in new territory, facing the conflict of three common company quests: increasing employee fulfillment, enhancing employee engagement, and ensuring performance accountability.

Before we get into how best to navigate this new terrain, let's briefly explore what was the wind-of-change that took traditional accountability off the map.

A Quick Historical Overview

During the American Industrial Revolution, new industries created new economic possibilities for American families. Whole towns seemed to develop around a single industry, like Detroit, the Motor

City, or coal mining in Virginia, which offered new jobs promising steady work with a steady paycheck.

This new form of security was in high demand, and even with the growing industries, the job supply was still comparatively low. Jobs were sacred, sought after, and a means for survival. Employees didn't ponder if they were happy, fulfilled, or reaching their true potential in their work — they were grateful to be employed in this burgeoning period of American industry.

From this time grew an institutionalization of employee accountability as a means of ensuring performance. Accountability was derived from the real threat of job loss and the lack of other employment options.

If an employee lost their job at Ford in Michigan, where else would they go? Management knew *accountability was simply built into the fear of being fired*. It was a time when both employers and employees paid little attention to our modern notions of a fulfilling workplace culture or the "employee experience."

Employees were loyal out of necessity, but companies were not always loyal in return. Rick Wartzman explains this concept in his book *The End of Loyalty* (2017). When a depression or recession hit, companies put profits first and swiftly laid off loyal employees. Employees' dreams of stability were often shattered and their families were quickly and negatively impacted. When companies stopped being loyal to their employees, employees followed suit. Employees' children witnessed and learned a powerful loyalty lesson: companies put themselves first, so put yourself first, too.

Logically, we know companies need to look out for their profits, so they can persevere — put your own oxygen mask on first, after all. However, this doesn't change how employees-as-humans also default to **self-protection** when their financial safety or wellbeing is threatened. Morale drops when leadership revolves around threats of firing and, worse, proves itself insufficient for inspiring *real* employee accountability and loyalty.

During and after the Great Recession of 2008, companies downsized again. Employees' fear of survival spiked. This ultimately created "working managers," who had a full-time job plus the responsibility of managing a team. This new role often left leaders overworked and underperforming, with very little capacity for becoming the effective and inspiring leaders most wanted to be. Employees sought structure and guidance from their leaders, but leaders struggled to keep their heads above the flood of increasing demands of their companies, their own leaders, and their employees.

Then came the millennials who unapologetically shifted the focus to the employee experience. They grew up under a social media microscope where they felt connected to others by mutually sharing their feelings moment-by-moment through text and emojis. Younger employees are rumored to be the least loyal because, quite simply, they don't need to be thanks, in part, to technology.

There are so many non-traditional job opportunities today: working in-person, remotely, for others, or for themselves. Their boldness in asking for what they want branded them as an "entitled" generation, a common descriptor cited in *Forbes'* 2015 article, "Is 'Millennial' A Dirty Word?"

While this attention on how one *feels* in the workplace had older generations scoffing, it also simultaneously gave *all* generations permission to care about and advocate for their own workplace experience.

The New Competitive Advantage

It's official. Obligatory loyalty is *out* and feelings are *in*. Employees want their time at work to matter, personally and professionally. With buzzwords like "happiness," "self-care," and "best self" popping up on inspirational mugs, paired with incessant books, vlogs, and podcasts pressuring content consumers to "do work you love," an unsupportive and unhappy workplace is quickly becoming intolerable both personally and socially.

The irony is, in the midst of the pressure this creates for both companies and employees, employees also want a culture of accountability. Cultures with a poor accountability structure create a toxic work environment that under-values star performers, incorrectly rewards poor performers, and leaves leaders feeling confused and overwhelmed. In the end, the best employees leave for a culture with greater accountability so that they are no longer adopting the slack of employees who are not being held sufficiently accountable.

This rise in employee expectations has elevated the quality of the employee experience to become today's competitive advantage in hiring. Companies seek the best employees with the promise to create the best results, but those top-tier employees also seek an exceptional experience at work. Improving both employee experience and results are now irrevocably intertwined.

All this leaves leaders like you stuck — wanting to help but not knowing how.

Overworked and frustrated, leaders are often left with little support themselves. They may end up destructively attempting to *demand* better results from employees because they don't know how to improve engagement, accountability, and results in this new, human-centric environment. They struggle to get employees engaged and accountable, and too often they get pigeonholed into the role of the "bad cop," an outdated idea from the time when accountability meant being the bearer of bad news, pointing out problems, or attempting to motivate change by hanging over an employee's head the implicit (or explicit) threat of firing.

Instead of staying stuck in the outmoded tradition of leading in the workplace, which focuses on what's in the way, let's instead *explore what's possible.*

Improving Results and Employee Experience — What's Possible?

Is it possible to meet demands for results while improving the employee experience?

Yes, it absolutely is.

The answer is not giving employees everything they ask for and crossing your fingers. Optimism is important, but hope is not a strategy. You probably know companies who have tried to take care of their employees' well-being hoping to boost overall efficiency, productivity, and results, but to no avail. So, what's been missing in companies who have unsuccessfully tried to increase results while improving the employee experience?

Companies need a functional culture of accountability. This does not mean hastily demanding accountability or relying on an overflow of perks and parties.

Rather, the key is in *inspiring a clear, consistent, and compelling structure of accountability* that keeps employees *engaged* in their work, *receptive* toward accountability, and *resourceful* toward results.

What if the same human traits that are responsible for the lack of loyalty, engagement, and accountability in some employees are also an asset toward improving those factors to get results? What if the answers are not in fighting the problem but in using these challenges to inform solutions?

As we'll discover in the proceeding chapters of *Inspiring Accountability in the Workplace,* in today's professional climate, having a modernized sense of accountability with an understanding of neuroscience and human dynamics will help you navigate the demand for better results while improving the employee experience along the way.

Do You Need Inspiring Accountability?

If your employees are self-regulating their accountability to your standards, then you don't need to change anything. Fantastic!

But if they're not, it's first and foremost in *your* best interest to change your leadership approach, and Inspiring Accountability as a methodology offers you the strategies and tools to productively do so.

One of the most unrealistic assumptions about employee accountability is that employees should and will be completely accountable on their own because "that's what they are paid to do." While ideal, waiting for that assumption to manifest into new behavior prevents real results from coming to fruition.

Accountability can be your best development tool, making it continuously easier to get better results. If your team is not cultivating development to produce the results you need, you can begin using Inspiring Accountability so you can finally stop guessing what to do and start inspiring your employees to become an efficient, engaged, and productive team.

CHAPTER 1

Inspiring Accountability: Origination and Overview

"If it's worth doing, it's worth getting started. Do
your best, then learn, and do better."
—MELANIE DULBECCO, CEO OF TORANI SYRUPS

An Origin Found in a Chocolate Banana Latte

I stood at the drink counter in the coffee-making station of Torani Syrups' office, excited to be having a latte with Torani's CEO, Melanie Dulbecco.

I was building my employee engagement and leadership development business, so I was delighted Melanie agreed to meet with me. I'd recently seen her speak about the innovative road to growth for this popular flavored syrup company. I was certain I could learn a lot from her. I found myself staring at the rows and rows of the signature red, yellow, and blue labels that offered endless latte possibilities when I asked Melanie for her favorite flavor combinations. It was an easy choice for me — a chocolate banana latte.

She hopped over to the espresso machine, packed the grounds, and started steaming the milk. It was as if she was a covert barista and not the successful CEO of the ubiquitous and creative B-corp flavored syrup and sauce company for the last twenty-seven years.

That was not a typo: that's *twenty-seven years*.

But don't let Melanie's long tenure at the 100-year-old company fool you. She leads Torani with the same energy and enthusiasm as a day-one CEO. She exudes a magnetic vibrancy, the curiosity of an innovator, the patience of someone who is grounded in trust, and an unquestionable love for the people who help make Torani a great place to work.

A few years ago, Melanie and her VP of People and Culture, Catriona Wiley, faced one of the most unsolved company mysteries: performance reviews. They knew the process was disliked and lacked effectiveness. In 2014, they launched "Contribution Management," an approach that changed everything that didn't work about performance reviews into an effective and enjoyable experience that supports development, empowers employees, and drives results.

"It's fairly simple," Melanie explained. "The team member is in the driver's seat. Each individual is accountable for how they contribute to the company's success and their own growth. Of course, this is achieved with the support of their leader."

Melanie is both an optimist and a pragmatist. She's positive and patient. When Torani decided to adapt and implement Contribution Management, Melanie set a three-year goal of experimenting with this concept. "I thought we should give ourselves three years to get good at this. I wanted to see the horizon of where we're heading, and I also wanted some forgiveness if the journey there took some twists and turns. When you trust people, you can figure it out as you go," Melanie expressed.

At the start of Torani's Contribution Season — in January and February — leaders share company goals directly with their teams. "We make sure everyone knows what we're doing for the year." Afterward, each team member reflects on how they contributed to the past year's goals with forms they fill out. Each team member then meets with their leader to discuss their feedback, staying in the driver's seat of their own development.

During meetings, team members present how they see their contribution for the previous year and how they'd like to contribute to the next year. Leaders aren't there to judge — they're there to listen. They acknowledge employee successes and ask questions to guide development. In total, the conversations last about 60-90 minutes with each individual.

"Our team members know the company mindset is to always grow every year," Melanie said. "They know we value, focus on, support, and expect development. Feedback is always through the lens of development and unearthing undiscovered contribution potential. Growing Torani is interwoven with supporting our team members' development for their own personal and professional fulfillment."

In Torani's Contribution Conversations, team members focus on sharing answers to:

- How I developed myself toward continuous improvement
- What I could have approached differently
- What I need to develop
- What I'm planning to contribute
- Other projects that interest me

The leader then becomes a supporter that acknowledges and guides contribution and looks for opportunities to support the employee's development and interests.

Melanie elaborated about the type of relationship managers must have with their employees for these meetings to work. "There has to be trust to have these conversations. Feedback can't be a surprise. As leaders, we are here to support our team members' development and unearth greater contributions they haven't even discovered yet."

Melanie's ability to hold to commitments and drive results is equal to, if not dependent on, her commitment to developing her people with such heart. Her ability to balance caring about people and caring about results opened the door for what I began to see was possible.

Under Melanie's leadership, the company has averaged 20% year-over-year revenue growth in the last two decades and expanded distribution across the U.S. and to over fifty countries, from Korea to Norway.

On her ongoing success, she has this to say: "If it's worth doing, it's worth getting started. Do your best, then learn, and do better."

Being in Melanie's presence left me unquestioningly believing her professed trust in people and her commitment to employee development. She inspired me to realize that the annual performance review, one of the oldest and most dysfunctional tools of traditional accountability, could be reinvented to meet the needs of the modern workforce. Was it possible that performance reviews could actually inspire accountability instead of demand it? How else could this concept be expanded and applied?

My meeting with Melanie about Torani's Contribution Management strategy energized the beginning of *Inspiring Accountability in the Workplace*, which started as a mere mindset pointing toward employee contribution as a means of empowerment, and it soon developed into the accountability models, strategies, and tools in this book. Before I even finished my last sip of latte, I committed to explore how companies and leaders can inspire employee happiness, wellbeing, and results.

Inspiring Accountability in the Workplace substantially expands upon the spark of inspiration from Torani's innovative approach. This book will provide you with a foolproof toolbox of strategies that will give you **actionable clarity**, or knowing exact steps, tools, and strategies to get the results you want from your employees. So, let's get started!

Seeking Accountability Solutions

During my first career as a VP of marketing, I was on all sides of the "results" issue. I've been the manager knowing I could do better by my team but drowning in my own excessive workload and frustrated by the company's poor organizational structure, lack of support, and guidance.

I've also been the employee desperate to have a better experience, hoping an expensive essential oil blend behind my ears and positive quotes on Post-it Notes would help me overcome the wear-and-tear of a company culture that enforced instead of inspired results.

I've both received **triggering** performance reviews and nervously given performance reviews that I hoped kept my employees feeling receptive, resourceful, and engaged instead of anxious, unseen, or unappreciated.

I've seen executives inelegantly demand results in ways that corroded company culture, employee engagement, and accountability.

I've seen countless employees that really care about their work and colleagues leave a company in search of a more fulfilling culture and leadership, and I could see that this failure of retention was completely avoidable.

Mostly, I've seen leaders that want to improve the employee experience with the hope of also improving results, but these leaders lack the time, skills, or support to do so effectively.

These issues led me to investigate the difficult, stubborn questions of accountability: How do we maintain an experience where employees and leaders alike feel rewarded because they are seen as competent, important, and contributing meaningfully? How do we drive results and hold employees accountable without it coming with a discouraging, demanding, and disengaging approach?

Most people want better experiences at work and for their work to be more successful with better results, but old ways of driving results compromise this experience. *What is the solution?*

I started with the human brain, the control center for human behavior. I knew that leaders who understand how to work with the brain and its proclivity to produce stabilizing behavior patterns create more fulfilling workplaces and achieve better results from employees.

So, I set out with one important goal: to create the content, strategies, and tools that now form *Inspiring Accountability in the Workplace*.

Don't get me wrong — it wasn't a simple, quick fix for me. It was quite a journey to get here. Years of therapy, backpacking South America for three months, having a bank account depleted from creating a failed app designed to connect people through shared inspiration, studying inspiration and happiness to write my first book, *Happiness is Overrated — Live the Inspired Life Instead* (2015), and becoming certified to practice Neuro-Linguistic Programming. I needed all of this to finally step out of my **"trigger trenches"** and create, with actionable clarity, tools that give leaders modern strategies to answer: "How do I inspire accountability and get results while keeping my employees inspired, engaged, and fulfilled?"

The answer is the Inspiring Accountability methodology.

The Traditional Approach is Not Working Today

When leaders aren't getting the results they want from their team, they often turn to traditional methods of holding employees accountable. Traditional accountability methods are typically employed after a result is missed, an ask goes neglected, and, most importantly, *after it's too late for the employee to have done better.*

Traditional accountability is activated by a leader's understandable feelings of frustration and exasperation of how to get better results. The easiest response is to express the frustration in hopes that it's "enough" to get through to the employee and necessitate change.

Unfortunately, that traditional approach triggers employees into a defensive, unreceptive, and unresourceful state, leading to resentment and disengagement.

Notably, *this is the opposite of what accountability is supposed to accomplish.*

Much like how traditional performance reviews actually decrease performance, as reported in *Psychology Today*'s 2011 article entitled, "Why CEO's Need to Scrap Employee Reviews," traditional accountability hinders our ability to sustainably get better results and keep employee engagement and satisfaction high.

But enough about what's in the way. Rather, let's explore what's possible.

Outlining Inspiring Accountability

When we say we want employees to be more accountable, what we really want is to have more reliable and successful results. We want employees intrinsically inspired to provide their full effort without leaders having to worry about what's being done, constantly follow-up out of concern, or expend energy pushing or pulling for effort.

When a leader is entrenched in the latter, they usually turn to accountability as the tool to "fix it," but there are two sides to the accountability coin. You can use accountability to address problems, but there is a second option. The goal of accountability is to get better results, and you can also use accountability to *prevent* problems by getting the result you want the first time.

Instead of relying on the "dealing with the problem" side of the coin, Inspiring Accountability methodology approaches accountability from two perspectives: 1. Successful accountability is ensuring the right result the first time, and 2. Being able to productively manage when the result is missed. These two perspectives are referred to in this book as:

> **Proactive accountability:** Ensuring the result is met the first time, preventing a need for responsive accountability.

> **Responsive accountability:** Responding in the most productive way if the result is not met to better achieve the result in the future. The "most productive way" includes maintaining employee engagement, receptiveness, and resourcefulness.

From here, the Inspiring Accountability methodology redefines accountability into clear and actionable objectives to work toward.

When it comes to responsive accountability, leaders have long been searching for a positive way to turn uncomfortable confrontations into conversations that inspire action. **In Part II, The Results Model: The Ultimate Accountability Tool,** the Results Model helps you to take action on the top accountability pain points with ease by:

> ☑ **Setting Clear Expectations:** How efficiently and effectively can an employee focus their effort?

☑ **Clearing the Path to Success:** How clear is the path to getting the result?

☑ **Being Solution-Focused:** How much initiative are employees applying to creating a better future for the company and customers?

☑ **Regular Revisiting:** How often are employees regularly revisiting the impact of their contribution toward a result with you to calibrate, adjust, and continuously improve?

When it comes to proactive accountability, you want to create an essential foundation of employees being engaged, receptive, resourceful, empowered, and rewarded. **In Part III, Proactive Accountability: Inspiring Effort and Engagement,** you'll learn how to effectively contribute to how much an employee is:

☑ **Engaged:** How much are employees feeling seen as competent, important, and contributing meaningfully? And how much effort are they offering?

☑ **Receptive:** How receptive are employees to feedback, improvement, and accountability?

☑ **Resourceful:** How resourceful are employees toward solutions, focusing not only on what's in the way but also what's possible?

☑ **Empowered:** How empowered are employees to contribute toward solutions?

☑ **Rewarded:** How satisfactorily are employees being rewarded and celebrated for their effort and contribution?

These nine themes make up Inspiring Accountability's top leadership contributions that offer you the best chance to achieve optimal performances from your team. In addition to the tools in **Part IV, Inspiring Leadership in Action: Applying Concepts for Better Results,** each of these themes is transformed into tools that allow you to confidently take action to improve results. As you begin putting them into practice, this list will become more and more achievable, eventually saving you crucial time and undue stress once integrated into your leadership approach and team culture.

You will find all these themes seamlessly support and often overlap each other throughout the book with the presented models, tools, and strategies available to you now, culminating into a practical leadership approach that will get you results without having to use outdated, traditional accountability.

One way Inspiring Accountability is easier than other methods is that instead of looking at all the ways employees are different and having to track different personalities and work styles — which absolutely can be beneficial when time allows — we go one level deeper to the basics of what makes us all human and what unites, drives, and rewards us universally: our human brain. Our brain wiring creates our experiences, determines how engaged we are, and triggers us to feel resentful, shut down, and unresourceful.

Neurologically humans are actually quite predictable. Our brains run behavioral and experiential patterns in much the same way a software program runs, designed to automate the connection between a specific input and a predictable response. Our brains establish these patterns, or "loops," to create predictable responses that save precious conscious processing power and also keep the oldest and most reactive part of our brains feeling "safe."

Feeling safe thousands of years ago looked more like running from woolly mammoths. Today, in the workplace, we are protecting our fundamental human needs to be seen as contributing, competent, and important. When these needs are generally fulfilled, we are engaged and inspired to go above and beyond. When these needs are threatened or neglected, we get triggered, leading to disengagement, defensiveness, and shutting down.

With this book, you'll be able to forgo traditional accountability, which often leaves employees feeling triggered into negative emotional responses, and instead inspire accountability with **actionable clarity**, knowing exact steps and best practices to create a results-rich environment where employees feel valued.

To do this, you'll start by learning how the brain releases neurochemicals which create our experience and engagement (or disengagement) in the workplace, what triggers this response, and what leaders can do to support a positive response that keeps employees receptive, resourceful, and engaged.

Next, we will examine the practical and powerful Results Model that improves both the leader and employee's experience and effectiveness for contributing to results and receiving feedback. You'll then learn how to convert general Desired Results to clear expectations using the **Accountability Anchor Conversion Checklist**.

You'll learn how to apply the Results Model, how it will inspire accountability with greater ease, and how employees will participate.

We then move into proactive accountability tools, learning about the Hierarchy of Human Needs in the Workplace and the Employee Engagement and Experience Loop. You'll learn what inspires employees to engage and what triggers them to disengage, with tools to navigate how to inspire optimal effort.

After a solid foundation of how the brain creates our experience at work, you'll learn Engaging Leadership Language, powerful linguistic nuances to help you get the answers, engagement, and the accountability you want from your team. Additionally, we'll expand upon how to intentionally infuse positive neurochemicals into your employees' daily work experiences.

Filling your leadership toolbox, you'll learn how to hold employees accountable for mindset, attitude, and behavior by upgrading company values to Culture Values and Action Steps (CVAS).

To close, you'll learn the Inspiring Accountability approach to other tools, including performance reviews and Proactive Accountability Measures (PAM's) so that you can inspire performance.

All of these tools make *Inspiring Accountability in the Workplace* like a reference manual disguised as a book. Each clearly defined chapter is packed with its own set of tools and progressively adds context to the previously mentioned nine themes and mindsets. Absorb and apply lessons from each chapter at a steady and practical pace that works for you. When you get stuck in a leadership challenge, make this one of your go-to resources. Take notes or highlight sections that inspire you so you can find a solution quickly.

While much of this book is focused on understanding your employees, often you will find an understanding of your own experience comes first. These concepts will also apply to you and your experiences on any given day, both when you are leading your team and when you are personally responding to your managing entity.

Once you understand how to work with the brain's default operating mode, you can't unlearn it. You will notice it in yourself, and you will notice it in your employees. Many of my clients cite the value of the presented tools and methodology as helpful in personal relationships with their partners, family, and even children. If you read this with the mindset of, "How else can I apply this to improve my life?" you will inevitably discover countless ways.

A Very Important Note: Navigating this Book

I assert that leaders are not solely accountable for an employee's engagement and accountability but that leaders are *100% accountable to contribute positively and productively* to their employees' engagement and receptiveness to accountability. This book contains numerous resources you can use when you're not getting the results you need from your team. Additionally, you can find supplemental materials on my website: www.inspiringaccountability.com.

While I encourage commitment and consistency to build trust, a great way to begin is by trying a new tactic as a trial to see what works best — and being transparent about it with your employees.

Of course, you'll want to find your own way to use these tools with your specific team and in your unique workplace. If you find yourself getting stuck in what won't work for you, shift your thinking to what's possible to make it work for you. I help my clients customize their own practical integration and use of the Results Model to fit their unique teams, and you will be able to do the same if you keep asking yourself: "Given our available time and resources, what's possible for me and my team to get the most value from these tools?"

Once you begin to see the outlined needs and patterns in your employees and yourself, you will be empowered to navigate challenges by working with what makes us human instead of resisting it.

Initially there may be a slight increase in your effort while learning and implementing these new strategies, but you will soon reap the benefits — including efficiency and your sanity — in spades.

Keep in Mind

If you want healthy plants, you have to pull the weeds and add nutrients to the soil. Then you get to enjoy the bounty with much less effort through less demanding, ongoing maintenance.

Similarly, spending a little time up front to establish these new tools, pulling the weeds and nourishing the soil, will help your employees become rooted in being more self-reliant and engaged, giving you more time in your day-to-day future. Their engagement and accountability will grow with much less effort from you.

Additionally, the more you help employees be engaged, prepared, and fulfilled upfront, the more you will enjoy less stress and more personal and professional fulfillment. You no longer have to use severity, anger, or frustration to hold an employee accountable when you have trusted accountability tools.

We Begin in the Brain

The secret to inspiring accountability and engagement starts with asking:

- What makes us human?
- What drives us toward or away from tasks?
- What inspires us to give our best?
- What motivates us to shut down?
- What, exactly, determines our happiness and fulfillment at work?

We begin in the brain, where all experience and engagement begins. Are you ready to change your experience as a leader? It starts right now.

Use the Glossary

Important terminology is bolded throughout *Inspiring Accountability in the Workplace* and can be found in the Glossary at the back of the book.

Find additional resources, content, and support

online at www.inspiringaccountability.com

CHAPTER 2

Neurochemicals in the Workplace: Engagement Tools and Disengagement Triggers

"I've learned that people will forget what you said, people will forget what you did, but people will never forget how you made them feel."

—MAYA ANGELOU

In this chapter, we'll explore what creates our experience at work, including:

- Neurochemicals, otherwise known as "engagement and experience indicators"
- How "positive" neurochemicals act as engagement tools
- How "negative" neurochemicals act as disengagement triggers
- How and when neurochemicals are released (and how you, as a leader, can stimulate them)
- How neurochemicals affect your employees' performance

Along with the classic Maya Angelou quote that opens the chapter, science supports that how we *feel* becomes our primary memory, and how we *feel* creates our experience. In the workplace, our experience determines our engagement. Employees that feel great get great results, and great results make employees feel great.

So, what creates these feelings of engagement, happiness, and productivity? And what happens when an employee is negatively triggered or disengaged? As a leader, you can express to your team how important a result is, you can outline the best strategic practices, and offer specific execution guidelines, but if your employees don't feel good about what they're doing, their brains simply won't operate at peak engagement. Therefore, it benefits you to understand the brain's role in helping achieve the results the first time.

The Correlation Between Happiness and Productivity

The more engaged and fulfilled employees are, the better their performance, making engagement an excellent proactive accountability tool to help you achieve optimal results the first time.

As it turns out, happiness has commonly been linked with engagement and performance:

- **Companies with happy employees outperform the competition by 20%** (Entrepreneur.com, 2014, "It Really Pays to Have a Rich Company Culture").
- **Employees who report being happy at work take 10x fewer sick days than unhappy employees** (*Wall Street Journal*, 2011, "The Five Drivers of Happiness at Work").
- **A decade of research proves that happiness raises nearly every business and educational outcome: raising sales by 37%, productivity by 31%, and accuracy on tasks by 19%, as well as myriad health and quality of life improvements** (*Harvard Business Review*, 2011, "The Happiness Dividend").

In addition to these statistics, you probably intuitively know that happiness matters in the workplace — but what, exactly, is "happiness" and "fulfillment"?

When we talk about employees *being* engaged, we generally omit the most important nuance of engagement — that employees actually *feel* engaged. In this chapter, you will learn about how neurochemicals create predictable ways for employees to feel happy and fulfilled — the kind of fulfillment that inspires engagement, accountability, and results. Learning how neurochemicals act as engagement tools or disengagement triggers will have a profound impact on how you can influence your employees' ability to stay engaged, receptive, resourceful, and rewarded.

What are Neurochemicals?

Neurochemicals are chemicals, or hormones, like dopamine, serotonin, and oxytocin, that the brain releases in response to incoming sensory information. These chemicals affect the nervous system, health, and sense of wellbeing in a variety of different ways. Perhaps most importantly from a leadership perspective, they create the feelings that reward and incentivize effort and behavior.

Think about it…what let's you know you're feeling good? It is hard to put your finger on it. You just…feel good! But there is science behind this elusive process, and without being scientists, we can still understand through our own daily experience how neurochemicals provide incentive and reward for engagement.

Inspiring Accountability refers to these as **engagement and experience indicators** because they indicate how we experience work and determine if we feel positively or negatively about our work and work environment. These indicators greatly affect if and how much we engage with a task, project, or person. When we work on a project where positive neurochemicals are present or expected, our engagement and resourcefulness increase. When we feel negatively triggered, and positive neurochemicals are lacking or negative ones (such as adrenaline, cortisol, and norepinephrine) are present, engagement and resourcefulness dramatically decrease. These feelings of negativity then threaten engagement, receptiveness, and resourcefulness.

Thus, *neurochemicals are always acting as engagement tools or disengagement triggers.* They inform our ability to give 100%, to be inspired by a company vision, to connect with clients, and to creatively collaborate. They can also be engagement enemies, jolting us into a defensive self-protection mode and triggering our brain to limit our resourcefulness.

These non-negotiable neurochemicals are rewards in themselves and can be the best way to create engaged and accountable employees. Let's learn how to positively leverage these neurochemicals to create happier employees that get better results.

Positive Neurochemicals

The three "engagement tool" neurochemicals are **dopamine, serotonin**, and **oxytocin**. These can be referred to as "positive" neurochemicals because they generally create a positive experience.

When you help employees have opportunities to experience these positive neurochemicals, you significantly elevate your leadership effectiveness. You'll find that it can be free, easy, and rewarding to help employees experience more positive neurochemicals in their daily work experience, and you'll inspire engagement that gets results easier and more effectively.

DOPAMINE — "I did it!" Reaching the Goal, Getting it Done

There is enough research to conclude that emotions and emotional behaviors are caused by neural activity. According to Daniel M. Cable's (2018) *Alive at Work: The Neuroscience of Helping Your People Love What They Do*, there is still exploration around *all* emotions being caused by architecturally and chemically distinct circuits in the brain. Yet, neuroscientists tend to agree that one of the most basic emotional systems pertains to an identifiable neural circuit that depends on dopamine for motivation.

Dopamine is the "*I* did it!" neurochemical. Dopamine is a neurotransmitter that plays a key role in the limbic system, which is involved in emotional function and control. Dopamine is also involved in cognitive processes associated with movement, executive function, body temperature regulation, and, most importantly in the workplace, motivation and reward. When dopamine is low in employees, so is motivation. Conversely, when dopamine is high, employees are naturally more engaged and motivated.

In the 2017 *Huffington Post* article, "Hacking Into Your Happy Chemicals," Thai Nguyen writes: "Dopamine motivates us to take action toward goals, desires, and needs, and gives a surge of reinforcing pleasure when achieving them. Procrastination, self-doubt, and lack of enthusiasm are linked with low levels of dopamine. Studies on rats showed those with low levels of dopamine always opted for an easy option and less food; those with higher levels exerted the effort needed to receive twice the amount of food." Dopamine provides that motivational endurance and desire to put in necessary effort for the biggest reward.

Therefore, when it comes to maximizing employee effort, healthy doses of dopamine are key. A dopamine dose is the natural reward for achieving a result of one's personal effort, generally confirming a sense of competency and satisfaction. Dopamine then rewards us for favorable behaviors and motivates us to repeat them.

Dopamine is what makes it feel good to beat a level of *Candy Crush*, finish a 5k race, or finish weeding an over-grown front yard. In the workplace, it's why it feels great to cross something off a to-do list, gain a new client, or successfully launch a new product.

Generally, the greater the challenge, the more rewarding the dopamine dose. But smaller goals get more frequent celebratory boosts of dopamine, which contribute more frequently to engagement, the priority for leaders. A mix of both is important to keep incentivizing engagement, and there are many references on how to infuse positive neurochemicals into your employees' experiences throughout this book.

Unlike the following two "positive" neurochemicals (serotonin and oxytocin), experiencing dopamine doesn't require or involve anyone else. However, as a leader, you can facilitate more circumstances for employees to experience it. You can help employees track items in ways that show a clear achievement and allow for a ceremonial or celebratory completion, like visible to-do lists that are triumphantly crossed off, sharing achievements in weekly meetings, or ringing a gong when milestones are met. Internally knowing you completed something is less rewarding than a clear moment of celebrating it.

Whether you have a gong culture or not, you can fuel employee engagement by finding ways to "high five" small wins. As a leader, you will also receive a dopamine boost when you contribute to employees experiencing neurochemical benefits.

As we'll learn in Part III on Inspiring Effort and Engagement, dopamine is also responsible for the *anticipation* of reward, which creates incentive to continue engaging in the future.

SEROTONIN — "You did it!" The Crowd Cheer, The Trophy

Serotonin is the "*You* did it!" neurochemical. Serotonin is a monoamine neurotransmitter that plays a regulatory role in mood, sleep, appetite, body temperature regulation, and other processes.

For the most part, serotonin is required to feel "happy." In the aforementioned 2017 *Huffington Post* article by Thai Nguyen, Princeton neuroscientist Barry Jacobs is cited, explaining that most antidepressants focus on the production of serotonin, making serotonin essentially a non-negotiable neurochemical for humans.

Serotonin sparks feelings of significance when we get recognized for doing a good job or completing something successfully, equivalent to, "You did it!" As the most important, if not only, source of meaningful recognition in the workplace, leaders have substantial influence over how much serotonin their employees experience. Being recognized and seen as contributing, competent, and important all infuse serotonin into our employees' workday, which you'll learn more about in Chapter 9 on Workplace Rewards and the Hierarchy of Human Needs.

In addition to being the most important neurochemical that leaders can influence, employees with high levels of serotonin also maintain rational decision-making and exhibit a more stable mood — a win for all.

In her 2015 blog entitled, "Serotonin — Miracle Drug at Work," Dr. Ellen Weber, MBA Leadership professor and author, writes: "Sometimes called the molecule of wellbeing, serotonin is the chemical that transforms *gunner* into *giver*, *lazy* into *learner*, and *victim* into *victor*. For individuals or teams, serotonin chemicals add focus, support innovative or disruptive solutions, increase motivation and can even transform stress into success." The workplace is one of the best sources for serotonin fulfillment. Leaders can offer this important human experience through the simple yet essential act of acknowledgment.

Serotonin is the leadership neurochemical. While all neurochemicals are important in the human experience at work, serotonin is most important to the Inspiring Accountability methodology and employee engagement. It's the neurochemical most within your influence to create a better employee experience that naturally leads to getting better results.

OXYTOCIN – "We did it!" The Team Win

Oxytocin is the *"We* did it!" connection and trust neurochemical. Oxytocin creates the feeling of friendship, love, and connection. It creates togetherness.

In his 2014 book, *Leaders Eat Last*, Simon Sinek explores neurochemicals as an important concept in leadership. He explains: "We feel it when we do something nice for someone or someone does something nice for us. Without oxytocin, we wouldn't want to perform acts of generosity."

In the workplace, oxytocin is released when we have a valued and trustworthy connection with our manager or coworkers, a productive collaborative effort, or a team or company win that was achieved collectively. Workplaces that cultivate oxytocin are marked by effective, collaborative, and celebratory teams.

Oxytocin also creates the feeling of "deep trust" — essentially knowing that our manager and co-workers have our backs. Sinek (2014) concludes, "The less colleagues and leaders look out for us, the less we look out for them." Understandably, when we trust our manager and colleagues, we exhibit greater loyalty and effort. Dr. Paul J. Zak, author of *Trust Factor: The Science of Creating High-Performance Companies* (2017) calls this neurotransmitter "the chemical foundation for trusting others," and states that it "motivates us to work together for a common purpose."

Similar to the adage that people do business with people they like and trust, employees go the extra mile for leaders they like and trust *and feel liked and trusted by*. Oxytocin goes both ways, reinforcing when the feeling is perceived mutually.

But not all neurochemicals make us feel good. There is another set of "negative" neurochemicals that are generally released as a response to "negative" experiences. These neurochemicals result in feeling like we need to protect or defend ourselves, trigger the fight-freeze-flight response, and can also create anxiousness that interrupts efficient effort, none of which help employees feel safe to be accountable or resourceful to get better results. When an employee experiences these, engagement, receptiveness, and resourcefulness become limited.

Negative Neurochemicals

Adrenaline, Cortisol, and Norepinephrine — "I failed."
The Over-Protective Engagement Saboteurs

While perfectly helpful in times of physical danger, our brains' threat-response system treats an unexpected curt email from a manager as if we're being charged by a massive woolly mammoth.

Designed to improve our physical ability to stay alive, the 200,000-year-old **creature brain** boasts a timeless **threat-response system**, the physiological process the creature brain uses to protect and defend against threat. It includes the fight-freeze-flight response, feeling **triggered**, and the effects of adrenaline, norepinephrine, and cortisol. Originally supporting early humans' ability to physically respond to danger, this well-established process is disproportionately out-of-date for workplace threats. It also limits access to useful parts of the rational human brain, leaving us less receptive, less resourceful, and easily triggered from the most common day-to-day workplace threats to our emotional safety, like perceived damage to our dignity, which is defined in Chapter 9 as being seen as contributing, competent, and important.

It begins when a threat is perceived. The brain's amygdala sends a distress signal to the hypothalamus, which alerts the rest of the nervous system to increase the top survival tools: breathing, blood pressure, and heartbeat.

To increase these physical survival tools, the adrenal glands receive the signal to start pumping the hormone epinephrine, commonly called **adrenaline**, into the bloodstream. Adrenaline is a hormone secreted by the adrenal glands, especially in conditions of stress, that increases rates of blood circulation, breathing, and carbohydrate metabolism, all preparing muscles for exertion.

Here, the fight-freeze-flight response is engaged as blood gets pushed to the muscles and away from the rational part of the brain. Our senses sharpen, and blood sugar and fats are released from temporary storage to provide a surge of energy to all parts of the body.

Norepinephrine, a hormone similar to adrenaline, is also released to help the physical and sensory systems become more responsive, shifting blood flow to areas like the skin and muscles.

While this might be helpful if you're running from a puma, it's less helpful if you're trying to stay calm and collected through a nerve-racking presentation. But the oldest creature part of the brain that triggers this response system doesn't understand the difference between a puma and a presentation. It simply registers "threat," focusing an inordinate amount of attention on the threat, and correspondingly limiting activity in the prefrontal cortex, the human brain's star advocate for rationality.

As reported by *The Science of Psychotherapy* in 2017, "The most typical psychological term for functions carried out by the prefrontal cortex area is executive function. Executive function relates to abilities to differentiate among conflicting thoughts, determine good and bad, better and best, same and different, future consequences of current activities, working toward a defined goal, prediction of outcomes, expectation based on actions, and social 'control' (the ability to suppress urges that, if not suppressed, could lead to socially unacceptable outcomes)." The prefrontal cortex is not found in reptiles and is supremely developed in humans, so for simplicity, *Inspiring Accountability in the Workplace* will refer to the rational part of the brain as a function of the "human brain" and the threat-response controller as a function of the "creature brain."

This threat response initiates so quickly and efficiently that it begins before the brain's visual centers even have a chance to fully process what is happening, classifying this system as one of our oldest and most powerful involuntary responses.

Putting this all together: when the creature brain function has flagged a threat and the threat response initiates, the priority goes to physical survival and away from the human brain, meaning all of those valuable attributes of the prefrontal cortex are diminished.

A bit overkill for the workplace, isn't it?

And yet, the threat-scanning creature brain function we've been operating with since the beginning of humankind is as active as ever.

To help regulate this temporary intensity, **cortisol**, a steroid hormone commonly called "the stress hormone" is released. Cortisol curbs functions that would be nonessential in a fight-freeze-flight reaction. It alters immune system responses and suppresses the digestive system, the reproductive system, and other growth processes. With these well-being systems dialed down, the brain can activate other systems that can more usefully and urgently respond to the threat.

When the threat passes, cortisol levels fall and the body begins to return to its baseline. Amit Sood, M.D., director of research at the Complementary and Integrative Medicine and chair of Mayo Mind Body Initiative at Mayo Clinic, is quoted in the 2013 *Huffington Post* article, "Adrenaline, Cortisol, Norepinephrine: The Three Major Stress Hormones, Explained," citing that it could take anywhere from half an hour to a couple of days to return to a normal "stress free" resting state.

But this response that has kept our species alive also causes unnecessary, outdated (and sometimes unending) stress in our modern-day lives. In today's "too-much-to-do" workplaces, sometimes the stress level is re-activated before it is de-activated, creating an unending release of negative neurochemicals.

Being in a continuous state of cortisol-related stress and feeling triggered is bad for our physical health, limits our mental health, and decreases our ability to be engaged, receptive, and resourceful in the workplace. If we continuously focus on problems, subconsciously translating these problems to workplace threats, the body can *continuously* release cortisol.

Chronic elevated levels of cortisol can lead to serious health issues. Perhaps the most destructive is that chronic cortisol exposure weakens or suppresses the immune system, which of course makes us more susceptible to any ailment. The Australian Spinal Research Foundation website notes another major concern: "Cortisol depletes serotonin and dopamine levels. It actually damages the receptor sites of these neurotransmitters."

Additionally, according to the Mayo Clinic website, the long-term activation of the stress-response system and subsequent stress hormones increases the risk of:

- Anxiety
- Depression
- Digestive problems
- Headaches
- Heart disease
- Sleep problems
- Weight gain and obesity
- Memory and concentration impairment

In the workplace, it's easy to see how minimizing stress hormones helps contribute to a healthier, happier, and more productive work experience and environment. Therefore, leaders must contribute to reducing triggering events if they want to get the best from their teams.

The aforementioned 2013 *Huffington Post* article also states that there are many additional brain factors that affect how each individual reacts to stress, including estrogen, testosterone, dopamine, and serotonin. Additionally, diet, exercise, and other established brain patterns play a role in the evocation and recovery from stress. But the classic fight-freeze-flight reaction is mostly due to adrenaline, cortisol, and norepinephrine.

Our 200,000-year-old threat-response system, tried-and-true as it is, still drives our behavior and reactions. Although the workplace is no exception, leaders play an influential role in preventing this threat-response system from being triggered in the first place.

Next, you'll learn more about how we experience being triggered in the workplace so you can learn how to prevent it.

Note: future references of "safety" refer to whether the creature brain feels "safe" (when the negative neurochemical response is not activated) or feels threatened and unsafe (triggering disengagement, shutting down receptiveness, and limiting resourcefulness).

Getting Triggered in the Workplace

Britt Andreatta, author of *Wired to Resist* (2017), explains that the modern-day equivalent of a fight-or-flight response can be to resort to criticism, sarcasm, withdrawal, defensiveness, or stonewalling. None of these, of course, are conducive to maintaining engagement, receptiveness, or resourcefulness.

When we become triggered in the workplace, our threat-response system reliably kicks in. We become subconsciously self-protective. More often than not, we immediately lose access to being resourceful toward what we'd rationally like (being calm while presenting) or rationally need (being able to problem solve, avoid responding defensively, or accepting accountability instead of looking to blame others).

Imagine you're talking with a co-worker about a project. You're collaboratively problem-solving, on the verge of a solution you're confident your manager will approve. You're nearing the "I did it!" dopamine, "You did it!" serotonin, and "We did it!" oxytocin. This is shaping up to be a great day!

During this positive and fulfilling conversation, the front human brain function where your ability to evaluate rationally and problem solve creatively lights up with activity. Michelle Masters, an esteemed NLP Marin instructor I studied under while becoming certified in Neuro-Linguistic Programming, explains that on a brain scan while active and untriggered, the rational and resourceful part of the brain would be "lit up with activity, like flying over Los Angeles at night."

Lit up.

You can imagine that your successful brainstorm is keeping positive neurochemicals flowing, and you're 100% engaged and feeling great! But then, it happens. Your office phone rings. You see your manager's name on the caller ID and pick up promptly. You hear your manager curtly say, "I need to see you in my office *right* now," followed by an abrupt hang up. If you're wired like most of us, your brain instantly interprets this to mean something is wrong.

As you hurriedly end your meeting to go to your manager's office, your creature brain function hits the big red threat alert button. Now those lights representing the rational part of the brain are having a city-wide power outage. On a brain scan, the activity in the rational human brain would go almost dark, but the creature brain now shows the primary activity. The threat-response system is activated and negative neurochemicals are released. Rational resourcefulness, something that would be most important when meeting with your manager, is getting harder and harder to access with each anxious step down the hall.

The creature brain is now in control. The fight-freeze-flight center has been activated, consuming much of the energy on your brain's power grid. In the workplace, our best option is often to freeze and comply. Flight usually feels like a desired choice, but we weigh the cons of dramatically leaving the office. When enough of the "I want to flee" moments build up, we start looking for a job. Fighting (even verbally) is likely going to get us fired, so instead we persevere as we walk toward the manager's office in a "triggered" and essentially frozen state.

There you are, with limited rational resourcefulness, heading into a daunting meeting where you'd be better able to contribute productively if the human brain was in charge.

This natural human response happens to leaders and employees alike. So, what can be done?

Your goal as a leader should be to increase the experience of positive neurochemicals and decrease the experience of triggering negative ones. When you practice **Possibility Thinking**, which is built into the upcoming Results Model, you'll move quickly from "what's in the way" to "what's possible," and you can retrain your brain to problem solve instead of panic. When you no longer need to rely on frustration or agitation to communicate the weight of a problem, you will inherently give permission and create safety for your employees to stop panicking and start problem-solving.

Before we close this foundational introduction to how neurochemicals impact our employees' engagement in their work, receptiveness to feedback and accountability, and resourcefulness toward solutions, let's first understand how neurochemicals are released.

How Neurochemicals are Released

Neurochemicals are released in response to **sensory input**, what we consciously or subconsciously notice with our five senses. Interestingly, the brain is built to automatically save processing power and create predictability by recognizing, creating, and relying upon patterns. The brain then releases neurochemicals in *expectation and anticipation* of "positive" or "negative" stimuli, as well as in *reaction* or *reward* to sensory input and experiences.

To illustrate, we'll learn what happens in the brain of Ralphie the Friendly Lab Rat as he navigates a maze to get a reward of cheese at the end. Over pizza at a charming lunch spot in Berkeley, California, Dr. Vivienne Ming, theoretical neuroscientist, entrepreneur, and author, offered a useful meta-analysis of studies that highlight how dopamine is released. Dr. Nathaniel Daw, Professor of Princeton Neuroscience Institute and Psychology, also confirms countless studies similar in nature prove the same basic relationship between dopamine, reward, and expectation of reward.

While this study references dopamine activity, we can also extrapolate the process to the release of "You did it!" serotonin, our main focus as leaders.

Let's see how these concepts are revealed in Ralphie the Lab Rat's experience in a maze, and then how it applies to our experience in the workplace.

Ralphie's Adventure in Dopamine Land

One day, Ralphie the Friendly Lab Rat was hanging out in his usual cedar-chip tank when a hand scooped him out and dropped him in front of a maze.

Whether it was compulsion or curiosity, Ralphie travelled through the maze, making right and left turns, right and wrong turns, until he took a corner, and then another corner, and then BOOM! Ralphie got a surprise dose of dopamine when he discovered a piece of cheese at the end of the maze.

The second time he was put in front of the maze, he travelled through, making right and left turns, right and wrong turns until he saw that corner he recognized *just two turns away* from the cheese he got last time. BAM! Ralphie received that feel-good dopamine hit when he *recognized* those last two corners in expectation and anticipation of the cheese to come. Once he took those two corners, he then got another small dopamine hit when he actually got the cheese.

The third time he was put in front of the maze, BOOM! He recognized the maze (familiar sensory input now associated with expected reward) and experienced a dopamine hit (patterned response). Already flooded with dopamine, he travelled through, with fewer wrong turns, taking those last two corners, and getting to the cheese for another smaller hit of dopamine.

The final time Ralphie was put in front of the maze, BOOM! He recognized the maze (associated with expected reward) and experienced a dopamine hit. He traveled through and reached the end, anticipating and expecting cheese. But this time...there wasn't any cheese.

Ralphie's dopamine plummeted, dipping below the normal baseline. This drop is especially devastating because his brain, expecting cheese, was already experiencing dopamine in anticipation of the reward. When this expectation was not met, *the experience was much worse than if Ralphie had never expected cheese initially.*

You can see the relationship between the primary dopamine impact and one's baseline, the sensory input that becomes associated with expecting the reward (**cue**), and experiencing (or not experiencing) the reward itself.

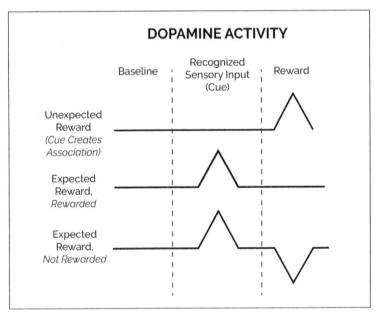

Figure inspired by "Reward prediction and subsequent dopamine activity model" by Rebecca Clements.

One clear explanation of how dopamine is released in response to reward prediction and learning is from Trevor Haynes, a research technician in the Department of Neurobiology at Harvard Medical School. In his 2018 article, "Dopamine, Smartphones and You: A Battle for Your Time," Haynes writes, "Unexpected rewards increase the activity of dopamine neurons, acting as positive feedback signals for the brain regions associated with the preceding behavior," like when Ralphie unexpectedly discovered cheese. Haynes continues, "As learning takes place, the timing of activity will shift until it occurs upon the cue alone," like Ralphie getting the dopamine boost from seeing the maze, "with the expected reward having (little or) no additional effect. And should the expected reward not be received, dopamine activity drops, sending a negative feedback signal to the relevant parts of the brain, weakening the positive association." Haynes highlights that the dopamine reward system works off of *anticipation* and *reinforcement* of the association between a particular stimulus or sequence of behaviors and the feel-good reward that follows.

He explains, "Every time a response to a stimulus results in a reward, these associations become stronger through a process called 'long-term potentiation.' This process strengthens frequently used connections between brain cells called neurons by increasing the intensity at which they respond to particular stimuli or sensory information."

Haynes states that this neurological feature is why individuals continue to play casino games. If you've ever played slots, you'll have experienced the intense anticipation while those wheels are turning — the moments between the lever pull and the final reveal provide time for our dopamine neurons to increase their activity, creating a rewarding feeling within the anticipation, simply by playing the game. This keeps us engaged in playing.

But eventually, as negative outcomes accumulate, the loss of dopamine activity incentivizes us to disengage. Haynes concludes: "Thus, a balance between positive and negative outcomes must be maintained in order to keep our brains engaged." We must experience enough good rewards to keep enduring disappointment of "failure." So, how do we apply Ralphie's maze journey to the workplace?

In the workplace, being put in front of the maze is like being put in front of our manager, a task, or a project. Before we begin, are we expecting something positive or negative? The Ralphie the Lab Rat study and casino example highlight common neurochemical response patterns, and here is how those may be reflected in the work environment:

- Employees' anticipation and expectation of a good outcome, reward, or result is as powerful as actually achieving it and helps a good outcome occur.
- Employees experience dopamine when expecting a good outcome, fueling engagement and feeling good throughout.
- Employees must receive enough "reward" to keep enduring disappointment or "failure," or they give up and stop engaging.
- Positive surprises, like an unexpected employee bonus or thoughtful gift, offer the best neurochemical reward. Negative surprises, like surprise negative feedback or an unexpected poor rating on a performance review, are the most neurochemically destructive.
- When employees expect a good outcome, reward, or result, and do not achieve any, it is more damaging than if there was never an expectation. It starts to de-stabilize and disincentivize engagement and effort.

Studies prove that it neurochemically *feels worse to expect and not receive than to not have expectations at all*, but not having any expectations leads to an apathetic and unmotivated workforce. Humans' brains, by nature, create expectations to establish predictability. Fulfilled positive expectations bring humans a sense of excitement, engagement, and optimism. You want employees to predict positive outcomes to incentivize engagement and inspire proactive accountability, which you'll learn to do in upcoming chapters.

An Aside: The Neurochemical Effects of Working Alone

I was coming up on my first year of working for myself, which at the time also meant working *by* myself. As a natural extrovert and "people person," I was having a tough time with the isolation. I was generally unhappy; I felt something was missing, and I thought something was "wrong" with me.

I was working on a client's training presentation, inputting the neurochemical concepts that were previously outlined, and BAM! It hit me: *This* is what is wrong! In this moment of connecting concepts I'd been writing and training on with my personal experience, it all made sense. I was lacking:

Dopamine: Because I was now working on long-term projects — developing trainings that were months out and writing a book that was still almost two years away from completion — I was in a major dopamine deficit because my "I did it's!" were few and far between. My to-do list was hardly the fast-paced "check, check, check" that I had in the marketing world. My opportunities for "I did it!" were coming far less frequently.

Serotonin: Similarly, I was only getting a serotonin boost when I finished a training. After a training, understandably, the acknowledgment was usually, "That was so great! Thank you so much!" I had to wait many months to learn how the new tools implemented in the training were making their workplace better. Working alone offers fewer and less satiating "You did it!" opportunities than working in a team and for a manager.

Oxytocin: I enjoyed connecting with clients and training participants, but that was only a sliver of my working hours. Mostly I was in my office working solo. I was used to being very close with my former team and sharing in many collaborative wins, almost daily at times. This major shift blindsided me as I found myself in a proverbial desert, thirsty for more connection and collaboration.

If, for whatever reason, you're in a similar neurochemical shortage, you'll have to look for ways to intentionally refuel neurochemically inside or outside of the workplace.

The Workplace is a Neurochemical Goldmine

In conclusion, the workplace offers a wealth of opportunities for leaders to boost employees' dopamine, serotonin, and oxytocin. And your awareness of creating and making the most of these opportunities is a key difference between "happy" employees and employees lost in the desert, looking for another workplace to quench their thirst.

In the book, *Never Split the Difference: Negotiating as if Your Life Depended on It* (2017), author and former international hostage negotiator for the FBI, Chris Voss, shares that "When people are in a positive frame of mind, they think more quickly, and are more likely to collaborate and problem-solve (instead of fight and resist). Positivity creates mental agility in both you and your counterpart." Voss validates the value of keeping employees in a positive mindset to maintain their resourcefulness, among many other beneficial workplace wins.

In alignment with Maya Angelou's opening chapter quote, the foundation of being an unforgettable leader who inspires engagement, accountability, and results is all in how you influence your employees to (neurochemically) *feel*.

Integration Questions:

1. What is a workplace example that you personally relate to feeling the "I did it!" dopamine? How about "You did it!" serotonin, and "We did it!" oxytocin?

2. What are some workplace examples of when you've felt triggered or in fight-freeze-flight? Which of the three is your default response?

3. Which neurochemicals do you think your team members are most in need of to improve their ability to be engaged, receptive, and resourceful?

Key Take-Aways:

1. There are "positive" neurochemicals that are released in our brains: dopamine ("I did it!"); serotonin ("You did it!"); and oxytocin ("We did it!"). These are important engagement tools.

2. There are "negative" neurochemicals that are also released in our brains: adrenaline, cortisol, and norepinephrine ("I failed," or "My value or competence is threatened."). These are disengagement triggers.

3. Leaders can increase positive neurochemicals in the workplace, making employees *feel* happier and reduce negative neurochemicals, which inspires employees to be more engaged in their work, receptive to feedback and accountability, and resourceful toward solutions.

4. The more engaged and fulfilled employees are, the better their performance, making engagement an excellent proactive accountability tool to help your team get better results the first time.

5. Employees must receive enough good rewards to keep enduring disappointment or "failure."

6. When employees expect a good outcome, reward, or result, and do not achieve any, it is damaging. It starts to de-stabilize and disincentivize engagement and effort.

7. Positive surprises offer the best neurochemical reward. Negative surprises are the most neurochemically destructive.

CHAPTER 3

Traditional Accountability vs. Inspiring Accountability

"If you want to change something,
you have to change something."

—UNKNOWN

In this chapter, we'll be covering the compelling differences between "Traditional Accountability" and "Inspiring Accountability," including:

- Traditional Accountability: triggering, past-focused, problem-oriented
- Inspiring Accountability: engaging, future-focused, solution-oriented
- How is accountability different from ownership?
- What is a leader's role in accountability?
- How do you inspire employees to care more about results?

Being Accountable for Bringing Home A Pizza is *Not* Inspiring

There is no better source of motivation than the one at our most basic level: survival.

The survival-focused part of our brain, introduced in the previous chapter, ensures we protect ourselves and our loved ones by any means necessary. It's the fight-freeze-flight construct we're hardwired with. Attack the eleven-foot woolly mammoth or run?

It would appear we've evolved beyond that limited binary. We have mortgages, rent, at-home grocery delivery apps — not a mammoth in sight. Much of our basic needs have been met, but the original fight-freeze-flight wiring still fires with the same intensity. That ancient part of the brain has just found other aspects of life to deem threating.

In the workplace, then, our source of motivation isn't a basic means of employment for survival but also the protection of our value, dignity, and self-worth. More specifically, we are motivated to be seen as a competent, important, valuable contributor.

Before work happened in factories and skyscrapers, we used to feel our value and purpose by spending a day hunting or foraging, triumphantly bringing back the bounty. Or perhaps we felt satisfaction tending to the well-being of our community, spending the day taking care of and providing for the kids and the elders. All this was *enough*.

Today, the vital tasks necessary for survival have been diluted to mundane expectations. While we still have the ancient creature brain, the impressiveness of our value and purpose is quickly depleted when we can order dinner with the touch of a button and have daycare to allow working parents to contribute outside of the house. So how else do we get a sense of purpose and self-worth when we aren't valiantly celebrated for our ability to bring home a pizza?

Our need to feel that we are competent, important, and that we contribute meaningfully has shifted to completely different activities that suit the modern workplace. Without a sense of these, there's not much to drive employees to be inspired or enthusiastic about their work.

Employees invest their effort and energy in a company, and the currency they hope to receive in return, which is much more satiating than a paycheck, is this sense of dignity, value, and purpose.

When employees feel set up to succeed, they love working. Work becomes a major source of personal fulfillment and satisfaction. Generally, employees would prefer to engage in meaningful and proportionately challenging work rather than to sit at their desk and scroll on social media all day. Employees want to put their abilities to use when the impact is seen and celebrated. They want that bucket of berries they foraged for to be noticed and enjoyed by others. Otherwise, what is the purpose? They want to experience how good it feels to meet expectations and be seen as contributing, competent, and important. It's how we're wired.

People are inspired to be accountable for contributing meaningfully to successful results. We're less enthused about being accountable for contributing to unsuccessful results. Meaning, the more we achieve successful results through meaningful effort, not just bringing home a pizza or doing a mundane task at work, the more we enjoy being held accountable for contributing to those solutions. This is the positive side of accountability. Relatedly, the more we look at problems, set-backs, and "failures" as being *in progress toward inevitable positive results*, the more we become comfortable with accountability.

Inspiring Accountability Foundations

Let's imagine you have to lead a department meeting to address how your team missed hitting your quarterly numbers. Your goal is to leave this meeting with your employees understanding that the results from the last quarter were down and must be improved.

If you open the meeting by saying, "It's time for more accountability in this department," you can expect to see a loss of eye contact, fidgeting in seats, and an inordinate increase of nervous ticks.

Your employees will undoubtedly be worrying about what this means for them, and they may be thinking things like:

"Does he think it's my fault?"

"Doesn't she know it was Joe who has been slacking, not me?"

"Am I going to have to work longer hours?"

"Am I going to get fired?"

"Am I going to work longer hours and *then* get fired anyway?"

Traditional accountability is triggering. It jolts us with negative neurochemicals into self-protection, defensiveness, and disengagement.

Why do we tend toward such an unfavorable reaction to the concept of "accountability"? Our answer could be in the embedded meaning in Google's definition of the word:

> **(traditional) ac·count·a·bil·i·ty:** 1. (of a person, organization, or institution) required or expected to justify actions or decisions. *Synonyms*: responsible, liable, answerable; to blame.

To suggest that an employee must "justify their actions or decisions" would immediately make them defensive.

The notion of "blame" would make anyone averse to conversations about accountability. Further, many people may be triggered into defensive behavior during accountability discussions because they're traditionally focused on perceived problems instead of solutions and possibilities.

Using outdated methods of triggering **traditional accountability** with your team compels them to *avoid* instead of *engage*, become *discouraged* instead of *empowered*, *stuck* instead of *innovative*, and *resentful* instead of *inspired*.

No matter what your role, you can likely relate to feeling this way at some point in your own career when a manager tried to hold you accountable, especially for something you didn't feel was within your power. We often rely on other people, departments, and companies to complete a project. When we feel we gave our best effort and still didn't get the result, being held accountable for what seems like impossible circumstances disregards the positive effort we put in and leaves us discouraged, disengaged, and demotivated.

Think of, for example, someone in charge of fulfilling orders, and holding them accountable when the product is delayed from another plant. For a bank teller, it looks like holding a friendly and helpful employee accountable for a crabby customer, even though the teller offered empathetic service. For a software engineer, it looks like missing a deadline after working overtime every day to try to finish. Accountability is not incentivizing when used as a synonym for fault or blame. Our employees are instinctively aware of this, and as leaders we need to be, too.

Still, we need our employees to be accountable. We need them to be responsible for their work and subsequent results. We can't have employees doing whatever they want like a chaotic game of tag where everyone is trying to be "not it." So, how do we effectively and positively ensure everyone performs at a level that meets the organizations' vital performance needs and expectations?

We first must understand that *the intended purpose of accountability is to get results*, ideally the exact results that meet leaders' expectations.

With that purpose in mind, we can seek a more positive and productive approach to accountability from an updated definition:

In·spir·ing Ac·count·a·bil·i·ty: 1. (*noun*) A modern leadership methodology that includes proactive and responsive accountability strategies that inspire employees to be engaged in their work, receptive to feedback and improvement, and resourceful toward achieving results. 2. (*verb*) The act of implementing the methodology resulting in employees who are inspired, engaged, receptive, and resourceful.

Without a need to "justify" actions or a sense of "blame" that focuses on the problem instead of the solution, we can already begin to see how this definition is more desirable for managers and employees.

So, About Traditional Accountability...

Before we get into Inspiring Accountability, let's break down traditional accountability. Rather than being a useful morale-booster, traditional accountability is often blame-focused and competence-crushing. This triggers employee disengagement. It also triggers the aforementioned fight-freeze-flight response.

A triggered employee may attempt to "flee" the situation by avoiding it in any way possible. They may "freeze" like a deer in headlights, essentially shutting down, contributing the bare minimum. They may attempt to "fawn" by buttering up the manager and exaggerating or falsifying results, or they may become openly hostile in an attempt to "fight" the triggering accountability.

Worse, once triggered, the employee we want to do better actually has less ability to do so because the brain is under siege from those negative **neurochemicals** that reroute our impulses and zap resourcefulness. None of these responses get us closer to the results we need.

But why is traditional accountability so triggering?

Unfortunately, it's often experienced as a confrontational accusation of blame that extends further than the temporary situation or a momentary behavior. It feels like a personal attack on who we are, not what has happened.

For the employee, accepting traditional accountability feels like a proclamation of general incompetence. For the leader, demanding traditional accountability feels like a grasping attempt to enforce compliance and performance instead of, say, inspiring effort, engagement, and subsequent results.

There are three distinctions between leaders using traditional accountability and leaders using Inspiring Accountability.

Traditional leaders and teams tend to focus on...	Inspiring leaders and teams tend to focus on...
Blaming and shaming to teach a lesson (triggering disengagement)	Empowering for long-term improvement (keeping employees receptive and resourceful)
The *problem* in the *past*	The *solution* in the *future*
Results only (rarely in the employee's total control)	*Effort* toward results (always in the employee's control)

Let's review each distinction in more detail.

1. Traditional Accountability Distributes Blame Instead of Sharing Contribution

Traditional Accountability is triggering. It's fraught with blame, as defined by Google:

Blame: assign responsibility for a fault or wrong. *synonyms: hold responsible, hold accountable, hold liable, place/lay the blame on*

There's nothing demeaning in this definition of blame, yet being blamed feels triggering because it's usually delivered along with its corresponding cousins: retribution, shame, and guilt. To understand how damaging these forms of traditional accountability can be, consider the following Google definitions. Notice the triggering language used.

Retribution: punishment inflicted on someone as vengeance for a wrong or criminal act.

Shame: a painful feeling of humiliation or distress caused by the consciousness of wrong or foolish behavior. A loss of respect or esteem; a person, action or situation that brings a loss of respect or honor. As a verb, (of a person, action or situation) make (someone) feel ashamed.

Guilt: a feeling of responsibility or remorse for some offense, crime, wrong, whether real or imagined.

The "feeling of responsibility" associated with guilt sounds positive, but employees don't need to endure guilt to motivate improvement. In fact, guilt and its related companions become triggering impediments. Managers turn to using blame, shame, retribution, or guilt when they feel helpless about influencing results. The power of shame is used as a frustrated, last-ditch effort to make the employee feel the weight of their poor contribution in hopes the damage will be so unforgettable that it will never happen again.

Shame can falsely equate the quality of the person with the error made. Instead of focusing on correcting and learning from a specific mistake, the employee feels humiliated. Nothing positive comes from humiliation. Employees who feel badly about themselves never do optimal work.

In the workplace, while shame can be an effective short-term motivator that jolts an employee to attention, it's denigrating and dangerous to long-term engagement. The shame involved in traditional accountability blocks receptiveness to improve and corrodes the quality of a worker and the workplace.

Traditional accountability is often used as a response to a problem, like when someone's action or inaction affects our clients, reputation, effectiveness, or results. Then, in a traditional team meeting, accountability gets portioned. Traditional leaders present a savory "accountability pie" seasoned with rancid blame that they *insist* must be eaten. So, employees push it around the table taking as little as they can. Negative neurochemicals are waiting to pounce on whichever unfortunate employees get stuck with a piece of the accountability pie on their plate. No one is hungry for punishment, especially when punishment is equated with publicly declared failure and incompetence.

Quite differently, Inspiring Accountability empowers employees to improve by avoiding the blame and shame game. When an employee's dignity is maintained, they are better able use the mistake as a growth opportunity.

Blaming, shaming, and guilting takes time away from creating solutions. Sometimes, employees will use getting stuck in guilt to prove how sorry they feel. Guiding your employees to care about the solution is a more productive way for them to show this concern.

2. Focusing on the Problem in the Past vs. the Solution in the Future

You may have noticed that the definitions of blame, retribution, and shame all reference a response to "wrong" behavior. Considering workplace mistakes as "wrong" instead of as opportunities for development and progress triggers a negative response in employees.

Additionally, focusing on the past and what went wrong may seem like a necessary step to understand the problem and prevent it in the future. But similar to Albert Einstein's suggestion that "You can't solve a problem with the same thinking that created the problem," teams and leaders that focus on problems are stuck in the same thinking that created the problem.

If the saying, "Energy goes where attention flows," carries any truth, do you want your employees' attention and energy stuck in the unchangeable past, exploring what didn't work, or engaged, exploring what can be improved and done better? Which is likely to more productively improve results? Which option better inspires engagement and action?

When employees don't have to undergo blame and shame before contributing to solutions, dignity is kept intact, along with engagement, receptiveness, and resourcefulness.

One more shortcoming of traditional accountability is that past failures are useful in showing employees what not to do. Simply providing negation doesn't translate to productivity.

If your manager came in and said, "I need you to create a report. I don't want you to include past sales, current sales, or estimated sales." The likely next question would be, "What would you like me to include?"

With Inspiring Accountability, we similarly skip over spending time and energy on what *not* to do and move directly to the effort we *can and will do* to more productively get the result.

When your company's mindset is **Possibility Thinking,** leaders and employees move quickly past "What's in the way?" to "What's possible?"

Quick Tip: Allow Natural Consequences

Often, a manager will protect their own sense of competency by not allowing an employee to fix a problem "so it can't get worse," but this puts additional burden on the manager and keeps the employee locked in shame.

The better way: let employees respond to the natural consequences, and let employees be accountable for the solution.

Natural consequences are issues that naturally occur when a Desired Result is not met. Natural consequences simply exist and don't require criticism, judgment, or punishment to empower an employee to start fixing them. Natural consequences offer opportunities for the leader to empower an employee to correct a situation, whereas punishment doesn't actually relieve or compensate.

Natural consequences support dignity, whereas punishment degrades dignity. Being empowered to navigate natural consequences allows an employee's guilt to move and be resolved, whereas removing the ability to "make it right" locks guilt in place. Employees can then maintain their vision of how they can contribute, be competent, and be an important part of crafting the solution. Being able to contribute to the solution repairs their dignity, keeping the employee in an inspired, engaged, and resourceful state.

Punishment is the traditional accountability alternative to natural consequences. Punishment could include withholding the ability to make it right, exaggerating the problem, or using criticism, harshness, or shame to prove "wrong doing." It operates under the misguided assumption that the harsher the punishment, the more the person will learn. Employees who feel poorly about themselves rarely produce inspiring results. Future situations that trigger a fear of punishment create a fresh wave of low performance and productivity.

The question then becomes, how can you utilize natural consequences after a problem occurs without resorting to punishment?

Think about when parents ask their teenager what they feel would be a fair consequence of a certain action. This allows the teen to assess the appropriate consequence that will balance out their guilt. Usually, this approach is far less triggering. When done appropriately, it can be empowering and respectful. It honors the reality that humans make mistakes and that it's what one does to amend that mistake that counts.

In the workplace, we likely won't ask employees what they think is a fair consequence. A better question is, "What's possible to solve this problem or make it right?" Now you have your employee accepting accountability for the solution and focused on future possibilities rather than mired in past failures, and now is the time to empower them to contribute to the solution.

A lack accountability often indicates a lack of empowerment. An employee may not be in a role that allows them to take the action to make it right, but you can still let them "project manage" to completion.

Leave the natural consequences with the employee, allowing them to contribute to the solution as much as they may have contributed to the problem; the guilt and shame can be naturally absolved and amended, freeing the employee to move forward productively having made it "right."

Remember the key distinction: traditional accountability uses punishment to create a fear of repeating a past mistake, whereas Inspiring Accountability allows natural consequences to occur and empowers employees to be accountable for solutions in the future.

3. Holding Accountable for Results vs.
Holding Accountable for Effort Toward Results

Inspiring Accountability believes that each individual is 100% accountable for the *effort* they contribute, regardless of the result.

Have you ever put in 100% effort and still didn't get the result? If yes, then you know there's nothing that will make an employee check job listings faster than being held accountable for something that was beyond their full control.

To avoid this unnecessary and damaging aspect of traditional accountability, Inspiring Accountability is *focused on results* and is designed to incentivize, reward, and hold employees accountable *for their effort and contribution toward results.* After all, getting full and consistent effort from employees provides the best chance at getting consistent results, regardless of how many unforeseen outside circumstances continue to get in the way.

With Inspiring Accountability, **effort** is defined as the conscious and subconscious choice to apply an amount of capability through attention and action. Trying to hold someone accountable for not getting the result when they've put in 100% effort *does not acknowledge effort contributed,* discouraging the most important behavior you need from any employee. It also doesn't acknowledge factors outside of the employee's influence, creating resentment and disempowerment. This misguided approach is the ultimate engagement killer.

This is why Inspiring Accountability is results-*focused*, but it's not results-*based*.

Additionally, no one can provide more than 100% effort. If someone gave 100% effort and didn't get the result, trying to hold them accountable for that discourages them from giving their best in the future, creating lower engagement for next time. Being held accountable in this situation teaches the employee that their best isn't good enough and that they can't win at your company or with you as their leader. To be engaged, *employees always need a way to win with you.*

Instead, inspiring leaders expect employees to put forth 100% effort continuously calibrated toward a specific result, keeping the incentive and reward on what is actually within the employee's control.

This also means that we don't say employees are accountable *for* results. Instead, we say employees are accountable for *contributing toward* results. *Toward* is always in motion, allowing for the continuous improvement mindset that we'll develop using the ultimate accountability tool, the Results Model, introduced in the next chapter.

Example: Improving Engagement

Let's examine the differences we're highlighting, including previews of concepts you'll learn in this book.

Imagine your traditional accountability manager tells you that you need to increase employee engagement by 25% by your next performance review. If you don't improve by 25%, you get the sense you could be replaced. Your manager casually says, "I don't care how you do it. Just do it."

While this might seem like empowerment (full range to do or try anything), it's also not supportive for a big, new, and elusive goal. Your manager is removing any of his or her accountability and contribution to the result, leaving you solely accountable for a result that has many factors (and people) beyond your control. This flippant form of delegation makes the task feel more like a threat.

If you put in full effort throughout the year, but your manager is disappointed at your next performance review, what options would you have? You were not set up for success, your valuable effort feels negated, and your enthusiasm is extinguished.

Now imagine how an Inspiring Accountability leader would approach this.

Markus, a CEO of a software company, is having his regular monthly **Innovation and Efficiency Meeting** with Melinda, the company's tenured VP of People and Culture. He says, "Melinda, you've mentioned that you see opportunities to increase employee engagement to improve productivity and create a more compelling company culture that attracts and retains great employees. I'd like to support you with this initiative for this next year. What do you think would be a good engagement goal or result to set for twelve months from now?"

Melinda lights up and responds, "I'd love to focus on this initiative! Can we put some money in a budget toward this? I'd need to do research on what would be needed, but a friend that works at a similar company put $25,000 toward a goal of increasing engagement by 25%. I don't know if they hit the mark, but I'm willing to work toward that result. How does that sound?"

From here, Melinda and Markus go into defining the result with **actionable clarity**, a clear idea of exactly what the first action step is, and a crystal-clear concept of what success looks like when expectations are fulfilled.

Using the tools you'll learn about in this book, Melinda adds this clear Desired Result to her **Results List.** They begin using the Results Model to explore what could get in the way and what's possible at each one-on-one meeting. This helps Markus stay informed and helps Melinda stay engaged, supported, and resourceful when challenges arise. They continue to use the **Accountability Anchor Conversion Checklist** to upgrade Desired Results to those that offer proof of progress and create achievable, neurochemically-rewarding, and bite-sized goals.

If you hold employees accountable for effort, and also explore what got in the way in a non-punitive approach using the Results Model, you will keep them focused on what's in their control and keep them problem-solving for what isn't. *The most predictable way to get results is with consistent 100% effort*, and the upcoming Results Model will virtually guarantee you will be able to get that effort.

Accountability is Owning Outcomes, Not Being An Owner

One of accountability's popular synonyms is "ownership," as in, "I need my employees to take more *ownership*." You may want employees to "own" outcomes; however, asking employees to take greater "ownership" without greater specificity can be destructive.

Outside of employee-owned companies, employees are *not* owners. They will not have as much on the line as owners, and they're not compensated appropriately to do so.

It's unhelpful and frustrating to expect employees to care and sacrifice as much as those higher on the ownership ladder. It can create confusion, discouragement, and resentment to insist on cultivating a feeling of "ownership" when employees are rarely empowered enough to take initiative and make decisions without being overridden or undermined by higher ups.

Even if an employee does "take ownership," you might find that translates to having a difficult or obstinate employee. Do you know an employee that acts like they're the owner, makes decisions without consulting management, and takes great pride and responsibility in their work? These employees get resentful if the decisions *they owned* aren't upheld. They get frustrated and discouraged if their work, of which *they took ownership,* wasn't actually what management wanted and gets disregarded or criticized. After all, how many more levels of "owners" are above them? Everyone can't be owners unless everyone's influence and empowerment is equal.

But not enough "ownership" leaves owners and leaders frustrated and employees under-utilized, unempowered, and uninspired, thinking unproductive thoughts like, "I just do what my manager tells me to do," and "I didn't think to try that because no one told me to."

When I hear leaders say they want employees to take more ownership, it is a red flag that:

- The leader is not productively holding the employee accountable, or
- Employees do not have a sense that they are empowered.

The framework of wanting more ownership falsely lets leaders off the hook because "it's a problem with the employee." Once stated, it ends curiosity and concludes with a finger pointing at the employee to shape up or ship out. As long as a leader is characterizing the problem as the employee not taking ownership, I know the leader either doesn't want to contribute to the solution or, more likely, they simply don't know how.

The request of more ownership is too vague to be successful and needs to be broken down into actionable and achievable clear expectations (with the Accountability Anchor Conversion Checklist, introduced in Chapter 5).

And finally, there is likely a real or perceived lack of empowerment. Ownership doesn't have much of a sliding scale of empowerment. Do they get to make and maintain all decisions under their role's purview *or not?* Do they have access to needed resources without climbing the ladders of approval? Just like accountability, *a lack of ownership often indicates a lack of empowerment.* In my experience as a leadership consultant, the amount of empowerment needed is often not supported within the structure of office hierarchy.

So, if the amount of empowerment needed is unrealistic or unavailable, then "ownership" is not the problem or the solution. There is a more specific goal or desired behavior that can serve as an accurate and productive way to describe the issue, which you will create using the Results Model in Part II.

Furthermore, ownership often has an inherent comparative nature:

- They'll care as much about quality *as I do.*
- They'll come to work as engaged *as I am.*
- They'll be dedicated enough to come to work early or stay late *like I do.*

Caring about quality, being engaged, and being dedicated are important culture and employee attributes. However, your employees care about your company for *their* reasons, not yours, and they engage in their work for *their* reasons, not yours.

But employees can take initiative. They can care deeply about their contribution. They can come to work engaged. They can create solutions themselves. These are all very achievable goals; they need your help creating a conducive structure and environment for empowerment and accountability.

Let Inspiring Accountability's strategies and tools help you create a culture that effectively holds employees accountable for and inspires employees to take initiative, care deeply for the quality of their work, feel engaged, and be excited to actively problem-solve.

A Leader's Role in Inspiring Accountability

Usually, leaders want employees to be accountable *to themselves,* so the leader doesn't have to feel like a "babysitter" or expend energy getting what's needed from the team. But employees need you to offer leadership to help calibrate and adjust their efforts to ensure their contribution is as effective as possible. The goal is to do so in a way that costs you less energy to lead, which is possible with the Results Model.

Summed up, Inspiring Accountability methodology asserts that leaders are accountable for *contributing* toward an employee being **engaged** in their work, **receptive** to feedback, improvement and accountability, and **resourceful** toward results.

You are the Difference

Peter Senge, author of *The Fifth Discipline: The Art and Practice of Learning Organization* (2006), says that "People don't resist change; they resist being changed." Humans welcome change when expecting it will lead to a positive outcome. Inspiring leaders understand that inspiring change within employees starts by working with the brain's natural question: "What's in it for me?" Employees can easily be inspired to change when it's seen as helping fulfill greater potential and contribution, both a win for employees and their leaders.

However, humans resist change when they are uncertain or pessimistic about how it will affect their lives. If the brain perceives the demand for change originates from a leader's critical judgment or selfish preferences, the brain's natural defense will be resentment and resistance.

As a manager, you *are* entitled to demand changes and enforce subjective preferences — but *inspiring* change, where the drive sprouts from within the employee instead of externally, is a much more successful and enjoyable approach. Yes, you're authorized to assert the idea of "Because I said so," and while this heavy-handed approach will get the job done, it does not inspire a magnetic culture to attract lasting engagement or employee retention.

Trying to hold an employee accountable with a traditional approach is like trying to hold a stream accountable for changing how it flows. You can't yell at a stream to make it change, but you can remove and rearrange rocks and boulders in its path to "inspire" the stream to adapt and move in the direction you want.

When we want an employee to be more efficient, we remove boulders. When we want an employee to be more proactive and creative at problem solving, we help them accept what boulders are currently immovable and ask how they can work around them. Leaders can use Inspiring Accountability to help employees adapt around natural obstacles instead of ceasing effort when feeling stuck.

Leaders' Contributions Toward Employee Receptivity

Other chapters in this book dig deeper into the ways in which leaders can contribute positively to employee receptivity and feedback. Your ability to get results using Inspiring Accountability tools will depend on:

- How consistently you utilize the Results Model (Part II)
- How much your employees feel seen as contributing, competent, and important (Chapter 9)
- How well you're clearing (or not clearing) what's in the way (Results Model, Part II)
- How well you are using Engaging Leadership Language (Chapter 13)
- If you are triggering employees into self-protection mode (Chapter 11)
- How effectively you acknowledge and reward to fuel engagement (Part III)
- If, when providing negative feedback, you can go from a confrontation to a conversation (Chapter 13)

This book will continue to lay out the specific areas you can enhance to meet employee needs and get the very best effort from them. Keep in mind that *there is no right or wrong amount of effort from you.* There's only the result you want and what effort you want to contribute toward influencing and inspiring your team to better achieve that result.

With this specific mindset and the evaluation tools provided, you'll have the power and actionable clarity on how to inspire more accountability, employee engagement, and productivity. These will steadily and reliably increase your ability to get results from your team. Given the introduction to Inspiring Accountability, are you getting curious about what's in the way of getting the best results from your team? And more importantly, what's possible to get better results positively and productively? These two questions are the foundation of the Inspiring Accountability approach and Results Model, the ultimate accountability tool, up next.

Integration Questions:

1. How have you relied upon traditional accountability methods, like focusing on what went wrong or using guilt or shame to get an employee to care enough to improve? Have you valued results more than effort?

2. What outcomes were you hoping for in previous uses of traditional accountability methods? What were the results?

3. What possibilities are you most open to in letting go of traditional accountability methods and trying new Inspiring Accountability methods?

Key Take-Aways:

1. Traditional accountability is focused on problems of the past. It utilizes punishment, retribution, shame, and guilt.

2. A traditional-style postmortem of the problem is completely unnecessary to getting better results in the future.

3. Inspiring Accountability is focused on creating solutions in the future. It honors employee dignity by allowing natural consequences and letting an employee "make it right," thereby restoring dignity.

4. You do not need to punish an employee with the past to inspire them to improve their participation in the future.

5. Inspiring Accountability is *focused on results* and is designed to incentivize, reward, and hold accountable for an employee's effort and contribution toward results.

6. Effort is the only aspect fully within an employee's control.

7. Leaders are accountable for contributing toward employee engagement.

8. Leaders are also accountable for contributing toward employees being receptive to feedback, improvement, and accountability, and being resourceful toward results.

9. A lack of ownership often indicates a lack of empowerment.

10. Fear-based lessons that demand proclaiming incompetence do not keep employees engaged, receptive, or resourceful. It triggers shutting down and self-protection, decreasing all three of these three valuable goals.

PART II

THE RESULTS MODEL

The Ultimate Accountability Tool: The Results Model

"A good tool improves the way you work. A
great tool improves the way you think."

—JEFF DUNTEMANN

**This chapter introduces the ultimate accountability tool: the
Results Model, along with its leadership benefits and an overview of the steps.**

Now it's time to work with the Results Model, your ultimate accountability tool. It may sound like a bold statement, but I have not met
an accountability problem the Results Model and its corresponding
methodology can't improve.

The Results Model retrains the brain to think and communicate
in a way that effectively inspires the attitude, mindset, and behaviors
that get results and improves receptivity to accountability.

It converts Desired Results into clear expectations and concrete
success criteria. It will teach your employees' brains to take initiative
and be more comfortable making changes and receiving feedback.
Most importantly, it will prevent employees from feeling stagnated by
obstacles and, instead, to start imagining what's possible.

A brief overview of some of the leadership benefits of using the
Results Model include:

- **Engagement:** You are engaging employees in the process of contributing toward results. You are creating opportunities to improve the employee experience by infusing positive neurochemicals. You'll also have opportunities to fulfill an employee's need to be seen as contributing, competent, and important — explored further in Chapter 9 in the Hierarchy of Human Needs in the Workplace.

- **Receptivity:** The Results Model keeps employees' brains receptive by using non-triggering language, primarily in asking, "What's in the way?" This simple question provides a platform to investigate problem areas that keep employees' brains receptive to exploring, without the usual defensive responses to questions that insinuate, "What's wrong with *you*?" You're also creating a regular and expected pattern of receiving feedback, keeping employees more receptive because what's normalized through repetition feels safer to the protective part of the brain.

- **Resourcefulness:** Accountability conversations are known for being triggering, and as you now know, the rational part of the brain can go "offline," diminishing the capacity to generate ideas and contribute to solutions. The Results Model is designed to reduce triggering employees to help maintain resourcefulness.

- **Clear Expectations:** You will set clear expectations when articulating Desired Results by qualifying each with the **Accountability Anchor Conversion Checklist**. Clear expectations allow employees to know exactly how they can be successful and for what specifically they are accountable, which also maximizes neurochemical rewards and incentives.

- **Clear Path to Success:** You will explore, "What's in the way?" to proactively identify what can be improved upon or cleared to fast-track a result. Employees will also leave with a clear next step, so they may take action confidently and fully engage through the duration of the ask, task, or project.

- **Solution-Focused Thinking:** By asking, "Given what's in the way, what's possible?" leaders and employees no longer become mired in problems. As employees learn to ask themselves this question, they will more naturally look toward solutions until it becomes their regular way of thinking. You will establish a more balanced and cooperative relationship with your employees. You'll require and allow them to problem solve, reducing their dependency on you to problem solve for them. This dynamic empowers employees to take initiative, and this solution-focused mindset leads to continuously better results.

- **Regular Revisiting:** The Results Model is designed with built-in revisiting to regularly assess the impact of employee contribution, providing the opportunity to calibrate and adjust in order to continuously improve. The Results Model method of **Revisiting** lets the brain know, "This is important!" and worthy of extra attention. This connects to the concept of **Accountability Attention,** an increase in attention toward Desired Results simply because there is expected and non-negotiable Revisiting. The brain wants to avoid being seen as incompetent when this Revisiting happens, so it subconsciously flags the ask, task, or project as a priority and more willingly gives it extra attention. Regular Revisiting keeps Accountability Attention focused on the results, ensuring that it is inevitable to meet expectations.

- **Addressing Issues:** *What you don't address, you approve.* The Results Model makes it easier and more comfortable for you to address issues in a positive and productive approach.

- **Built-In Rewards System:** Though the focus is ultimately on getting results, it is the employee effort and contribution that ultimately achieves them. Busy managers find it challenging to know enough about what employees do each week to acknowledge employee effort satisfactorily. Now, you'll have a framework to learn the details about how employees are contributing. This will provide more opportunities to neurochemically reward and celebrate employees' efforts, keeping them expecting and experiencing positive feelings of engagement before, during, and after efforts. This is covered in more detail in Chapter 10.

- **Inevitable Results:** When followed consistently, the Results Model makes getting the results you need inevitable. With regular Revisiting and calibration on the biggest problem areas, it unpacks both overt and hidden obstacles to productivity and accountability. Be it related to behaviors, changes, outcomes, or goals, success is inevitable when Revisiting is unavoidable.

The Results Model encompasses the best of Inspiring Accountability's methodology. Taken in tandem with the models discussed in later chapters — such as the Hierarchy of Human Needs and the Engagement and Experience Loop — you will be provided with the proper tools to bring accountability to your team in a positive and productive way. These key concepts add substantial power and influence to what may appear as a simple model.

Introducing the Results Model

The Results Model consists of seven important steps that can be utilized for success in companies of two, 2,000, or 200,000.

Let's take a look at the Results Model, see it in action, and outline each step.

The Inspiring Accountability Results Model is a process to get better and better results from your team (**proactive accountability**), as well as a positive and productive method to respond when results aren't met (**responsive accountability**).

As a leader, you'll use the model to Revisit during **Results Conversations** on their own or as part of one-on-one meetings with your employees. You'll be able to use the informal method of asking, "What's in the way?" and "What's possible?" in every accountability conversation you have.

INSPIRING ACCOUNTABILITY IN THE WORKPLACE
RESULTS MODEL©
Your Ultimate Accountability Tool to Getting Results

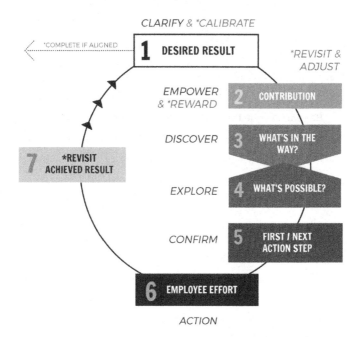

CLARIFY & *CALIBRATE

*COMPLETE IF ALIGNED

1 DESIRED RESULT

*REVISIT & ADJUST

EMPOWER & *REWARD — **2** CONTRIBUTION

DISCOVER — **3** WHAT'S IN THE WAY?

7 *REVISIT ACHIEVED RESULT

EXPLORE — **4** WHAT'S POSSIBLE?

CONFIRM — **5** FIRST / NEXT ACTION STEP

6 EMPLOYEE EFFORT

ACTION

Steps of the Results Model — A Quick Breakdown

Let's look at a brief summary of what's accomplished in the seven steps of the Results Model. Consider these an overview to see the big picture, and the following chapters will provide more detailed discussions of the concepts and how to implement the steps.

**Step 1 – *Clarify the Desired Result* as a Clear
Expectation with the Accountability Anchor Conversion
Checklist, helping you answer questions like:**

- What is the Desired Result for which the employee is accountable?
- How can you offer the Desired Result with **actionable clarity** (enough clarity for your employee to take action and exactly meet expectations)?
- How can you offer the Desired Result in a way that incentivizes the brain to engage and persevere until the result is achieved?
- **Benefits:** Vague Desired Results get vague achieved results. Clear expectations are required for employees to successfully meet those expectations. The Accountability Anchor Conversion Checklist creates a strong "anchor" to revisit and calibrate against, keeping employees closely aligned with the Desired Result.

**Step 2 — Empower and Reward Contribution,
helping you ask questions like:**

- "How can you contribute to successfully achieve the Desired Result?"
- **Benefits:** Empowers employees to create the plan of action because more initiative is taken when employees conceive strategies. This step removes the unnecessary burden of you generating the solutions. It also leaves accountability in the hands of the employee.

**Step 3 — Discover What's in the Way,
helping you ask questions like:**

- "What's in the way of getting the Desired Result?"
- "What *could* get in the way?"
- **Benefits:** Employees naturally think of what's in the way, often referred to as "excuses." Yet, without asking, you may not learn what they perceive as a barrier to successfully achieve the Desired Result. If you don't know what they perceive as a

barrier, you can't help clear the path, which is one of the most appropriate forms of leadership.

Step 4 — Explore What's Possible, helping you ask questions like:

- "Given what's in the way, what can possibly be cleared or improved upon?"
- "Given what's in the way, what's possible to still get the Desired Result?"
- **Benefits:** By moving quickly through what's in the way to what's possible, employees put their attention on solutions. They are no longer impeded by obstacles as they wait for you to problem-solve. Rather, they take more initiative and become accountable for the solution instead of the problem.

Step 5 — Confirm First or Next Action Step, by simply asking:

- "What will be your first action step toward achieving the result?"
- "Where can you start?"
- **Benefits:** A hesitancy on *how* to move forward creates hesitancy *to* move forward. Helping employees start this new effort with confidence, clarity, and optimism increases their engagement and chance of success (as you'll learn about in Part III on Inspiring Effort and Engagement).

Step 6 — The Employee Takes Action, Applying Effort Toward the Result:

- Up to this point, you have been 100% accountable for how you've set up your employees for success. Now that you've offered a clear expectation, the employee is responsible for their effort toward achieving it. You will learn more mindsets, tools, and strategies to help inspire effort and engagement in Part III.
- **Benefits:** Effort is what gets results and is required to fulfill a meaningful sense of contribution.

Step 7 — Revisiting the Achieved Result to Calibrate and Adjust.
We Revisit the steps of the Results Model, this time in a reflective format to uncover the post-effort experience of working toward the Desired Result and planning for the next round of effort:

- **Step 1 (Revisiting):** *Calibrate* how aligned the achieved result is to the Desired Result, answering how successfully the employee met expectations.
- **Step 2:** *Reward* contribution by asking, "How did you contribute successfully toward the Desired Result?" and acknowledging the effort.
- **Step 3:** *Discover* what got in the way.
- **Step 4:** *Explore* what's possible to get the result more efficiently next time (if achieved) or what's possible to still get the result now.
- Naturally adjust or further clarify any aspects of the Accountability Anchor Conversion Checklist, clear more of what's in the way, or contribute to greater possibilities as is deemed useful throughout the Revisiting process.
- **Step 5:** *Confirm* the next action step toward the Desired Result.
- **Step 6:** Employee executes effort toward Desired Result.
- **Step 7:** Continue the Revisiting process until the Desired Result is successfully or satisfactorily achieved.
- **Benefits:** Accountability always requires revisiting. Results Model Revisiting provides the process and feedback for an employee to more precisely and consistently achieve results. Because it will be done regularly, the employee comes to expect this accountability, improves engagement in the effort toward the Desired Result, maintains receptivity to the feedback and opportunities to improve, and becomes more resourceful toward seeing possibilities and creating solutions. The Results Model is a process that continues to cycle through until the Desired Result is achieved, making success inevitable.

Each step builds upon the other, creating a simple yet powerful framework for holding regular Results Conversations that keep attention on being accountable for their effort toward the Desired Result. In addition to what you've learned about neurochemicals, Part III on Inspiring Effort and Engagement offers more science-based strategies that confirm and increase the effectiveness of the Results Model process.

What Lies Ahead

In the next few chapters, we will cover a step-by-step breakdown of the Results Model that explores the concepts in-depth. The order of the steps *is* important, and it is recommended you read through each step in a linear order to parallel how you'll use this tool with your employees.

In true "teach a person to fish" spirit, the best part about the Results Model is that the questions you'll be asking your employees are the questions you're teaching them to ask themselves. Although you'll lead Results Conversations at first, soon your employees will expect to be asked, "What's possible?" and will then begin to explore solutions before presenting issues to you. You can create a results-oriented, obstacle-navigating team consistently engaged in imagining possibilities, enabling them to work through issues with less time and attention needed from you.

Integration Questions:

1. Can you think of any behaviors from your employees that you have neglected to address (and have thereby been approving)?

2. Can you remember a project where you failed to offer clear expectations? What was the result?

3. Given the benefits shared so far, which employee or project do you imagine would benefit most from using the Results Model?

Key Takeaways

1. The Results Model is the ultimate accountability tool, offering actionable clarity through a clear expectation, empowering employees to take confident action, and offering you a positive way to hold employees accountable for their effort toward a Desired Result.

2. Accountability always requires revisiting. The Results Model offers a practical format for leaders to reference an expectation in a way that keeps employees inspired and engaged to keep working toward it.

3. What you don't address, you approve. The Results Model will help you address issues with a more productive a positive approach.

4. The Results Model is a process that continues to cycle through until the Desired Result is achieved, making success inevitable.

5. The Results Model can be used exactly as is, or the foundational components can be used in less formal Results Conversations.

6. The Results Model is effective for companies and teams of any size.

7. The Results Model offers you questions to inspire accountability while inherently coaching your employees what to ask themselves.

CHAPTER 5

The Results Model: Clarify the Desired Result

"Without an anchor, we can be drifted to any shore."

—LAILAH GIFTY AKITA,

THINK GREAT: BE GREAT! (2014)

In this chapter, we'll learn the important process of using the Accountability Anchor Conversion Checklist to create clear expectations that meet Inspiring Accountability's criteria.

The **Accountability Anchor Conversion Checklist** makes it easy to clarify Desired Results into expectations explicit enough for an employee to exactly achieve.

Many leaders' directives are too vaguely phrased for employees to achieve results efficiently and effectively. Julie Dirksen offers a relevant example in her book, *Design for How People Learn* (2015) when she states, "It's like saying 'Meet me in Africa.' It's a destination, but it doesn't help you book a flight."

Getting the exact results you want begins with establishing actionably clear expectations. Let's learn the Inspiring Accountability process for creating clear and effective expectations for your team.

The Results Model — Clarify the Desired Result
Using the Accountability Anchor Conversion Process

The Accountability Anchor Conversion process creates a clearly defined Desired Result that an employee works toward and by which a leader calibrates the employee's success. The converted Desired Result becomes an effective accountability tool. A leader can then effectively "anchor" the employee to a clear expectation, closing the distance between the actual result and Desired Result.

Much like a ship at sea, the Desired Result keeps the employee tethered to the ask, task, or project and is a clear point of reference for what is expected and what defines success.

Desired Results with vague success criteria lead to equally vague results. If you want specific results that meet your exact expectations, you start by clearly defining these expectations for your employees. Employees feel it's unfair to be held accountable for a missed result if they misunderstood an expectation that could have been clarified.

Without an anchor, employees can drift, and drifting employees don't know if they've made progress. Employees should know how well they are meeting expectations to remain incentivized to engage. Desired Results are only strong "accountability anchors" when they are clear enough to calibrate specifically how far an employee is from where you want them to be. Employees should always be able to return to the anchor when they need clarity and direction, and you will return to the anchor to keep them accountable and on track. The goal is to create a Desired Results so clear that, when used in the Results Model, it becomes inevitable that an employee will successfully achieve it.

To inspire accountability (and engagement), employees must know the following four components, all of which the Accountability Anchor Conversion Checklist clearly addresses with actionable clarity:

- What you expect
- Why the ask or improvement is worth doing
- What details will ensure expectations are exactly met
- How to start

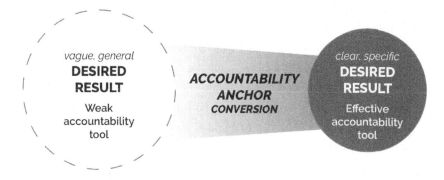

vague, general
DESIRED RESULT
Weak accountability tool

ACCOUNTABILITY ANCHOR CONVERSION

clear, specific
DESIRED RESULT
Effective accountability tool

Once you have mastered establishing strong accountability anchors, you will create a more productive and rewarding environment that saves everyone time and energy.

The Accountability Anchor Conversion Checklist

Take a moment to think of a current challenge you'd like an employee to improve upon or Desired Result you'd like to see an employee achieve. Use this as a working example as we go through the following process to clarify your Desired Result into an effective accountability tool, starting with this overview checklist:

- ☑ **1.** Identify the Desired Result
- ☑ **2.** Is there a clear moment of achievement?
- ☑ **3.** Is it achievable within three months or less?
- ☑ **4.** Is it stated as what you want (not as stopping what you don't want)?
- ☑ **5.** What are the Actionably Clear Expectations and Specifications?
- ☑ **6.** What is the contribution context?
- ☑ **7.** Is it confirmed in writing?

1. Identify the Desired Result

Whether it's an ask, task, project, or behavior, start with the Desired Result you want the employee to achieve. For your employee, the Desired Result is a positive synonym for a new expectation or request for change.

Start applying one of your real asks to get the most out of reading this chapter. In addition to your working example, let's walk through a challenge for Mary, a manager, who has been struggling to hold her employee, Mario, accountable for showing up to meetings late.

Mary's Desired Result is for Mario to "stop being late to meetings." Let's watch the evolution as we go through the Accountability Anchor Conversion Checklist to qualify this as an Inspiring Accountability-approved request.

Desired Result:
Stop being late to meetings.

2. Is there a clear moment of achievement?

How will you know your ask has been precisely fulfilled? How will your employee know he or she has successfully met the expectation, worthy of acknowledgment and neurochemical celebration?

Take, for example, smart watches and activity trackers. These capitalize on the value of tracking something specific because it feels good to know you fulfilled your chosen metric. "Moving more" doesn't have a clear success indicator — but getting in 10,000 steps a day does. Imagine the difference in getting a notification of, "Congratulations, you moved more today!" versus, "You completed 10,000 steps!" Clear expectations facilitate clear moments of achievement, which offer the best neurochemical rewards.

A Desired Result often starts as something general, like taking more initiative, being more detail-oriented, demonstrating a value, or not being late to meetings. Stated as such, these Desired Results don't offer an opportunity for clear completion, creating issues where:

- Desired Results are slower to achieve and less accurate.
- There's low accountability because there isn't a clear anchor to compare and calibrate against.
- A clear sense of accomplishment is less available, therefore limiting engagement-incentivizing neurochemical rewards.

A clear moment of achievement allows for more effective progress tracking, greater reward and motivation, and a clearer reference to adjust habits and patterns.

To determine a clear moment of achievement, you can ask yourself:

- Where is the first place I'd like to see evidence of this success?
- How will my employee and I both know the expectation has been exactly met?
- How can I be more specific about what successful completion looks like?
- What definitions are being assumed or would benefit from clearer definition?

Let's loop back to Mary and Mario.

Mary must clarify the moment in which Mario will know that he has successfully met expectations of being "on time" to meetings.

To do this, Mary will clarify any preconceptions that would benefit from further definition. Different people define "not being late" with slightly different meanings. Both Mary and Mario benefit from Mary being precise with her expectation.

Mary decides that Mario being "on time" means that he is seated, prepared, and ready for the meeting to begin when the clock strikes the calendared start time. This eliminates Mario from disruptively rushing in at 9 a.m. when what Mary really wants is everyone to be ready to start at 9 a.m.

For Mario, it may be understandable that arriving exactly at 9 a.m. would meet expectations. If he made the effort to do this and was met with frustration because Mary actually wanted him settled in his seat at 9 a.m., it would result in triggering disengagement because he put in effort and thought he met expectations.

Mary's clearly defined Desired Result becomes: Mario is in his seat and ready to begin at the meeting time.

Note, she is not micromanaging Mario by requesting he be there five minutes before, which would disempower him from judging how long it will take to be ready. Filling in "the how" for an employee is different than providing a Desired Result. Providing the micromanaging "how" does not inspire accountability. In Mario's case, it would likely leave him feeling punished as he sits in the conference room for five minutes until the meeting start-time. Mary isn't telling him *how* she thinks he could be successful; she's simply clarifying the result she wants, and he's empowered to discover his "how" as he puts effort toward the Desired Result.

Clarified Desired Result:
In your seat, prepared, and ready for the meeting to begin at the calendared start time.

3. Is it achievable within three months or less?

If successfully achieving the Desired Result is going to take longer than three months, it does not qualify as an effective Desired Result. Once the timeframe edges out past about three months, it becomes too long term and not urgent enough for the brain to warrant the same effort as more "important" priorities. Anticipated neurochemical rewards are too distant to be incentivizing, so you create a dull Desired Result.

Luckily, this is a simple step with a quick answer: can your Desired Result be successfully completed within three months?

If not, ask yourself questions like:
- What's the soonest indication I could see that my employee is making progress?
- What is the first evidence of success or sign of progress that can be completed within three months?

In the case of Mary and Mario, the answer to this question is clearly, "Yes, this is achievable within three months." If the answer had been "No," she would have simply asked herself, "What is the first aspect or evidence of success that can be completed within three months?" until she found a success milestone for Mario to begin working toward as a step toward the longer-term result.

Desired Result Qualifies as Achievable —>
Desired Result Remains the Same
In your seat, prepared, and ready for the meeting
to begin at the calendared start time.

4. Is the Desired Result framed as what you want (not as stopping what you don't want)?

Stating what you *don't* want is rarely as helpful as stating what you *do* want.

Say you're pressed for time but want to bring in lunch for your team to celebrate a big win today. You quickly ask your team what they want, and you hear:

- "I don't want pizza. I just had pizza last night."
- "I don't want burritos because I'm trying to watch my calories."
- "I don't want to go to that Greek place again. I didn't think it was that good."
- "I don't want sushi because it's not filling enough."

It is more helpful and efficient to state what is wanted. **To make sure your Desired Result is stated as what you want, ask yourself:**

- Is what I'm asking for reflecting the result, behavior, or change I want to see? Or, is it a result, behavior, or change I want to stop?

Before starting the Accountability Anchor Conversion Checklist, Mary's Desired Result, "Stop being late to meetings," stated a behavior she didn't want to see. As we dug deeper, we crafted a positive Desired Result. Now Mario knows exactly what's expected of him, "Be in your seat, prepared, and ready for the meeting to being at the calendared start time," and his brain is focused on demonstrating the desired behavior. The brain — particularly the powerful subconscious — thrives off what it focuses on, and Mary wants Mario to focus on the positive direction toward the desired behavior.

Desired Result Remains the Same
In your seat, prepared, and ready for the meeting
to begin at the calendared start time.

5. What are the Actionably Clear Expectations and Specifications (ACES)?

If an employee is missing specified details on deliverables, you can create an **Actionably Clear Expectations and Specifications (ACES)** checklist.

ACES provide a clear reference sheet for the exact Desired Result requirements needed. ACES take into account the details, format, and specifications necessary to successfully meet expectations.

Successful ACES eliminate an, "I didn't know that!" excuse and prevent unproductive efforts. Leaders can maintain an ACES checklist to have in meetings to quickly evaluate details, especially if important specifications are forgotten from time to time. Much like a job aid or requirements checklist, ACES can simplify expectations even on the busiest days, making it easier for employees to be successful.

Your ACES list may be long, short, or not needed, depending on the specific Desired Result. ACES may be technical in nature or more behavioral. The included specs may vary from role to role.

ACES proactively remind you and your employee to include what's needed the first time, ensuring that you don't hear during Revisiting, "I didn't know I needed to include that," or "I didn't know that's what you wanted."

To discover helpful ACES, you can ask yourself:
• What does the employee need to include to be successful?

- Is there anything they've often forgotten to include or to be in compliance with?
- Is there anything I tend to forget to include that would be useful to ask for proactively?
- What else will I need to see from the employee to be 100% satisfied they've met my expectations?
- What words have I already included that could be better defined?

For each position or department, you can maintain and grow an ACES checklist to quickly scan for what needs to be included with each Desired Result. This ensures everyone is on the same page and avoids miscommunication. There's no need to reinvent ACES for each ask, task, project, or behavior if there is often overlap.

Here are some possible ACES that you could consider providing:

- Deliverable date
- Other indicator dates and deadlines
- Format, what to include/ensure (for example: Excel spreadsheet with columns, supporting data, printable to one page)
- What to exclude
- What rules or regulations must be adhered to or checked
- What must be included per client contract
- How it's delivered (for example: emailed, presented with PowerPoint, written, in a meeting and who will attend the meeting)
- Restrictions or things to avoid
- What to double-check before submitting (like if a content writer often confuses "to" and "too")
- Whatever has previously been incorrect or forgotten

Note, including what is required is not the same as how to do it. Mary, in this case, would resist her inclination to share her ideas on how Mario can be on time because the expectation is simply that he will be on time. Employees are accountable for "the how," and leaders are accountable for empowering employees to discover it themselves.

Mary quickly checks to see if she's missing any exact requirements Mario will need to successfully meet expectations. In meetings, Mario sometimes brings project updates, a notepad, and a pen — but when he's rushing, he tends to forget at least one of these items. Mary realizes "ready" could be better defined, so she adjusts her Desired Result to include: "Ready means with project updates, notepad, and pen" as ACES required for him to meet her expectations.

Sometimes you may not have any ACES, other times you'll have many. The quantity is not important. What's important is that you've reviewed this prompt to ensure you've set up your employee with the requirements needed for them to efficiently direct their effort toward your Desired Result. This accountability anchor is now starting to have some weight to it.

Desired Result Remains the Same; ACES get added

In your seat, ready for the meeting to begin at the calendared start time. ACES: Bring project updates, notepad, and pen.

6. What is the contribution context?

If you have ever been irritated by the phrase from an authority figure, "Because I said so," then you probably understand that it is not the ideal way to inspire engagement toward Desired Results. We are more incentivized to invest effort and engage in required action when we understand the impact of our efforts.

Providing **contribution context** intentionally and proactively communicates why an ask, task, project, or behavior is important. This sets the stage for employees to be seen as contributing meaningfully, which naturally incentivizes engagement.

To identify the contribution context, you can ask yourself:

- Why does the Desired Result matter beyond personal preference? What is important about the Desired Result? To whom or what does it meaningfully contribute?
- What is the negative impact of not having the Desired Result currently? To whom, what, when, how or where does this negatively contribute?
- What is the expected positive impact of having the Desired Result fulfilled? To whom, what, when, how, or where will it positively contribute?
- How will fulfilling this help the employee meet his or her need to be seen as contributing, competent, and important?

Let's look again at Mario. To inspire him to be on time and to engage his brain's attention in this commitment, Mary would benefit from sharing why it matters and what the impact is in the workplace.

To complete the Accountability Anchor Conversion Checklist, Mary comes up with the contribution context to include when she presents this new Desired Result.

Final Desired Result; ACES and Contribution Context included:

"Mario, I'd like you to work on being on time to meetings. This matters because you are an important contributor, and I want your input in meetings. Because our team is busier than ever, I'm going to start meetings on time, and I don't want you to miss anything. Although coming in late is mildly disruptive, more importantly, I need your input and so does the team. I don't want you to miss your opportunity to contribute or our opportunity to get your valued input.

I'm asking you be seated, ready to begin meetings with your project updates, notepad, and pen at the calendared start time."

How wonderful and non-triggering is that? It took less than 60 seconds to deliver this significantly more effective ask. Who wouldn't be inspired to show up on time when presented with this context?

Mario will not be triggered with this new behavior request, and, if anything, will feel inspired to make this change, staying receptive to this new expectation and resourceful toward how to meet it. He also begins this change feeling important and valued, which inspires greater action than feeling criticized or demeaned.

First, Mary introduced the ask with the quick version of the positively stated Desired Result, then she explains why it matters. Mary saves the clear ask with ACES for last. This order helps prime the brain to first hear the context of the new request (what to expect), why it matters, and then what exactly is involved.

Much like warming up a car on a cold winter day before you drive it, you want to prime the brain's receptivity before giving a detailed expectation. This expectation, after all, is a request for change, and when abruptly launched, can easily trigger defensiveness and close-off receptiveness. The contribution context adds warmth to all the mechanics that can more easily guide the car in the right direction. Sure, you can turn on a car in freezing temperatures and jolt it into action, but you might do some damage in the process. We want this car, and our employees' engagement, receptivity, and resourcefulness, to run smoothly.

You are now ready to present an effective accountability anchor, and, pending our final requirement of also providing this new expectation in writing, you are ready to enter into the Results Conversation, up next in Chapter 6.

7. Is it confirmed in writing?

Having the Desired Result and it's corresponding contribution context written down is *imperative* to accountability. When the Desired Result is in writing, it serves as an inarguable agreement. Offering the new expectation in writing constructs a clear success milestone, completes the anchoring of this precise expectation, and offers something for you and the employee to point to, revisit, and calibrate toward.

As you'll learn in Chapter 8: Using the Results Model, the employee will maintain a Results List of the few Desired Results they're actively working toward. This will inherently be in a written format, digital or otherwise, so that all the specifications and expectations are clearly available for you both to refer to at any point.

As you began learning in the Chapter 2 on Neurochemicals, specific achievements in writing also give us something to ceremoniously cross off, offering more neurochemical rewards than those just remembered. Goals that are vague, half-remembered, or misconstrued provide negligible neurochemical incentive and reward.

Troubleshooting: "Why didn't my employee just ask if they didn't know?"

While employees ideally would feel comfortable asking questions until they are perfectly clear on all points, there are many reasons — like protecting competency — that employees won't lead the clarity conversation. Often, they simply don't know what they don't know.

If you have an employee who isn't good at asking clarifying questions, rest assured that with the Results Model consistently applied, you'll create an environment more conducive for employees to ask questions. In addition, the components of the Results Model begin retraining their brains, and yours, to think about questions more proactively.

Stay with it, and lead the way!

Accountability Anchor Conversion Checklist — A Quick Reference

Use this section as a reference guide to convert a Desired Result to an effective accountability tool, and soon this process will occur more naturally with very little time and effort.

☑ **1. Identify the Desired Result**
- What do you want?
- What do you want to be different?
- What will it look like when it's different?

☑ **2.Is there a clear moment of achievement? What is the clear moment when the employee will know "I did it!" and where you can offer "You did it!"?**
- Where is the first place an employee can see evidence of this success?
- How will my employee and I both know the expectation has been exactly met?
- How can I be more specific about what successful completion looks like?
- What definitions are being assumed or would benefit from a clearer definition?
- Remember, this is clarifying what it looks like when the result is fulfilled, not how to get there.

☑ **3. Is the Desired Result achievable within three months or less?**
- What's the soonest indication I could see that progress has been made?
- What is the first evidence of success or sign of progress that can be completed within three months?

☑ **4. Is the Desired Result stated as what you want (not as stopping what you don't want)?**

- Is what I'm asking for reflecting the positive result, behavior, or change I want to see versus want to stop?

☑ **5. What are the Actionably Clear Expectations and Specifications (ACES)?**

- What does the employee need to remember to include to be successful?
- Is there anything they've often forgotten to include or be in compliance with?
- Is there anything I tend to forget to include that would be useful to point out proactively?

☑ **6. What is the contribution context?**

- Why does the Desired Result matter beyond personal preference? What is important about the Desired Result? To whom or what does it meaningfully contribute?
- What is the negative impact of not having the Desired Result currently? To whom, what, when, how, or where does it negatively contribute?
- What is the expected positive impact of having the Desired Result fulfilled? To whom, what, when, how, or where will it positively contribute?
- How will fulfilling this help the employee fulfill the need to be seen as contributing, competent, and important?

☑ **7. Is it confirmed in writing?**

- Add to their Results List or offer in accessible and agreed upon writing.

Congratulations, you've upgraded your expectation to a clear Desired Result!

As mentioned earlier, this chapter is meant to be a deep dive into the mechanics of converting Desired Results into effective accountability tools. Future iterations of this step (Step 1) will only take a few minutes as you become accustomed to easily clarifying expectations.

If you followed along with your own example, now you're ready to share a clear expectation with your employee to complete Step 1, and proceed with Steps 2 to 5, all covered in the next chapter.

Integration Questions:

1. How quickly can you convert a Desired Result to an effective accountability tool using the Accountability Anchor Conversion Checklist? If you didn't already go through the process with your personal working example, make the most of what you've learned by applying the checklist now or schedule time to go through it.

2. What ways can you see the Actionably Clear Expectations and Specifications (ACES) checklist work for you and your employee?

Key Take-Aways:

1. The Inspiring Accountability Results Model is both a process to get better and better results from your team (with proactive accountability), and a method to incorporate positive and productive approaches when results aren't met (with responsive accountability).

2. The first step of the Results Model involves crafting a strong "accountability anchor" that will clearly answer four key components for your employee:
   - What you expect
   - Why the ask or improvement is worth doing
   - What details will ensure expectations are exactly met
   - How to begin

3. Accountability always requires revisiting, and Desired Results, qualified through the Accountability Anchor Conversion Checklist, are what you will use the Results Model to Revisit.

4. Clear expectations keep employees on target, on track, and set up for success every time. Employees come back to this anchored Desired Result when they need clarity, and you'll regularly revisit it to calibrate feedback until it is achieved.

5. Actionably Clear Expectations and Specifications (ACES) checklists can be useful to maintain if you have frequent missed deliverable specifications or easily forget to provide direction on specifications.

6. The Accountability Anchor Conversion Checklist to convert Desired Results into effective accountability tools includes (full guide provided on pages 92-93):

    - ☑ **1.** Identify the Desired Result
    - ☑ **2.** Is there a clear moment of achievement?
    - ☑ **3.** Is it achievable within three months or less?
    - ☑ **4.** Is it stated as what you want (not as stopping what you don't want)?
    - ☑ **5.** What are the Actionably Clear Expectations and Specifications?
    - ☑ **6.** What is the contribution context?
    - ☑ **7.** Is it confirmed in writing?

7. Some facts about vague Desired Results:

    - Vague goals produce slower, less accurate results.
    - Vague goals have low accountability because there isn't a clear anchor to compare and calibrate toward.
    - Vague goals offer fewer neurochemical rewards because you only experience neurochemicals when you clearly accomplish or successfully contribute to something.

CHAPTER 6

The Results Model: Requesting a New Result

> "Motivation is what gets you started.
> Habit is what keeps you going."
> —JIM ROHN

In this chapter, we'll be covering:

- Entering the Results Conversation, a continuation of the Results Model process
- The three core accountability questions to empower contribution, discover what's in the way, and explore what's possible
- The necessity of confirming next action steps
- Putting it all together with an example conversation assigning a new Desired Result

Now that you've qualified your Desired Result as an **accountability anchor**, you're ready to bring it forward to your employee in the **Results Conversation**. The Results Conversation is dedicated time in one-on-one meetings to conversationally present a new Desired Result or revisit an active one, using the Results List to guide the conversation. It can also be used in teams, which is addressed in Chapter 8.

The Results Conversation is where we begin to reframe how we discuss and approach Desired Results in an effort to create a habitual way of thinking about problems and solutions.

But how do you present requests for improvement in a way that maintains engagement, receptiveness, and resourcefulness? How can you help your employees to be inspired and motivated to get results?

To answer that, here is the conversational part of engaging your employee to work toward this new Desired Result.

Introducing the Results Model
Process for the First Time

If you are new to using the Results Model and having Results Conversations with your employee, it's important to acknowledge that you're trying a new process. I recommend you share that you're optimistic that this new process will be more supportive to your employee's success in meeting expectations.

Deliver the introduction in a way that feels most authentic to you, ensuring you include:

- An overview of the process and the Results Model
- Details you think your employee will want to know
- How they will benefit from the process (much like contribution context)

You can omit describing the Accountability Anchor Conversion process since creating an "accountability anchor" is internal speak and an internal tool for leaders, not employees. In addition:

- Share your optimism to set a positive expectation (being stern or too serious will communicate this is more punitive than positive)
- Leave time for questions and conversation
- Keep employees receptive to trying it, maintaining you want to try the new process for, say, three months, and then determine together if it's been useful

INSPIRING ACCOUNTABILITY IN THE WORKPLACE
RESULTS MODEL©
Your Ultimate Accountability Tool to Getting Results

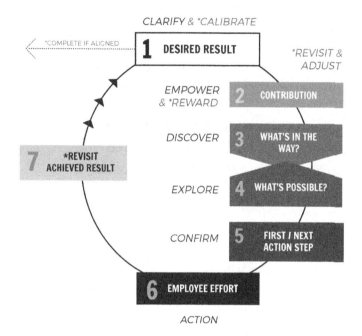

CLARIFY & *CALIBRATE

*COMPLETE IF ALIGNED

1 DESIRED RESULT

*REVISIT & ADJUST

EMPOWER & *REWARD **2** CONTRIBUTION

DISCOVER **3** WHAT'S IN THE WAY?

7 *REVISIT ACHIEVED RESULT

EXPLORE **4** WHAT'S POSSIBLE?

CONFIRM **5** FIRST / NEXT ACTION STEP

6 EMPLOYEE EFFORT

ACTION

For sample ways to introduce the Results Model process with your employees, visit www.inspiringaccountability.com/bookresources.

The Results Model: Step 1 —
Share the New Desired Result

Now that you've upgraded the result you want through the **Accountability Anchor Conversion Checklist**, you're ready to present it to your employee.

The thoughtfulness and intentionality you've brought to clarifying the Desired Result is going to make it easy to present this new ask while keeping your employee receptive to the change and clear on how to succeed.

Share the "ask" as respectfully as you can, similar to how it was outlined at the end of the previous chapter. Be sure to include that valuable contribution context to answer why it matters to your employee to inspire instead of enforce the change.

Although the "ask" is actually a non-negotiable expectation, a conversational tone is important to keep your employees engaged, receptive, and resourceful, and to keep their dignity intact.

The Results Model: Step 2 — Empower by asking, "How can you contribute to successfully achieve the Desired Result?"

To initiate the conversation, you'll share the Desired Result with its corresponding contribution context, like Mary did with Mario in the previous chapter. Now what?

To keep the focus on contribution and effort, we'll use the first of the three core accountability questions: *How can you contribute to successfully achieve the Desired Result?* Some variations to how you can ask this question include:

- "What can you do to successfully contribute to the result?"
- "What do you see yourself needing to do to achieve the result?"
- "What can you do differently to more easily achieve this result?"
- "What ideas do you have to make it easier to successfully achieve this result?"
- "What will you need to do differently to remember to [make the change necessary to achieve the result]?"

The value of these questions is that you're requiring your employee to brainstorm their contribution so that:

- You are not unnecessarily burdened with creating solutions.
- You are not micromanaging or disempowering them by providing the solutions.

- They are focused on their contribution instead of expecting others to be accountable.
- They are initiating the ideas, inclining employees to put more effort toward ideas they originate.

One can't be productively held accountable for something they were not empowered to do. Therefore, these questions empower employees to determine "the how," so they can take action.

In some cases, asking how one will contribute is unnecessary or redundant, but asking *what they will need to do differently to remember* will be valuable. Say, for instance, a social media manager is forgetting to post the required amount of posts each week. The original question: "How can you contribute to successfully achieve the result?" will likely get a flat response of: "Post articles to LinkedIn." This answer, however, doesn't get to the root issue of what needs to change. Instead, asking: "What will you need to do differently to remember to post four times a week?" will get an answer that will drive necessary change.

In our example of Mario being on time to meetings, Mary using this question will help Mario discover for himself how he can be successful.

In this case, Mary would ask Mario something like, "What do you think you'll have to do differently to be on time to meetings?" When Mario discovers for himself what could help him be on time, he will create the most accurate and meaningful options. The accountability is with Mario to determine "how" and requires him to ask for support or resources if he needs them.

This contribution question is often missing when I hear leaders complain about employees not taking ownership, initiative, or accountability. It indicates that the employee isn't coming up with the how and instead is purely executing. It indicates the employee isn't being engaged in a two-sided conversation about the Desired Result or how to achieve it. And above all, it indicates an employee is not feeling empowered in their role. When you ask how the employee can contribute, you are empowering them to take the lead in the solution and own their contribution, strengthening accountability.

From a neuroscience perspective, using this question requires the brain to undergo the following operations:

- The brain is engaged in active thought instead of passive listening.
- The brain puts attention on what's needed instead of waiting for others to change or solve it.
- The brain processes what proactive changes are necessary before they're needed, dramatically increasing the chance of practicing (and repeating) the new behavior.
- The brain starts to expect success, which has a massive impact on how we begin a task (you'll learn more about this in Chapters 10 and 12).

"How can you contribute to successfully achieve the Desired Result?" is the first of the three core accountability questions, and it naturally prepares the brain for the next question: "So, what's in the way?"

The Results Model: Step 3 — Discover "What's in the Way?"

Competing priorities. Not enough resources. Confusion of team roles. These are some of the culprits we confront in Results Model Step 3: Exploring What's in the Way.

When presenting a new Desired Result, we should proactively ask:

- "What's in the way of getting the result?"
- "What could get in the way of getting the result?"

Asking, "What's in the way?" in the present, proactive ("What *could* get in the way?"), and later the reflective ("What *got* in the way?") formats is, in part, about helping employees be heard. A *Forbes* (2019) article, "10 Timely Statistics About the Connection Between Employee Engagement and Wellness," cites, "Employees who feel their voice is heard are 4.6 times more likely to feel empowered to perform their best work."

Additionally, this question avoids using triggering questions equivalent to, "What's wrong with you that you haven't already done this?" or the rhetorical, "Is there any reason you can't get this done?"

Most importantly, "What's in the way?" is designed to elicit honest answers without triggering the employee to feel defensive, maintaining engagement, receptiveness, and resourcefulness.

"What's in the way?" is impersonal and assumes there are many reasons outside of one's own effort that can be an obstacle. Acknowledging that outside circumstances often get in the way more than one's competence maintains an employee's dignity and keeps employees receptive to improvement and resourceful while problem solving.

Leading your employees to discover "What's in the way?" identifies what can be *improved upon* or *cleared* to get to the result more easily and efficiently. What once seemed like accountability-avoiding excuses become results-getting gold. Once you hear what your employee perceives as obstacles, you can help the employee clear them, avoid them, or proceed despite them.

This question also crucially *acknowledges* what's in the way that can't be changed and that will remain a challenge for the employee. Often leaders are afraid to acknowledge what's in the way, like lack of resources or under-performing peers, because they think it will leave an employee free to avoid accountability. But with the Results Model, the opposite is true.

Excuses sound like avoiding accountability, but they actually let you know what you need to account for to successfully get the result. Excuses are like helpful road signs. They tell you what's ahead, so you can better choose how to get where you're going.

An excuse only remains a barrier to results when left unspoken. Only when what's in the way is brought to light can we ask what's possible. From here, excuses become an essential part of navigating the solution. Once expressed, excuses become a tangible tool to incorporate into the solution, either through removing, reducing, or adapting to what's in the way.

The more "excuses" you hear, the more you can clear the path or innovate solutions. Your simple acknowledgment of the obstacles can prevent your employee from feeling resentful or underappreciated. Simply stating, "I know this is going to be challenging considering [what's in the way], and I know you'll give it all you've got! Let's see what's possible," sets up your employee for success.

The Results Model: Step 4 — Explore "What's Possible?"

Employees and leaders too often get stuck on what's in the way. It's easy to focus on what's not working, creating loops and stories that stall productivity. It's as if an obstacle is reason enough to cease effort. However, after the obstacles have been revealed, the "What's possible?" follow-up questions prompt exploring innovative solutions despite what's in the way.

To support your employee with clearing the path to results, you'll ask and explore:

- Given what's in the way, what can possibly be cleared or improved upon?

Then, given what's remaining, to help your employee move from what's in the way to what's possible, you'll ask your employee:

- "Given [what's in the way], what's possible to [still get the Desired Result]?"

Some variations include:

- Given what's in the way, what else could be done?
- Given that big challenge, where's the first place you can start?
- Given that [this] didn't work, how else could we get the result?

- Given that you already feel like you have too much to do, what kind of commitment can you make to still contribute [to the Desired Result]?

Once "What's possible?" becomes ingrained as a response to an obstacle, your employee will automatically stop focusing on what's in the way and start moving toward possibilities.

Here's where traditional accountability, typically focused on past problems, differs greatly from Inspiring Accountability. By focusing on "What's possible?" the employee can begin problem solving. Letting your employees explore "What's possible?" acknowledges that the circumstances may not be perfect, but they're still expected to find innovative ways to keep working toward the Desired Result.

The Results Model: Step 5 — Confirm First Action Step is Clear

Hesitancy on *how* to move forward creates hesitancy *to* move forward. If the brain feels uncertain about the first action step, it can trigger anxiety about feeling incompetent. This **Anxious Effort** happens often and easily, and we escape that anxiety by switching to a task that has more actionable clarity. This natural human response is often dubbed as "procrastination" or "trouble focusing," and you'll learn more about it in Chapter 12: Inspiring Optimal Effort.

Additionally, how an employee begins a new task has a significant impact on how they engage and the likelihood of meeting expectations, which you'll learn about in Part III.

To set your employee up to easily engage in this new ask, task, or project, confirm they know the first action step they must take, so they begin their effort with confidence, clarity, and optimism.

To confirm the first action step, simply ask:

- "What will be your first action step toward achieving the result?"
- "Given [what's in the way], where can you start?"

Depending on if this is your first round with the Results Model or another regular check-in with the same Desired Result, asking your employee to confirm their first or next action step makes it easier for them to engage in the task with confidence and success.

The Results Model: Step 6 —
Employee Takes Action (Executes Effort)

Action and effort are in the middle of the Results Model, and represent the main step for which employees are accountable. Simply, this is where the employee takes action and applies effort between your one-on-one meetings.

This is the effort that you will then revisit, calibrate, and adjust in Step 7: Revisiting.

Integration Questions:

1. How can you become comfortable asking the three core accountability questions:
   - "How can you contribute to successfully achieve the Desired Result?"
   - "What's in the way?"
   - "Given what's in the way, what's possible?"

2. What could get in the way of using the Results Model given what you've learned so far?

3. Given what's in the way, what would make it possible to begin using the Results Model once you've completed reading this section?

Key Take-Aways:

1. One can't be productively held accountable for something they weren't empowered to do.

2. Step 1 of the Results Model is **Share the new Result.**

3. Step 2 is **Empower by asking about contribution:**

- "What can you do to successfully contribute to the result?"
- "What do you see yourself needing to do to achieve the result?"
- "What can you do differently to more easily achieve this result?"
- "What ideas do you have to make it easier to successfully achieve this result?"
- "What will you need to do differently to remember to [make the change necessary to achieve the result]?"

4. Step 3 is **Discover what's in the way:**

- "What's in the way of getting the result?"
- "What could be in the way of getting the result?"

5. Step 4 is **Explore what's possible:**

- "Given what's in the way, what can possibly be cleared or improved upon?"
- "Given what's in the way, what's possible [to still get the Desired Result]?"
- "Given that big challenge, where's the first place you can start?"
- "Given that [this] didn't work, how else could we get the result?"
- "Given that you already feel like you have too much to do, what kind of commitment can you make to still contribute [to the Desired Result]?"

6. Step 5: is **Confirm first action step is clear:**

- "What will be your first action step toward achieving the result?"
- "Given [what's in the way], where can you start?"

7. Once expressed, excuses become a tangible tool to incorporate into the solution, either through removing, reducing, or adapting to what's in the way.

8. Hesitancy on *how* to move forward creates hesitancy *to* move forward.

CHAPTER 7

The Results Model: Revisiting, Calibrating, and Adjusting

> "We are what we repeatedly do. Excellence,
> then, is not an act, but a habit."
>
> —ARISTOTLE

In this chapter, we'll be covering Step 7 of the Results Model: Revisiting, Calibrating, and Adjusting an active Desired Result. We will explore:

- Why Revisiting is necessary to inspire accountability
- How to Revisit an active Desired Result using the Results Model
- Accountability Attention and how the brain decides where to direct attention
- Alternative Results Model language that inspires possibility

Accountability always requires revisiting, and Results Model Revisiting is what solidifies a habit of excellent effort and productive **Possibility Thinking**, when the brain is retrained to think more about what's possible than what's in the way. Before going through the Revisiting process, let's clearly understand the value of Revisiting.

The Neuroscientific Reason to Revisit Employee Effort

Revisiting is the act of using the Results Model format to follow up on a previously introduced Desired Result. A leader specifically helps the employee Revisit the impact of his or her contribution toward a result to calibrate, adjust, and continuously improve.

During Revisiting, you and the employee discuss progress and obstacles regarding the Desired Result, and use this opportunity to explore what's possible. We do this because the brain acts differently with the promise of Revisiting. The promise of Revisiting alone helps employees better meet expectations through what Inspiring Accountability methodology calls **Accountability Attention**. The brain provides extra attention to specific efforts and their corresponding Desired Results *simply because there is anticipated and non-negotiable Revisiting.*

When an employee *believes* Revisiting will happen, this tells a powerful brain filter of ours, the reticular activating system, to code what will be Revisited as *important*. The **reticular activating system (RAS)** acts like a bouncer between our conscious and subconscious, deeming what is important enough to bring from our subconscious into our conscious awareness.

The conscious mind processes 40 pieces of information per second whereas the subconscious processes *11 million pieces* of information per second, as cited in Timothy Wilson's 2004 book, *Strangers to Ourselves: Discovering the Adaptive Unconscious.*

For example, if you are looking to buy a new model of car, you start seeing it everywhere. The RAS has deemed your interest in buying this car as important and begins both scanning for and revealing more of them to your conscious mind. There aren't more of these cars on the road, but your RAS is allowing you to consciously notice more of what's there. You'll learn more about how the RAS and similar systems contribute to our effort and engagement in Part III.

On a regular day, a request you make to an employee may briefly register in their conscious mind but not stick. You may have to make the same request many times because the employee's subconscious didn't code it as important compared to everything else he or she was doing. Your employee isn't being defiant; this is simply a function of the human brain. There is a solution included in the Results Model: you can use the promise and execution of Revisiting to help the subconscious assign your request greater importance.

When we trust we will be Revisiting an ask, task, or project (a.k.a. being held accountable), the brain codes the potential of being seen as incompetent as a threat. It then marks the Desired Result as important to protect from that threat.

Accountability Attention gets activated, and the brain prioritizes more awareness and effort toward this active Desired Result because not making progress or meeting expectations simply feels bad for the employee. Promised Revisiting naturally creates an impetus for the RAS to bring focus, information, and attention toward what's most important, making it easier for the employee to align with your priorities.

Similarly, if you ask an employee to make a behavioral change, like Mary asking Mario to be at meetings on time, it's unsupportive to not Revisit the issue. If the employee knows you'll be checking on this new Desired Result at each weekly meeting until the expectation is consistently met, the brain stays engaged, putting Accountability Attention on the issue because it knows compliance is prioritized and inevitable.

Too often leaders want to hold an employee accountable for a Desired Result expressed months or years prior without dedicated Revisiting, calibrating, and adjusting. This is unproductive. Realistic accountability — the kind that actually gets results — supports getting the result with regular Revisiting until the behavior patterns have changed to meet expectations. It's not usually obstinacy or carelessness that hinders employee improvement. We are creatures of habit, and it can take some repeated attention and adjusting to update our habits.

Revisiting is effective, in part, because it acknowledges progress, not only incorrect behavior. Often, the employee might do well the first couple of attempts because the brain is putting extra attention on changing old programming and patterns, but if that change goes unrecognized, it is reasonable to assume the employee may easily slip back into their previous patterns. As you learned in Chapter 2, recognition and rewards activate dopamine and serotonin, incentivizing the brain to stay motivated to keep doing that behavior to achieve a neural reward. With the Results Model, the employee's subconscious brain takes care of the heavy lifting because you promised and delivered on Revisiting until the new behavior becomes the default.

Based on processing power alone, we can see how trying to engage the conscious brain is vastly limited compared to the power of the subconscious. All Inspiring Accountability tools and strategies rely on working with the part of the brain that most effectively inspires engagement and results. This is not in relying on the conscious brain's limited ability to remember, but in the subconscious patterns we create that run automatically. Telling someone what to do hits the conscious brain; Revisiting re-writes the pattern subconsciously for lasting improvement.

There's no shortcut with Revisiting. Until your employee genuinely believes that Revisiting will happen, the Accountability Attention won't be activated and the subconscious may not support the change.

The Results Model: Step 7 — Revisiting the Result

Just like what you don't address, you approve, what you don't revisit, you approve. Revisiting is where the changes you want from your employees gain momentum. Revisiting with the Results Model returns to the steps we've already covered before employee effort, now in a reflective way post-effort. Through our core accountability questions, we look for useful adjustments to course-correct along the way, keeping the focus on the Desired Result while rewarding effort, progress, and contribution.

Revisiting Desired Results — What It Is

Successful Revisiting requires calibrating the achieved result with an already established Desired Result ("How close are we to that

INSPIRING ACCOUNTABILITY IN THE WORKPLACE
RESULTS MODEL©
Your Ultimate Accountability Tool to Getting Results

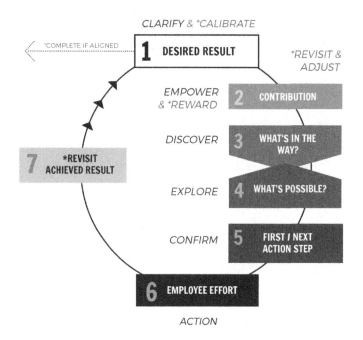

CLARIFY & *CALIBRATE

*COMPLETE IF ALIGNED

1 DESIRED RESULT

*REVISIT & ADJUST

EMPOWER & *REWARD   2 CONTRIBUTION

DISCOVER   3 WHAT'S IN THE WAY?

7 *REVISIT ACHIEVED RESULT

EXPLORE   4 WHAT'S POSSIBLE?

CONFIRM   5 FIRST / NEXT ACTION STEP

6 EMPLOYEE EFFORT

ACTION

anchor?"), rewarding contribution, discovering "What got in the way?" and exploring "What is possible?" Like in all Results Conversations, we close with confirmation of the next action step.

Feedback to adjust unproductive efforts is valuable and necessary. It is the Revisiting itself that creates the conversation for accountability to be achieved. Without Revisiting, your employee can only assume they are meeting expectations.

Here is the Inspiring Accountability Revisiting process:

Once the employee has made his or her initial effort, it's time to see what, if anything, needs to be adjusted to get the Desired Result.

Whether completing tasks, projects, goals, or demonstrating values, behaviors, service standards, or principles, you must Revisit so you can calibrate how the employee is doing and determine what to adjust so the employee can work toward better meeting expectations.

Revisiting mirrors the process of creating the Desired Result. In your regular one-on-one meeting, you'll begin the Revisiting process as part of the Results Conversation. Similar to the first half of the model, but now in a reflective context, we are asking:

- How did you successfully contribute to getting the Desired Result (or moving closer to the Desired Result) since our last Revisit?
- If the result was not met —> What got in the way of achieving the Desired Result?
- If the result was met —> What got in the way of achieving the result more easily or efficiently? (How can we innovate and build in efficiencies?)
- What obstacles can we clear to more easily achieve results in the future?
- Given what obstacles we can't clear, what can we do to make it possible to get the Desired Result more easily now or next time?

Relatedly, in the Revisiting check-in, we may adjust:

- The Desired Result
- Actionably Clear Expectations and Specifications (ACES)
- The amount of effort (if the employee feels they could have prioritized more or put in more time)
- The quality or direction of effort (if they feel they could have contributed more attention or action)
- What is in the way? (Were new roadblocks discovered?)
- What's possible? (What's still needed to achieve the result?)

Now let's break down these Revisiting steps, looping us back to Steps 1-5.

Revisiting Step 1: Calibrate What Was Achieved with the Desired Result

Calibration is where you review with your employee the Desired Result and the actual result achieved, determining if there's a difference between them. You're addressing how well the employee met expectations.

Take a look at the following examples:

- **Example 1**: "Great job! You successfully delivered the product design on time and to spec. Production is very happy and can get started right away!"
- **Example 2**: "I know you really worked hard on getting the product design done on time and to spec. It was almost exactly what they needed, but they found that it was missing one specific component."
- **Example 3**: "I know you've been swamped with many projects and missed the deadline on getting the product design to production because you were working on the other rush project."

Revisiting Step 2: Reward Successful Contribution and Effort

After sharing your calibration, we revisit the question: "How did you (the employee) contribute successfully to the Desired Result?" This is where you acknowledge their effort and the obstacles that they overcame.

Ideally, you start with what you noticed they did well. It will feel more meaningful when you notice their contribution, but if you aren't able to personally identify their contribution (many leaders aren't exposed to the day-to-day minutiae), you can ask them how they contributed successfully, listen to what they self-identify as important effort, and genuinely celebrate this progress.

This step includes:

- Acknowledging successful efforts you noticed
- Asking, "How did you contribute successfully to the Desired Result?"
- Genuinely acknowledging and celebrating their progress to reward and incentivize it

When you acknowledge what was successful about their effort and contribution, you provide serotonin-releasing feedback and confirm what you want to continue seeing, creating positive reinforcement.

Be specific. Vague acknowledgment provides weak reward. Point out one to three aspects that you want to continue seeing from them. Point out what worked about their contribution to the Desired Result. What is the most specific quality, trait, behavior, decision, or evidence of effort you can highlight? The more specific the positive acknowledgment is, the more meaningful and effective the reward will be.

It's important to lead Revisiting with rewarding language to provide the most neurochemical benefit and incentive to keep doing what is working. It also fuels the employee to persevere, especially if the Desired Result wasn't completely achieved.

Revisiting Step 3: Discover "What Got in the Way?"

Employees want to be seen as competent, and they want to meet expectations. It's likely that if they didn't meet expectations, something got in the way.

Now that you've positively acknowledged their effort, you can ask, "What got in the way?"

- **Example**: "The project got done on time, and it looks like all the numbers are right. Great job! You formatted the included information perfectly. What was missed is that we needed the dates with each item to be able to look back anytime to know if they're eligible to return an item. What got in the way of including these dates?"

Possible responses you may hear are:

- "I didn't know I needed to include dates with each item."
- "The system I exported from doesn't export them in a date format."
- "I don't have access to the dates."
- "I did have the dates from the Sales department, but I didn't think they were right, so I removed them."
- "I was going to include dates, but I ran out of time."

You want to give your employee space to answer. Just listen. You can even write down answers to reference. Although sounding like excuses, everything they share is golden, actionable information that you can leverage to get more accurate results next time and inspire more accountability.

As you listen, stay positive and receptive knowing that the more comfortable they are, the more you'll learn about what's in the way, so you can support your employee's development to create better outcomes in the future.

Revisiting Step 4: Explore "What's Possible?"

If the Desired Result was not met, respond with questions to help them discover for themselves what's possible to take action with each obstacle. This is where the change happens. This is where new possibilities, new thinking, new action, new system improvements, and new habits begin.

Here are some ways to revisit, "What's possible?":

Employee: "I didn't know I needed to include dates with each item."
You: "Given that, how could we better confirm what needs to be included next time?"

Ideally, you're already using an Actionably Clear Expectations and Specifications list, to which you'd respond, "I'll add it to our ACES sheet, so we don't miss it next time." (If it was already on the list, you could instead respond with, "Given that it was on the ACES list, what could be done to ensure you don't miss seeing it next time?")

Employee: "The system I exported from doesn't export them in a date format."

You: "Given that the system doesn't easily have that export option, what options might make it possible to still include the dates?"

Employee: "I don't have access to the dates."

You: "Given that you don't have access to the dates with the way the system is set up now, what else could be done to get access to the dates?"

Employee: "I did have the dates from the Sales department, but I didn't think they were right, so I removed them."

You: "Given that you didn't think the dates were right, what other options are possible to include accurate dates?"

Employee: "I was going to include dates, but I ran out of time."

You: "Given that you ran out of time, what else could have been done to still include them?"

From here, ask questions that remove the burden from you to solve any issues, and get your employees thinking about solutions. In addition to finding immediate solutions, the real goal is to train employees' brains to start thinking about solutions when obstacles arise in the future. *Remember, these are the questions you're teaching your employees to ask themselves.* Soon, they'll come to you ready to share what got in the way and what's possible without needing prompting. They'll become more independent problem solvers as they practice Possibility Thinking.

If the Desired Result was met, you still want to learn what got in the way or what's possible to uncover innovation opportunities.

Example: "Awesome! Since you met the Desired Result, what made it possible to meet this deliverable perfectly so we can keep doing it? Was there anything you discovered that was in the way that we should know or improve upon to make it easier next time?"

Step 5: Confirm Next Action Step

Similar to when you presented the new Desired Result, you always want to close the conversation with confirming their next action step. *Since hesitancy on how to move forward creates hesitancy to move forward,* we want to set up the employee to take clear and confident action to help make this new effort easier.

Step 6: Employee Effort

After your Revisiting conversation, it is then up to the employee to take action on the items you discussed.

Revisiting is a Discovery and Development Process

After a first round of Revisiting, if there is a lack of improvement, don't be discouraged! The Results Model is about discovering what's really in the employee's way and what can be done, whether in action or mindset, to persevere. There is valuable development that happens during this process that contributes to employees that take initiative, find a way to get the best results possible every time, and are accountable for their commitments.

Ideal Revisiting Frequency

An ideal Revisiting frequency for most active Desired Results is weekly. Whether it's a Desired Result of timeliness with deadlines, an issue with project management, or a larger interpersonal issue, a weekly check-in keeps employees tethered enough to the anchor that there isn't room to drift too far. With this frequency, Accountability Attention is strong. You also create availability to help clear obstacles and work through the issues with your employee.

Often, both leaders and employees have an unrealistic sense of what can be accomplished in a week or two. It's only with regular Revisiting that we begin to calibrate how much time and effort it takes to progress and change habits.

As one leader told me, she was concerned because she wasn't seeing improvement with her employee. The employee's lackluster performance eroded her trust and she responded by reviewing the employee's work more than usual, using valuable time that she didn't have to spare. I encouraged the leader to stick to the Results Model and reassured her it would save her time and sanity once it became ingrained with her employee.

When I checked in on her Desired Result, I realized its vagueness was being matched with vague improvement. I shared with the leader: "You both have to know the specific areas that need improvement. You need to be able to point to them directly and provide what you *do* want. Requesting your employee to be 'detail-oriented' isn't a strong enough anchor for either of you to drive or confirm improvement. We have to find more specific demonstrations of being detail-oriented so she can apply specific effort and eventually experience the reward of fulfilling that expectation. From there, you will continue to figure out, 'What's in the way?' and 'What's possible?' until the only path left is the one directly to the Desired Result."

Before the Results Model, the employee was confident she was working hard, citing "too much to do" and "feeling overwhelmed" as to why her performance was slipping. Upon Revisiting, the leader told me her employee realized she was serious about the necessary change, and the leader now had concrete comparisons to the employee's previous behaviors. The leader could compare what they both thought would happen alongside what did happen, therefore providing the real evidence of what got in the way. This created transparent accountability and an even more solid plan for the next week.

Very soon, the employee offered, "I realize I need to try harder." The leader was surprised by her employee's candor. The leader knew that pointing out that the employee needed to "try harder" would have been ridiculous, ineffective, and left the employee feeling unappreciated for the "overwhelming" amount of work she was putting her effort toward.

But using the Results Model and consistently Revisiting, the *employee* discovered that she needed to put more attention toward the items she was actively working on. She coded this aloud as "try harder," but what she really meant was that she had to *innovate* the way she was putting forth effort.

Revisit Until Complete

You lead rounds of regular Revisiting until your employee has achieved, fulfilled, or demonstrated the Desired Result satisfactorily. It's your approval that matters most. Only when your employees can "win" with you do they get full doses of "You did it!" serotonin. You retire the Desired Result when you can sincerely acknowledge that they have met the expectation fully and consistently enough to earn your full "excellent" rating, ideally in full celebration and without caveat.

Wouldn't you agree it feels great to fully meet expectations and feel you can truly win with your manager? Your employees deserve the opportunity to know how to win and fulfill expectations — and that feels good for everybody.

Alternative Results Model Language that Inspires Possibility

Everyone has their own style of asking the core accountability questions. You don't have to recite what I've included, as there are many ways to ask effective open-ended questions that inspire the same quality answers. It's important that you understand how to phrase questions to keep your employees thinking and engaged. Here are some common variations you can use while Revisiting in a Results Conversation:

Example 1:
> **You:** "What got in the way of including this detail?"
> **Employee:** "I don't know. I just forgot I needed to include it."
> **You:** "*What can you do to ensure* you don't forget next time?"

Example 2:

You: "What got in the way of including this detail?"

Employee: "Oh? You never said we needed that."

You: "*What can we do to better* be on the same page with deliverable specifications?"

Example 3:

You: "What got in the way of including this detail?"

Employee: "Gerald didn't get that to me on time, so I couldn't get it done."

You: "*Given that* he got this to you late, *what else could have made it possible* to still get it done in time?"

Oftentimes, what's "in the way" might be framed as other employees on the team or in other departments. To explore this, you could ask your employee:

You: "*How could we help ensure* they get their part of the deliverable done on time next time?"

Note that the phrase "help ensure" is best used when you're helping your employee explore possibilities that depend on someone they don't manage. Assist them getting into contribution mode, understanding that while he or she can't control this person, one can help contribute to the outcome by better working with or supporting the other person.

"How could we help ensure they get their part of the deliverable done on time?" keeps employees in a resourceful, empowered, solution-oriented place without holding them accountable for another's behavior.

In short, use variations of the core accountability questions to inspire possibilities and speak as if there are already many solutions waiting to be discovered. We're also using language to create momentum as if we're already in progress — because in the Results Model, we *are* always in progress toward the Desired Result.

Why the Results Model Works

Revisiting until the Desired Result is achieved is effective because it communicates that success is inevitable. It's not a matter of *if* but *when*. Utilizing the Results Model leaves no wiggle room for the brain to fail. Any resistance or defensiveness eventually melts away because employees realize the Revisiting step will continue until their inevitable success. It's like living somewhere with markedly different seasons. When it gets colder, we bring out sweaters and heavier coats. We don't think, "Well, if I just keep wearing my shorts, winter won't arrive." Rather, we adjust to the weather without much resistance because changes in weather are inevitable and changing our clothes to suit the weather is non-negotiable for our well-being. If we want to be warm and dry, we adapt.

Similarly, if employees want to be seen as contributing, competent, and important, which the overwhelming majority of employees do, their interest in adapting increases when they expect a positive effect on their well-being.

Another reason the Results Model is so effective is that it creates a safe environment to provide constructive or negative feedback. Having multiple rounds of Revisiting can become a regular method of providing feedback to your team members. As employees learn to expect regular feedback in this consistent format, what once was a triggering experience becomes normalized in the creature brain. This keeps employees receptive and resourceful.

Additionally, since employees are being asked, not told, what got in the way, the accountability conversation doesn't begin with leader-led accusations, triggering defensiveness.

The predictability of the Results Model structure creates an expectation of feedback, and expectations create familiarity and comfort, helping the brain feel safer. Employees become more comfortable and receptive to feedback and improvement. With regular Revisiting, meeting expectations moves from a hopeful invitation to an inevitable expectation when the brain realizes the best option is to adapt.

Integration Questions:

1. What is your favorite part of the Results Model and why?
2. What could be in the way of you using the model? Given what's in the way, what's possible to be able to use it? What customizations could you make to begin using it?
3. What is your first action step toward using the Results Model and its concepts to inspire accountability in your team?

Key Take-Aways:

1. Accountability always requires revisiting. Results Model Revisiting is what solidifies a habit of excellent effort and inspires the accountability that follows.
2. After an employee applies effort toward the Desired Result, you will Revisit using the steps of the Results Model process in a reflective format, calibrating and adjusting components along the way.
3. Revisiting is where we unearth what effort or action steps can be adjusted toward the Desired Result and create the new patterns and behaviors that more consistently get results.
4. Successful Revisiting requires a specific ask for a clear Desired Result, calibration ("How close are we to that Desired Result?"), and making useful adjustments ("What's in the way?" and "What is possible at this moment to achieve the Desired Result?")
5. Revisiting allows feedback to be seen as a helpful adjustment instead of criticism.
6. Revisiting allows the employee to be accountable for devising solutions.
7. Revisiting communicates that success is inevitable.
8. The Results Model creates a more conducive environment for employees to be receptive to developmental feedback and to receive positive recognition.
9. The brain provides Accountability Attention, extra attention to efforts and their corresponding Desired Results, *simply because there is expected and non-negotiable Revisiting.*

CHAPTER 8

Using the Results Model

"Problems cannot be solved by the same
level of thinking that created them."
—ALBERT EINSTEIN

In this chapter, we'll be covering what you need to know to successfully start using the Results Model to inspire accountability, including:

- How to use the Results List
- A sample Results List
- Unplanned and informal Revisiting and Results Conversations
- Team uses
- A sample Results Conversation

A Better Tomorrow is Unachievable in the Past

Similar to the opening Albert Einstein quote, if your leadership approach focuses on the problem, your employees might get stuck putting their attention on what doesn't work instead of deploying new strategies to discover solutions.

When we try to problem solve by focusing on past failures, we get stuck. If employees dwell on problems too long, it is your responsibility to move them toward creating solutions. When we imagine a better future coming from a place of dignity and curiosity, we can better access our resourcefulness — and even enjoy the process.

Now let's examine the nuts and bolts of how to successfully implement the Results Model.

Results List

To best utilize the Results Model and its benefits, every employee will maintain their own **Results List**. Consider this a list of one to three active Desired Results (which you've already qualified as effective **accountability anchors**) that they are working toward.

Employees bring the list to your regular check-ins or project meetings. The list can be digital or in whatever format they'd normally review a meeting agenda. It will feature the active Desired Results clearly stated with associated Actionably Clear Expectations and Specifications (ACES) and their version of the corresponding contribution context.

It's common for leaders to add new items to the Results List, and this should be a collaborative opportunity. Employees can add items, too, preferably in the realm of, "I'd like to work on this, so I'll add it to my Results List."

Is Every Desired Result Put on the Results List?

Definitely not. A Results List is not the same as a to-do list. An "active" result is something the individual is actively working toward "getting right." A "to-do" is something that needs to be completed. A Desired Result is about development, specifically developing new patterns, habits, or skills to meet expectations satisfactorily and consistently. It's been qualified as an effective accountability anchor through the Accountability Anchor Conversion Checklist.

A Results List features a doable amount of active Desired Results, limited to no more than three active Desired Results at one time, and this list is where progress will be tracked.

Recording in Writing

Regardless of where and how the meeting takes place, having a record of past Results Conversation agreements maximizes accountability. In alignment with the final criteria of the **Accountability Anchor Conversion Checklist**, accountability is best accomplished when the employee documents progress and revisions in writing. You'll have to determine what level of documentation is useful for each employee, as some may need more than others to stay on track.

One way this documentation can be done is for the employee to use Microsoft Word for the Results Conversation agenda and bring their preference of a printed or digital copy for taking notes during the meeting. After the meeting, the employee adds the revisions digitally, and then saves and sends it as a dated PDF to preserve the agreements.

If there is confusion about what's expected, these records are used for reference. This is just one way to maintain documentation. Find a practical and effective process that works for you and your team.

Because there should only be one to three items on the list, this should not be a long or cumbersome process, and the transparency of the written agreement creates a new level of accountability.

Capturing each step of the Results Model ensures the employee records:

- The active Desired Result (which you've qualified through the Accountability Anchor Conversion Checklist)
- Why it matters (the contribution context provided by you)
- How they plan to contribute (when applicable)
- What was cited as "in the way"
- The new possibilities
- Any Actionably Clear Expectations and Specs (ACES)
- The confirmed first or next action step(s)

Whatever format, it should be:

- Accessible to both you and your employee at any time
- Preserved and unchangeable for completed meetings

Here is a sample from the Results List from Mario who was asked to be on time to meetings. You'll see he took the upgraded Desired Result and corresponding contribution context provided and put it in his own words. As the leader, it's important to verify this conversion accurately reflects and includes all accountability and success components.

On the following page is a sample of an Active Desired Result on a Results List.

How does a new Desired Result make its way to the Results List? One option is for you to share the Desired Result (after clarifying it with the Accountability Anchor Conversion Checklist), explore the steps in the Results Model, and then have the employee summarize it into the Results List format before the meeting concludes or email it after for you to confirm.

If you're not meeting in person, another option is to email the Desired Result, including its contribution context, and have them add it to their Results List and email it back to you within 48 hours to ensure everything is concluded.

You may come up with a third way that works even better, and since an employee shouldn't be working on more than three active Desired Results at a time, this should not be a frequent or demanding process.

Lastly, to maximize important accountability buy-in, be sure the employee has an opportunity to ask clarifying questions before solidifying the agreement.

However you approach adding a new Desired Result to the Results List, this confirmation in writing serves as a two-way agreement for the employee to work toward this result with actionable clarity.

Employees Own Their Results

Employees own and manage their Results Lists. It should be written in their words, and they should bring it to your one-on-one meetings prepared to report their progress.

Results List

Desired Result: Be seated, ready to begin meetings at the calendared start time with my

- ☑ Project update
- ☑ Pen
- ☑ Notepad

Start Date: January 1   **Current Date:** January 12

Why it matters:
- My opinions are valued and might be missed if I'm late
- It's disruptive when I come in late

Actionably Clear Expectations and Specs:
Nothing additional to above

How I can contribute: Be on time and be prepared

What's in the way/what got in the way: I have a client call before team meetings that usually runs late.

What's Possible:
- I will ask the client if we can have the meeting earlier or let her know I have a hard stop ten minutes before the meeting.
- I will also make a calendar invite reminder for fifteen minutes before to leave five minutes to wrap the call.

First or Next Action Step:
- Send email to client requesting earlier meeting or requesting hard stop
- Adjust calendar invite reminder to fifteen minutes prior

Other Notes:

At the next Revisiting meeting, the employee will bring the Results List prepared with updates, ready to share progress, and poised to make adjustments for the coming week as needed.*

Although you will introduce the framework and review the different steps of the Results Model, it shouldn't take long after utilizing regular Results Conversations for your employees to naturally come prepared to report what's in the way and what's possible without your prompting. They know exactly what you're going to ask, so their brains become accustomed to reporting it.

This shift importantly indicates that *your employees are thinking this way on their own*, helping them become much more self-sufficient problem solvers and be more accountable for solutions. They learn to trust that if they come to you with a problem, you will ask, "What's in the way?" and "What's possible?" before you attempt to solve it for them, so eventually they will have already thought through these questions before you hear a knock at your door.

This built-in integration of accountability and Possibility Thinking is one of the top goals of Inspiring Accountability, and it only comes from your consistent adoption of the Results Model framework. Employees will be much more engaged and will feel a stronger sense of contribution when they're regularly thinking with this problem-solving mindset.

How Long Does a Desired Result Stay on the List?

In short, you will keep Revisiting a Desired Result until you feel the employee has achieved it satisfactorily.

Often, when discovering an employee has not been meeting expectations, a leader can lose trust. In this case, keep the Desired Result on the list until you've renewed enough trust that he or she is consistently demonstrating the result and meeting expectations.

Ideally, this will be the amount of time it takes for this new behavior or approach to become the default pattern. If the employee regresses at any time, you can re-activate the Desired Result.

---

* For a more thorough example of the process and its components, please visit

www.inspiringaccountability.com/bookresources.

Reminder: Frequency is Everything

As a reminder from the previous chapter, weekly or bi-weekly one-on-one meetings will be frequent enough to improve accountability and results. If your Revisiting frequency is too low, the speed of getting results will also be low and, at some point, possibly ineffective. Infrequent Revisiting doesn't sustain Accountability Attention, and a Desired Result can downgrade into a "thing I'm supposed to do, but it's not a priority."

Additionally, if your one-on-ones are spread too far apart, you're missing out on important opportunities to calibrate, engage, and infuse rewarding and incentivizing neurochemicals. Inconsistency of meetings or frequent cancellations can stall out and minimize Accountability Attention in the employee's brain.

For business structures that already have weekly one-on-ones, have your employee tackle one to three active results at one time. No employee wants a laundry list of 25 ways they need to improve. It's important that your employee feels optimistic about achieving the items on the Results List. As you'll learn in the upcoming section on Inspiring Effort and Engagement, being confident and optimistic about success is almost required to maintain engagement and achieve the Desired Result. If it doesn't feel doable, it won't get done. Triggering overwhelm will sabotage the effort.

If you're not currently meeting regularly for one-on-one's, if you want employees to be more accountable and get better results, weekly Revisiting facilitates the desired changes most effectively. If you meet with your employees every two to four weeks for one-on-ones, dedicate five-minutes for a results follow-up and schedule weekly five-minute follow-ups in between. You can keep it simple but structured in the framework of the Results Model so the employee knows what to expect.

Unplanned Revisiting versus Micromanaging

If you want to check your employee's progress before your scheduled Revisiting, you can, but it must be done without micromanaging.

Micromanaging occurs when a manager consistently monitors an employee's effort and actions, causing the employee to sense a distrust of his or her competence. If you instead check in with the intention of supporting the employee to stay on track to meet the result, the employee will likely sense the difference.

You can always do an unplanned check-in with casual language like, "Just checking in. How are you feeling about the progress of this task?" You can also ask, "What has come up that could get in the way of getting it done on time?" or "What else do you need to help meet the deadline, if anything?" It would be almost impossible for an employee to label this supportive approach as micromanaging, and you'll get that needed status-update.

While you're checking in, you can also add some serotonin into their day with some, "You did it!" recognition and gratitude for making it happen. "Thank you for ensuring this is getting done on time!" or "Excellent! Sounds like you're on track. Great work!"

If you sense the task is uninspiring to the employee, or you sense engagement is low, you can use the unplanned revisit to add contribution context:

> **Example:** "By creating this deliverable, we'll finally be able to get started on the new product creation! You're contributing to the most innovative product we've ever launched!"

What about Informal Results Conversations?

The format for Revisiting is up to you. Face-to-face human interaction offers a fantastic opportunity to provide neurochemical boosts, but sometimes you can't meet in person, so you'll have to improvise on the format of meetings. Whether it's via a call, an email, or even a quick walk around the building, do what works for you and your employee, maintaining the best practices outlined in this chapter.

Working with Teams

In addition to using the Results Model in one-on-ones, you can also use it with teams when challenges or missed deadlines arise. You might keep it formal and track it in writing, or you may use the format and its foundational questions to informally troubleshoot and innovate when the team experiences an obstacle.

When working with teams, remember that any "negative" feedback is best given privately. Depending on your team dynamic, it's important that "What's in the way?" doesn't become "Who's in the way?" Rather, use the Results Model as a way to teach your team how to think about their work and each other. If you're noticing personal attacks or defensiveness, steer directly to "What's possible?" Successful CEO and influencer Gary Vaynerchuk usefully reminds us to "attack the problem, not the person." Inspiring Accountability adds to then move from the problem to what is possible.

Daily Standups

If you really need a results revamp with your team, upping the Revisiting to a **daily standup** might be a great proactive accountability extension of the Results Model.

Daily standups originated from the **Agile Project Management methodology**, a popular format of managing projects from an almost real-time calibration of what's possible.

This involves teams meeting every morning for an agreed upon amount of time (often ten to fifteen minutes) before employees disperse to attend to the day's tasks. Each employee essentially runs through these three questions:

- What did you do yesterday?
- What will you do today?
- What impediments are in your way?

You could easily use the Inspiring Accountability framework to create a useful standup for your own team if it fits the nature of your work:

- How did you contribute successfully yesterday?
- What's in the way today?
- What's possible today?

With this frequency of Revisiting, the transparency of challenges, and the collective brainpower of your team supporting each other to determine what is possible, how can someone fall behind, dramatically miss the mark, or not put in 100% effort? Daily stand-ups don't fit every team or company, but more and more non-project management teams are adopting this style of an accountability-increasing check-in.

Don't Implement Retroactively

Leaders often get frustrated with employees who aren't taking initiative or improving their performances, but this behavior is only possible because there weren't effective accountability measures at the start.

What you haven't been addressing, you've been allowing. Having company values written on an office wall that you don't actively Revisit doesn't activate accountability. We can only productively hold people accountable for contributing to a specific result with a previously asked and agreed upon expectation paired with active Revisiting.

When you start using the Results Model, treat every Desired Result as a new expectation and new agreement. The regular Revisiting with and the questions within the Results Model will now act as a natural agreement that likely didn't exist before or results would have been achieved. Introduce this new format without resentment of past behavior. Focus on new opportunities to set your employees up for success with your new accountability tools.

You can open the conversation by acknowledging your own accountability, for example: "I know we talked about you being on time to meetings months ago, and I haven't been very good at Revisiting it. How about we start with this?"

Start fresh by shifting your resentments of unmet expectations to Desired Results, qualified as strong accountability anchors, and watch this new process empower employees to better meet your expectations.

Putting it All Together:
Example Results Conversation

Here's an overview of how using the Results Model will help you and your employees have more productive conversations to get better results and inspire accountability. Although this scripted example is exaggerated to highlight concepts, you can get a sense of how the basic framework of asking, "What's in the way?" and "What's possible?" and ensuring a next action step can be a practical and transformative addition to your accountability toolbox.

Michael and Adrian

Michael, Director of Product Delivery and Innovation, has his one-on-one Results Conversation today with his employee Adrian, a confident worker who has been with the company for eight months. Adrian has significantly grown his knowledge in his role, but, like most employees, he still has some performance gaps.

Adrian comes into Michael's office and brings his Results List, ready to Revisit the three active Desired Results he is working to improve. Michael already upgraded his expectations using the Accountability Anchor Conversion Checklist before presenting them as Desired Results to Adrian.

Michael greets Adrian and asks how his week has been.

Adrian replies it's been pretty good, but he's looking forward to clarifying some questions on current projects.

The Revisiting nature of the conversation commences. "So, Adrian," Michael asks. "How did you successfully contribute to your first result this past week?"

"For the New Feature Priorities Research (**Desired Result**), I was able to finish the first part and share it with the team on time. But I'm having trouble getting a response from Customer Service (**what's in**

the way), and it's taking me longer than I expected because Ana had that rush project she needed my help on **(what's in the way)**."

"That's great that you were able to do this. Well done! As for getting a response, when is the last communication you had from Customer Service, and who is your point of contact?"

"I first sent the request Tuesday to Mariska and followed up with a voicemail Friday when I didn't hear back," Adrian reported.

"Hmmm...okay. Given that Mariska isn't responding yet, what else do you think can do to get the information you need **(what's possible)**?"

Adrian takes a few moments to think. "Well, I could copy her manager, but that might be undermining her. But I really need the report. I could try putting 'Need by Thursday' in the subject line and email her again. I think I forgot to give her a requested delivery date in my original email. I'll ask her to acknowledge that she received my request and ask if it's possible to get the report by Thursday. I can mention that if I don't hear back in 24 hours, I'll check in with her manager instead."

"Okay, sounds like a solid plan." Michael now enters into informally creating a new Desired Result as this is a new request, beginning at step one. He skips the contribution question and usefully asks, "If I'm correct, I think you've been forgetting to include deadline dates in your email requests lately. What do you think gets in the way of remembering to do it **(what's in the way)**?"

"I'm usually working so hard in thinking about what to say that I forget some of these details sometimes."

"Okay, given that it hasn't been easy for you to remember in the moment, **what's possible** to help you remember every time?"

"Hmmm...I think I just need to see it somewhere and have a short checklist until it becomes a habit. I'll make a checklist **(ACES)** that I can see when I send 'request' emails to remind me to include these details consistently. I'm sure that will help it become habit in no time."

"Sounds like a great idea!" Michael acknowledges. He quickly runs this new effort through his Accountability Anchor Conversion Checklist, and says, "Let's add 'include deadlines in every request email' temporarily to the Results List as a new Desired Result, and we'll revisit it next week to check-in on your progress **(creating a clear Desired Result qualified through the Accountability Anchor Conversion Checklist, already having explored what's in the way and asking what's possible)**." Michael knows he can adjust the Desired Result when they revisit it next week if they discover other details that need to be included.

Michael continues: "So, to confirm: your first action step to remembering the details is…"

"Making a checklist where I can see it until it becomes a habit! I'll do it right after this meeting."

"Excellent! Back to the first result. You mentioned there was a rush project from Ana. Next time, if you're concerned that another project's priority is in the way of being on time, will you please email me? I think we're okay with this project, but it may cause challenges later, and I know it can be difficult when other managers ask for your help. Will you let me know next time?"

"Yes, I definitely will."

"Okay, thank you. What's next on your list?"

"Next is the Pantheon Feature Release Plan, which was completed yesterday."

"I saw that, congratulations! Your excellent attention to detail ensured it met all of our ACES. Very well done **(rewarding contribution)**."

"Thank you!"

"Have you thought about what might make it even easier in the future **(what got in the way/what's possible)**?"

"Hmmm…I think the only thing was it took longer than I expected to build out the software section because it was very new. Would it be possible next time for me to work with someone in design to ensure the language matches?"

"I think we can do that. I'll make a note to ask Raymond if he has someone on his team who could help. I think he has a newer employee who also might benefit from collaborating with our department. Do you have a need for that support on anything currently?"

"Yes, it would be helpful on the Ethereus Release Project I'm also working on."

"What date would you need this support and for how long?"

"I think in about two weeks, and I'd probably just need an hour or two."

"Alright, I'll check with Raymond today to see if that's possible."

Although idealized and exaggerated to highlight concepts, this excerpt of a Results Conversation highlights the style of communication that allows you to learn what's in the way and improves problem solving and efficiency over time. Notice Michael didn't need to problem solve, express frustration, or invest much energy in allowing Adrian to easily create action steps toward meeting the Desired Result.

Also notice the relaxed nature of the conversation. If you're worried about this new conversation feeling contrived, worry not. This new way of thinking and communicating might feel uncomfortable until it becomes familiar.

It's like learning a new language. At first, your accent is off, and you put thought into each word, carefully crafting each sentence. It takes practice to become more fluent and comfortable. Let the newness be a little strange to start, but keep finding your own way of authentically using the foundational concepts, and you will soon become comfortable and fluent in your own version of this new "language."

The initial feelings of newness are not a sign that you shouldn't embark on the change, but rather a sign that you are courageous enough to create change.

Language Tips As You Make the Results Model Your Own

You may have noticed the questions used in the Results Model begin with *what* or *how*. These prompts create effective questions that require more than a yes or no answer; they engage the brain to reply with an answer of substance.

Notice the difference between, "Is there anything you need?" and "What else do you need?" The first question invites the brain to determine if the answer is yes or no, and often the thought exploration stops here. Sure, it's *implied* that the employee will respond with something that is needed, but when the brain scans for a yes or no answer, as it does with questions that begin with *is*, *are*, *can*, or *do*, often the employee takes the easiest route to appease the manager. In this case, a quick "No, there's nothing I need," reply is likely.

Asking, "What else do you need?" instead prompts the brain to seek authentic, complete answers, bypassing the chance for a thoughtless answer. "What" or "how" questions engage and require the employee's brain to take initiative to problem-solve and uncover what's really in the way.

You'll learn more about asking effective questions that inspire accountability in Chapter 13 on *Engaging Leadership Language*, but for now, as you craft your own approach to asking Results Model questions, avoid questions that start with *is*, *are*, *can*, or *do*. Instead, get the answers, engagement, and accountability you want by asking questions that start with *what* and *how*.

Once you have learned, practiced, and become comfortable with the basic structure of the Results Model, you can discover how to usefully personalize and flex your own language to lead more productive accountability conversations.

Integration Questions:

1. Given what you learned about implementing the Results Model, how do you see these best practices being applied practically within your team?

2. What could get in the way of you implementing the Results Model?

3. Given what's in the way, what's possible? Where can you start?

Key Take-Aways:

1. An important goal of the Results Model is to get your employees to think about what's possible on their own, helping them become self-sufficient problem solvers and be more accountable for solutions.

2. We can only hold people accountable for contributing to a specific result with a previously asked and agreed upon expectation. The regular Revisiting with and the questions within the Results Model act as a natural form of agreement.

3. Do not hold employees accountable for problems or behaviors from the past. This is your opportunity to start fresh.

4. Move from the problem to what is possible.

5. For business structures that host weekly one-on-ones, have one to three active Results at a time. No one feels good about a laundry list of ways they need to improve. If it doesn't feel doable, it won't get done.

6. By asking the core accountability questions, you are teaching employees the questions to ask themselves.

7. Since accountability requires revisiting, weekly or bi-weekly one-on-one meetings will be frequent enough to improve accountability and results.

8. If your Revisiting frequency is too low, the speed of getting results will also be low and, at some point, ineffective.

9. Keep Revisiting a Desired Result until you feel the employee has achieved it satisfactorily or until you've renewed enough trust that they are consistently demonstrating expectations. Ideally, this will be the amount of time it takes for this new approach to become the default pattern, and if their behavior regresses at any time, you can always re-add it to the list.

10. In addition to using the Results Model one-on-one, you can also use it with teams when challenges or missed deadlines arise.

11. Some teams will benefit from holding daily standup check-ins, asking:
    - "How did you contribute successfully yesterday?"
    - "What's in the way today?"
    - "What's possible today?"
12. As you craft your own approach to asking Results Model questions, avoid questions that start with *is, are, can,* or *do.* Instead, get the answers, engagement, and accountability you want by asking questions that start with *what* and *how.*

PART III

PROACTIVE ACCOUNTABILITY: INSPIRING EFFORT AND ENGAGEMENT

CHAPTER 9

Workplace Rewards and the Hierarchy of Human Needs

"Reward and performance strategies need to be reimagined so they help fulfill employees' basic human needs of appreciation and connection."

—"SHRM/GLOBOFORCE SURVEY REVEALS HUMAN-CENTERED APPROACHES IN THE WORKPLACE HELP ORGANIZATIONS BETTER RECRUIT AND RETAIN EMPLOYEES" (2018)

In this chapter, you'll learn about what prompts the presence of positive and negative neurochemicals, including:

- The Inspiring Accountability Hierarchy of Human Needs in the Workplace
- The leadership currency in seeing employees as contributing, competent, and important
- What happens when employee needs are threatened or neglected
- Why an employee asking for more money is rarely about money

How well you meet the needs of your employees is your company's competitive advantage. According to *BusinessSolver*, a website dedicated to human resources, 92% of employees said they would be more likely to stay with an organization that empathizes with their needs. But that word — *needs* — can be frustrating to leaders and organizations that don't understand its meaning.

Yet, fulfilling these needs is what makes the workplace a potential neurochemical party. Your employees are neurochemically incentivized to be successful and be part of a successful team, all under your leadership.

But how *exactly* does a busy leader navigate being productively empathetic to the various needs of their employees in a simple, achievable way? Inspiring Accountability's **Hierarchy of Human Needs in the Workplace** will answer this question with actionable clarity and make fulfilling these needs practical, compelling, and a win-win for you and your employees.

In the workplace, positive neurochemicals are primarily released when our needs to be seen as **contributing**, **competent**, and **important** are fulfilled. Applying these needs back to what you learned about neurochemicals in the workplace in Chapter 2, when these needs are threatened or neglected, we can experience a void of positive neurochemicals and trigger negative ones, dramatically decreasing engagement, receptiveness, and resourcefulness.

Traditional accountability is challenging because employees feel that taking accountability will threaten their dignity, value, self-esteem, or move them toward losing their jobs. So, how do we make it safe (specifically for the protective and reactive creature part of the brain) to willingly engage in accountability when so much is on the line?

While humans might appear complex and unique, we're actually quite similar and predictable when we look at the Hierarchy of Human Needs in the Workplace. What makes us human precedes age, work style, or personality, making the Hierarchy a straightforward go-to when you need to inspire engagement, create accountability, and reward your team.

Inspiring Accountability's Hierarchy of Human Needs in the Workplace

Inspired by Maslow's "Hierarchy of Needs" which outlines human drivers in life, Inspiring Accountability's Hierarchy of Human Needs in the Workplace is an updated version tailored to address employees' most important needs in the workplace, giving you clear guidance on what to address when engagement and accountability are low. While it's still valuable to learn each employee's individual motivators and work styles, you can rely on the uncomplicated Hierarchy as your universal go-to when you need better results.

Let's examine how easy it can be to fulfill employees' needs. There are three key truths that will help us:

1. Humans engage in and make decisions based on what *feels best* (offers positive neurochemical incentive or reward).
2. As leaders, we are more available for others *when our own needs are already fulfilled.*
3. Specifically in the workplace, employees are available and willing to "put the company first" when they feel secure in their own need fulfillment.

The top three needs are being seen as contributing, competent, and important. These are the most relevant to accountability and engagement.

Leaders who inspire accountability acknowledge and enhance employee contribution, competence, and importance while nurturing connection, honoring belonging, protecting well-being, and ensuring safety.

Tending to these needs may sound overwhelming, especially since managers are expected to lead and attend to a full-time job as well. This straightforward and dependable model makes identifying and fulfilling needs easier.

Let's go from the bottom (level 5) of the Hierarchy straight to the top (level 1).

Hierarchy of Human Needs
in the Workplace©

Contributing
What value am I
creating for others?

Competent
How well am I able to meet expectations?

Important
How much does my leader value my role
and what I personally and professionally bring to it?

AND / OR

Connection and Belonging
Do I fit in this company culture? Do I connect with my leader, team, peers, customers?
Does my leader care about my well-being?

Safety, Health and Well-Being
Emotionally and physically safe work environment.
Fair and adaquate source of financial security.

Level 5: Baseline Safety Needs —
Safety, Health, and Well-Being

Primary Neurochemical: Negative neurochemicals when threatened (Adrenaline, Norepinephrine, Cortisol)

Primary Source: Company

Questions Asked by Employee:

- How emotionally and physically safe do I feel at work?
- How much do I feel a general sense of well-being?
- How fair and adequate is my paycheck (financial security) for the work I do?

Physically safe environments include standards like clean, running water, electricity, and a sense of security. An emotionally safe work environment, however, can be more subjective. An emotionally safe work environment is where an employee feels accepted and free from harassment and verbal abuse. It's no secret that everyone deserves to feel emotionally safe at work, and given that harassment training is required by law, there's great progress toward making this a given. Yet, until a company has strong values and a firm accountability system to adhere to those values, emotional safety may not be pronounced among employees.

When an employee is hired, they opt-in for their pay. Interestingly, when employees feel they are *fairly* and *adequately* paid, money is not the foremost need. You'll learn more about this later in this chapter.

Level 4: Baseline Culture Needs — Connection and Belonging

Primary Neurochemical: Oxytocin when fulfilled

Primary Source: Company culture, values, peers, hiring a "good fit"

Questions Asked by Employee:

- How well do I fit in this company culture?
- What do I need to do to belong?
- How will I know I belong?

My experience working with clients has revealed that the need for connection and belonging (and oxytocin) in the workplace varies individually more than any other need. I've seen connection and belonging with peers compensate for a manager not fulfilling the top three needs (covered next). This can retain an employee…for a while.

Take Gallup's controversial employee engagement survey question: "Do you have a best friend at work?" In Gallup's 2018 article defending the survey question, entitled "Why We Need Best Friends at Work," author Annamarie Mann cites, "Our research has repeatedly shown a concrete link between having a best friend at work and the amount of effort employees expend in their job."

Mann continues, "When employees possess a deep sense of affiliation with their team members, they are driven to take positive actions that benefit the business — actions they may not otherwise even consider if they did not have strong relationships with their coworkers."

But Mann also infers that this need for connection and belonging is secondary to managers meeting the basic engagement needs of their employees, explaining: "If employees don't know what's expected of them or don't have the opportunity to do what they do best every day, the friendships they do have at work are more likely to encourage gripe sessions. However, when basic engagement needs are met, friendships can take on a powerful dynamic in which casual, friendly banter turns into innovative discussions about how the team or organization can thrive."

In my experience, having a "best friend" at work is less important than a general feeling of belonging and connection both within the company culture and with co-workers. Therefore, Inspiring Accountability would ask, "How much do I feel I belong within my company?" or "How much do I connect and enjoy working with my co-workers?"

Companies with strong values, that hire in alignment with those values, and have a structure in place for ensuring those values are upheld, hire people who will connect with one another. You'll learn more about holding employees accountable for values, attitude, mindset, and behaviors, in Chapter 15.

Not a Foundation for the Top Three Needs

Contrary to what the triangle may infer, connection and belonging is not actually a foundational requirement for the top three needs. Connection and belonging are marked out separately because *sometimes* they can be a great foundation, and *sometimes* employees can survive without a strong sense of company belonging and connection *if* the top three needs are adequately fulfilled.

Have you ever stayed in a job because you experienced belonging and connection with your co-workers, despite you manager not fulfilling your top three needs? If yes, then you know it helped with retention, but something was still missing.

Connection and belonging are helpful for company morale, collaboration, and harmonious work environments, but they are not the most critical to our key accountability objective.

Ideally, leaders are the ones who best contribute to employee retention and proactive accountability by fulfilling employees' top three needs to be seen as contributing, competent, and important.

Levels 3 to 1: Baseline Engagement and Accountability Needs

The surest way to inspire accountability and engagement in employees is by fulfilling their following three needs:

- Being seen as **important**
- Being seen as **competent**
- Being seen as **contributing**

These top three needs are the superior results-drivers when fulfilled. Conversely, they're the most susceptible to become triggers when threatened or neglected.

Nothing will kill your engagement and accountability faster than neglecting or damaging employee importance, competency, and contribution. Without feeling a secure foundation of these, employees will be in self-protection mode, being triggered by negative neurochemicals that block opportunities to stay engaged, receptive, and resourceful.

When people are in **self-protection mode**, the adrenaline-triggered state so commonly associated with traditional accountability, they will spend their energy defending themselves instead of discovering possibilities and rational solutions. They will fight to prove they are good enough, valued enough, and important enough. They will choose to protect their needs instead of making decisions that protect what's best for your company and customers.

Proactively and responsively maintaining your employees' feelings of contribution, competence, and importance is essential to keeping them engaged, receptive, and resourceful. This gives you, as their leader, the incredible inside track you need to drive Desired Results through simply acknowledging and fulfilling these three human needs in the workplace. When employees get what they need, your organization gets what it needs.

A leader's minimum goal should be to meet employees' baseline needs.

Let's more closely examine these top three needs so that you can add these tools to inspire proactive and responsive accountability. You'll notice these needs primarily activate "the leadership neurochemical" serotonin, unlike the previous needs.

Level 3 - Being Seen as Important

Primary Neurochemical: Serotonin

Primary Source: Leader

Questions Asked by Employee:

- How much does my leader value my role?
- How much does my leader value what I personally and professionally bring to my role?
- How much do they care about my personal well-being?

The third most important need that influences and inspires accountability and engagement is being seen as **important**, a perception of being personally and professionally valued.

When we are seen as important, this creates a sense of:

- **Safety**: We are needed and relied upon at work, associated with continued work and stable income, in order to maintain housing and keep family safe.
- **Self-Esteem**: We feel valued and excited to contribute more.
- **Happiness and Fulfillment**: We have permission to feel good during the work day (our right to experience and express fulfillment).

We are inspired to engage and feel safe to acknowledge accountability when we have a solid sense that we're seen as important by our leader and our company. Having a solid sense that we are professionally valued, we trust that one hiccup in getting results won't get us demoted or fired.

When we know our leader values our role, it makes us proud to show up and fulfill it. While technically everyone is replaceable, when we know our leader values what we personally bring to the role, our unique gifts and skills that help us *feel* irreplaceable, this recognition and appreciation make us want to go above and beyond. When we feel our leader *cares* about our well-being, our sense of importance solidifies.

In addition to the "You did it!" serotonin, feeling seen as important also creates loyalty and trust that inspires effort, which generates oxytocin. Like the phrase, "People do business with people they like and trust," employees are inspired to provide more effort to support someone who likes and trusts them.

Leaders who help their employees feel important gain loyalty and naturally earn "followers." If there is one phrase I hear from employees that feel seen as important, it's that "I would follow him anywhere," or, "If she left, I would want her to take me with her."

Inspiring leaders whose employees feel important are rewarded with loyalty, trust, and above-average inspiration to put forth effort, keeping crucial serotonin and bonus oxytocin flowing and getting results.

Level 2: Being Seen as Competent

Primary Neurochemical: Serotonin

Primary Source: Leader

Question Asked by Employee:

• "How well am I meeting expectations?"

The second most important need that influences and inspires accountability and engagement is being seen as competent.

Inspiring Accountability defines feeling **competent** as being seen with the ability to meet expectations in any given moment. Note, this is different than actual **capability**, which we define as one's abilities and the current capacity to access and demonstrate these abilities. Competence is determined only in comparison to a leader's (subjective) expectations.

Humans, especially in the workplace, are emotionally and chemically driven to be seen as competent. We receive major serotonin and sometimes dopamine spikes or dips in response to how this need is fulfilled or threatened.

The question your employees are (secretly) asking to define competence in their roles is: "How well am I meeting expectations?"

Inherently within this core question is also a question of **confidence**, asking, "How confident am I that I will meet expectations?" Confidence is belief in one's ability to be successful, a phrase synonymous with the definition of competence.

Confidence significantly influences an employee's engagement and chance at actual success. Confidence, like competence, *is a perception,* one that leaders can almost completely construct. It's as easy to build it up as it is to tear it down, and you'll continue to learn compelling cases to use the Inspiring Accountability tools to build and maintain a sense of confidence and competence in your employees.

The Stakes

What's the number one need we are defending when we get triggered into self-protection mode in the workplace? Competency.

Competence can be one of the most triggering needs because of how deeply connected it is to our self-worth. It feels the least malleable in the moment. If we've given our best effort and are still seen as incompetent, we don't know what we can "do better" to be seen as more competent in our manager's eyes. If our best isn't good enough, then it feels like we can't win, which would leave anyone feeling a range of discouragement, helplessness, and hopelessness.

Without competency, we have a lot to fear. The thought of losing our jobs equivocates to a downward neurochemical spiral that includes threats to financial security, ability to provide, and a general sense of stability.

But these all pale in comparison to the biggest trigger our brains perceive when something threatens, damages, or neglects our competence: confirmation from another that we are not good enough. When it comes to competency, this is our deepest and worst fear. To our creature brain, the part that doesn't have the support of up-to-date rationality, not being good enough in the workplace feels like imminent death.

The self-protection mode connected to the previously discussed threat-response system is an accountability killer. Although fear of not being competent can be temporarily motivating, it's motivating for all the wrong reasons. We are likely being motivated by the negative neurochemicals, which actually deteriorate our resourcefulness, health, and well-being. Fear motivates employees to sabotage others, hold the company back to keep looking as competent as possible, or withhold information and opportunities.

An employee once confided in me that he would never hire a consultant for support because he was worried that having an expert on premises would reveal that he wasn't competent enough. He worried this would create a visible comparison that would expose that the company could hire someone much better.

That is self-protection mode in its purest form.

His self-protection did not allow him to put the company's best interest first, which would have included bringing in a consultant when needed. His creature brain could not take that chance.

The stronger one's sense of being seen as competent is, the more receptive to feedback and resourceful toward solutions one can be. These facilitate greater capability being accessed, gained, and demonstrated, benefiting company success.

Judging Competency is Destructively Triggering

There are far more productive ways to hold people accountable than to judge competency because doing so destroys engagement.

Author and professor Daniel M. Cable's 2018 book, *Alive at Work: The Neuroscience of Helping Your People Love What They Do*, cites Gallup polls which state that about 80% of workers don't feel that they can be their best at work, which means that employees identify their competencies as greatly under-utilized. Is it possible you have an employee you don't see as very competent, that's not meeting your expectations, that actually has under-utilized capabilities?

Evaluating competency is not the same as evaluating ability or capability. Competency is a reflection of how an employee generally meets expectations, which is not a reflection of their full skillset, capabilities, or ability to contribute. After all, so much outside of one's capability can get in the way of getting results.

When we judge or evaluate competency, it's usually received as if an employee's capabilities are fixed and finite. The label comes off as *judging the person on the entirety of what they can offer*, or even *who* they are, which triggers disengagement and, as a result, discourages one from expanding and demonstrating greater capability.

Some old school models encourage leaders to judge competency. If it's working for you and your employees — great! But if you think your employees would benefit by not being judged for this triggering concept, the Results Model is offered as a better way to keep employees accountable. You can stop judging competency while maintaining resourcefulness toward expanding their capabilities.

With all the popularized pressure to be one's "best self," live one's "best life," and do work one "loves," companies also feel that pressure as employees seek positive work environments to explore their potential. When employees are seen as competent, along with our top need of contributing meaningfully, many of these pressure-points get relieved.

Level 1: Being Seen as Contributing (Meaningfully)

Primary Neurochemical: Serotonin

Primary Source: Leader

Question Asked by Employee:

- "How meaningful is the impact of my work to clients/customers/ the company/my co-workers/causes I care about?"

At the top of our needs pyramid is the need that most contributes to engagement and accountability: being seen as contributing meaningfully.

Contribution is the action (effort) toward benefiting something or someone bigger than oneself in a valuable or meaningful way. To be fulfilled, employees must know how their work contributes (the resulting effect or impact), which is most often confirmed, communicated, or reinforced by their leader.

Employees need to feel they are contributing meaningfully to solutions and successes. Contribution is our means of being recognized and rewarded, and therefore becomes incentivized and required to earn positive neurochemicals.

When employees feel competent and confident in their ability to contribute, they take pride in their work. It's only when they feel their contribution doesn't matter or they don't feel competent (confident they'll meet expectations) that employees respond with apathy or defensiveness.

What inspires the action and effort in hopes of contributing meaningfully can be referenced with different terms. In Simon Sinek's 2009 book *Start with Why: How Great Leaders Inspire Everyone to Take Action*, he refers to what really motivates people into action is contributing to their "why."

Similarly, Daniel Cable refers to "purpose." In *Alive at Work* (2018), Cable writes that "physically, the feeling of purpose is good for us — it affects our health and life expectancy." He states a stark claim that supports how powerful this concept is to vitality, citing, "a relatively small increase in sense of purpose — only a 1 standard deviation improvement — substantially reduces the risk of dying over the next decade." So, it turns out, a sense of purpose is pretty important.

Inspiring Accountability asserts that contribution is the *answer to why* and the *filter of purpose*, which is how most of us strive to make sense of what we're doing in the workplace (and here on earth). How our contribution is recognized and communicated to us tells us how much our effort matters.

Cable also points out that in addition to the serotonin that is released when an employee personally connects to their own meaningful sense of purpose — a.k.a., meaningfully contributing — it also energizes with a dose of dopamine.

Through his research, Cable concludes, "When we have a personal experience that lets us develop a narrative and purpose about a certain activity...we engage ourselves even more in that activity."

Whether your employees regard it as their "why" or "purpose," we want employees to feel they are contributing meaningfully every day. If a task is worth doing, it means there is valuable contribution context waiting to be communicated. What greater success is your employee contributing toward that makes it worth doing in the first place?

Like the other top two needs, this need is also determined by how our manager perceives and communicates the value of our contribution. In addition to the section in Chapter 5, you'll learn how to effectively communicate this value through contribution context, a leader's most important contribution-boosting tool, in Chapter 14.

In the workplace, meaningful contribution is the answer to why our work matters beyond providing a paycheck. Given how many waking hours we dedicate to work, we would really like to know that our effort makes a difference. When we know it does, we are much more inspired to keep engaging. How would each of your employees answer the contribution question: "How meaningful is the impact of my work to clients/customers/the company/my co-workers/causes I care about?"

Summing It Up

The top three Hierarchy of Needs in the Workplace are encompassed in the word **dignity**, the sense of inherent worth that comes from being human.

A sense of dignity is exactly what is honored and protected when we feel that we are important, competent, and contributing.

When the integrity of the top three needs is threatened, one becomes **indignant**, feeling or showing anger or annoyance to prove one is worthy. This often looks like getting angry or resentful, grasping to prove one's self, acting out, disconnecting, or shutting down completely — essentially, every leader's most difficult employee.

No one is at their best when they are left without a sense of dignity. Fulfilling needs isn't catering to neediness: it's honoring what makes us human. It's filling up employees' fuel tanks so they can do their best work every day. When people feel truly supported and respected, amazing contributions soon follow.

Only Fulfilled by You

There's one important twist to the Hierarchy of Human Needs in the Workplace that's been alluded to but deserves its own emphasis: these needs can't be fulfilled by your employees. They must be fulfilled by *you*, their leader and primary source of "You did it!" serotonin in the workplace. Let's learn why this is true.

Meet Jacob. Jacob worked extra hours prepping a presentation on a new approach to a major company problem for the senior leadership team. He was only given ten minutes to present, and he knew he needed to make it count if he wanted to show the senior leadership team he has what it takes to be a major contributor at the company.

He shared his presentation with passion and had the figures to back it up. He walked out of the meeting feeling fantastic, knowing he nailed it, and glowing with the "I did it!" dopamine rush. Getting to his desk, Jacob is feeling confident and proud, basking in the glow of a clear demonstration of what a strong contributor he is to the team.

Just then, Jacob's manager comes in and closes the door, and without hesitation pointedly questions, *"What was that?"*

Confused and slightly alarmed, Jacob doesn't know what to say. His manager continues, "You went so fast, you didn't leave any room for questions, and you were clearly in your own world about this idea. Nobody understands it or thinks it's practical."

In the first moments of alarm, the threat-response system kicks in. Jacob's breathing quickens. He can feel the blood pumping through his body like a pulsating drum. His rational brain starts to go dark as the frenzied creature brain takes control. Wanting to fight and desperate to flee, he instead freezes, speechless.

As his manager keeps speaking, shock and shame flood through

Jacob, emotionally and physically. His face flushes uncontrollably with embarrassment and frustration. Firing on the inside and frozen on the outside, he stares at the floor. He's too ashamed to look up, still too shocked to move, and starts to shut down into numb defeat.

Jacob's once high dopamine has now plummeted below the baseline. Serotonin is nowhere to be found in the bleak disappointment of his manager.

Does it matter that Jacob thought he was competent when his manager doesn't agree? Does it matter if Jacob thought he was contributing meaningfully if his manager diminishes the value of his contribution? And is there any value in Jacob thinking he's important if the higher-ups don't agree?

No, it doesn't matter what Jacob thinks of himself if he isn't *seen* as contributing, competent, or important *by his managers*. Jacob's perception of himself is vanquished by his manager' perception of him.

No matter how hard any of us want to fulfill our own needs, it is our managers' perception that determines if these needs register as fulfilled.

Engagement Tools or Disengagement Triggers

Ask yourself: how is Jacob supposed to perform at his best when he feels terrible? How would *anyone*?

When Jacob's feeling defeated and depleted, the last thing on his mind is sustaining the company's vision or protecting the company. An employee's self-fulfilling dopamine won't stand against a manager's threat or neglect of needs. And the serotonin needed to feel happy, as we learned, is primarily created from a manager's acknowledgment of: "You did it!"

Jacob's confidence is crushed, and he now sits squarely in hopelessness. His best effort wasn't good enough. He is left without a way to win. His sense of despair evolves to disengagement.

An Inspiring Accountability approach would have been for Jacob's manager to come in and start with what Jacob did well, acknowledging the amount of time and effort put into preparing, the courage he had to present to senior managers, and his enthusiasm for solving problems to help the company grow — supporting Jacob's top three needs.

Only then could his manager productively explore different perceptions and opportunities to improve next time, instead of launching with criticism (getting stuck in the problem), followed by unproductively citing all the reasons it was terrible (digging a deeper trench to get more stuck in the problem). Because Jacob can't retroactively do better, bringing in blame for something he can't change mires Jacob in immovable shame, making it harder to see above the trigger trench and neurochemically recover.

Jacob can only respond to his manager's disappointment in two ways:

1. **Accept that he isn't seen as important, competent, and contributing.** This is a fairly hopeless stance that is almost impossible for humans to fully accept. Whether it's the imagined consequences of true incompetence or the threat of exclusion when we want to belong, both of these have been coded as intolerable for the creature brain to "survive." Although self-deprecation may be an initial phase, few people will accept feeling this way for long, eventually coping with it by converting it to anger and resentment, cuing up Jacob's second option:

2. **Decide that the person who doesn't see us as important, competent, and contributing is simply wrong.** This usually comes in the form of, "My manager is a jerk," or "My manager doesn't have a clue how much I do." It's probably no surprise that the latter is where most employees with neglected needs land. It's not personal; it's our human safety system protecting our needs.

Inspiring Accountability's methodology, strategies, and tools are designed to intentionally enhance opportunities to fulfill these needs while effectively reducing threats, preventing needs from becoming disengagement triggers.

The Money Myth: Money as a Need

To speak to a common question, you'll notice that needs related to money are not high on the list here. Everyone needs a fair working wage, enough to provide and survive, and many would like to have some aspect of a lifestyle that supports their happiness and well-being. Many studies have shown that once someone is making what they consider a "fair wage," money alone does not remain a motivator.

- **Money is not the problem**. In fact, according to the website CareerBuilder.com, only 12% of employees actually leave their job because they want more money.

- **89% of managers wrongly believe** their employees quit because they want more money, according to author Leigh Branham's book *The 7 Hidden Reasons Employees Leave* (2012). Interestingly, "poor management" is cited as the top reason employees actually leave.

- **71% of employees would accept a pay cut to get a better job** (which likely means a better manager), according to the 2017 U.S. Hays study: "What People Want."

Those are some pretty compelling statistics that infer that an employee's demand for more money is rarely about money. So what motivates employees to ask for money?

When needs go unmet, unacknowledged, or under-appreciated, money becomes the way to create tangible proof of one's contribution, competence, and importance. If they're not receiving enough proof in their day-to-day workplace, they'll ask for more money. Of course, if their worth was valued more, they wouldn't need to rely on money to confirm it.

Instead of money, Branham's book also offers four fundamental human needs on which to instead focus, compiled from 20,700 employee-exit surveys. These include sharing that employees need to feel **proficient** (competent), to feel a **sense of worth** (contributing meaningfully, feeling important, and being recognized and rewarded for these), to be **trusted** (perceived capability, upcoming in Chapter 14), and last but not least, employees need to **have hope** (optimism, a key engagement component, introduced later in this section and maintained throughout the rest of the book).

In the workplace, it's simply easier and less vulnerable to ask for more money than ask to feel more appreciated. Money becomes evidence that an employee is important. Asking for more money communicates that the employee wants to stay more than leave, but also that there's been too long of an appreciation drought. They're alerting you that their sense of feeling important, competent, and contributing is low.

It's much cheaper — and usually free — to improve recognition than to get in a salary war that won't actually solve the problem. If an employee is receiving a fair, industry-standard salary, providing financial compensation to remedy poor needs fulfillment will, at worst, solve nothing, and at best, buy you time.

When someone is seeking money to fulfill one of the top three needs, no amount will be enough. It's like throwing dollar bills on a campfire. It'll help it burn longer, but it doesn't provide lasting warmth. Possibly worse, if an employee asks for a raise and is turned down, you are confirming that the employee isn't seen as valuable. This will leave you with a disgruntled employee looking for a new job because staying in their position is daily proof that "No, you are not that important."

If you want to retain them, but can't offer an increase, what can you give them? Any concession is better than nothing while you concurrently put attention on discovering and fulfilling the needs in deficit. Give them guidance on what is possible to someday get that raise because they are valued and important.

Of course, if an employee has risen above their initial pay-grade, an increase makes sense. People should be paid fairly for their contribution and competency levels, which you'll learn about in Chapter 16.

With equal pay and pay scale transparency improving, this will help employers and leaders maintain fairness in the relationship between pay and roles, making it even easier to spot when a fair competency or contribution increase is needed or if your employee is, indeed, seeking evidence of being important.

To retain employees, the answer will almost always include improving the direct manager's ability to acknowledge and fulfill needs. This will drive improved engagement and results, growing a company that has more resources for all.

Needs and Getting Curious
About "What's in the Way?"

Having an employee that seems apathetic is a curious situation because that behavior goes against human nature. Since the human brain is hard-wired to seek, protect, and defend the need to be seen as important, competent, and contributing, it benefits you, as a leader, to be curious about what's in the way of an employee overtly pursuing these neurochemically-incentivized needs.

From here, we will adopt the assumption that when an employee is struggling with getting results and meeting expectations, *something must be in the way of them getting this need fulfilled*. Now, you can stop being frustrated and start being curious to find out what it is.

Consider this common example: you hired Rebecca, a new entry-level employee fresh out of college, who can't seem to hit her deadlines. She gets her work done, but not on time. In fact, she is turning in projects later and later, and the quality has begun to decline as well.

If we're curious about what's it the way of her competently meeting deadlines, we might discover that this young, ambitious employee struggles to see her "menial work" as contributing meaningfully to the larger goals of the company, which means she could be questioning if her entry-level role is important enough to warrant the effort.

Some employees respond to this scenario by trying to prove themselves, going above and beyond in their contribution with incessant attempts at proving competence, hoping to expand their importance. Usually, this gets annoying to managers who understandably can't match the effort with incessant gratitude. This stymies the employee because the manager's response is not neurochemically satiating enough.

When humans feel that our contributions don't reflect our dignity, we can react by doing *less* as a subconscious defense against doing tasks that, if fulfilled, might validate mediocre contribution, competence, and importance. You'll learn more about this concept of Self-Protection Effort Withholding in Chapter 12.

Back to Rebecca, whose growing apathy with deadlines is becoming a problem.

Without knowing any of this, you might get exasperated and confront her with, "Why can't you just complete your projects on time? Everyone else does!"

But most knee-jerk, blaming, and shaming reactions do nothing to address what is actually in the way, *particularly if the reason is that employees subconsciously don't feel valued enough* (that their work isn't meaningful or that they don't have competence beyond the menial task).

There is an infinitely more productive approach that maintains Rebecca's dignity and helps you both actually learn what is challenging this employee who wants to be successful. For example, you can open the discussion with:

"I've noticed that you seem to be struggling to meet your deadlines, and I want to support you in being successful. I know you're more than capable of doing this work well. Can you share with me a bit about what's getting in the way of submitting work on time?"

Your ability to initiate *conversations* instead of *confrontations* determines the engagement and accountability that follow. You'll learn more about approaching conversations in Chapter 13, helping you lead conversations that keep your employees receptive and resourceful, keeping their dignity intact, while also learning about what's in the way of their engagement.

When Needs are Neglected: Jessica's Furniture

I was at a luncheon sharing a table with a woman I'll refer to as Miriam, a business owner exasperated by an employee's recent behavior.

Jessica, her office manager, had been asked to help fill-in for the receptionist during her co-worker's maternity leave. I could tell by the way Miriam described the role that being receptionist was not well respected at this company. Jessica clearly resented that she was asked to take a role that, according to her company's unspoken opinion, was *less than*. Jessica was triggered.

Responding to the perceived threat of not being seen as important, competent, and contributing, Jessica demanded to be moved to where she wasn't seated at the front of the office (seen as a receptionist). Miriam obliged, and after IT and the movers came to make the move — which was certainly noticed and an inconvenient disruption in a smaller workplace — Jessica ordered some expensive ergonomic equipment from Amazon without clearing it with anyone. Jessica's brain was in self-protection mode.

In her mind, if she can't change how her manager or the company values her, how can she gain some control? As many employees do when they're in a position they feel lacks dignity, she grasped for evidence to prove she was valued. She compensated not being seen as important through the currency of the attention, financial expense, and effort spent to accommodate. She opted to purchase furniture that she saw as supporting her well-being to get proof that Miriam values her. That glimmer of hope was brusquely extinguished because Miriam was *furious*.

In this case, Jessica's real needs, only available from the Hierarchy, not Amazon.com, were still unfulfilled, despite the new desk band-aid. She likely didn't ask because she suspected Miriam would not approve the purchase, further proving that Jessica was not valued. Her creature brain was warning her that she was insignificant, so she indignantly tried to take matters into her own hands. It's not only children that act out passive aggressively, finding indirect ways to assert frustration or obtain what's wanted. This safety system feature is a built-in go-to feature for all ages.

Finishing her story at the lunch table, no longer caring who heard her frustration, Miriam escalated in her own self-protecting way to using sentences like, "I'm not her parent," "She's an adult," and "I'm tired of babysitting." Miriam promptly scheduled a meeting to, quote, "Rip Jessica a new one." This fateful meeting was to occur after Miriam returned to the office that afternoon.

Luckily, my across-the-table eavesdropping became less of a concern when Miriam broadcasted to the table a common management question, "Why don't employees just speak up and say something 'like an adult'?"

I asked if I could offer a possible answer. I'll share with you the same perspective I shared with Miriam:

> Quite honestly, at a certain point, it's about knowing someone pays enough attention to you to see that there's a problem, and that they care enough to acknowledge it. So while a great tactic for getting needs met would be honesty and asking for greater fulfillment of needs, in a dynamic of manager/employee inequity, it doesn't happen much. Registering this need with a more powerful manager comes with more risk. Today's work cultures rarely support a penalty-free, safe, or appropriate option to directly ask for our top three needs to be met. Plus, we're left incredibly vulnerable to be rejected. If we're already feeling unimportant, it feels like a huge, vulnerable risk to reach out if we don't know what we'll get back, especially in a workplace where feelings aren't supposed to be at the forefront. The inherent rules of the workplace don't make this a very viable option, and it has nothing to do with being "an adult." It also has nothing to do with ergonomic furniture. Would you say that the role of receptionist at your company is seen as highly respectable? How securely would you estimate Jessica feels seen as contributing, competent, and important? This answer will inform her behavior.

If we look through the lens of triggered workplace needs to see Jessica's viewpoint, it offers helpful clarity and better response options. After Miriam and I discussed this different perspective, Miriam decided to drop the (parental) punishment, and instead took it as an opportunity to offer a message of appreciation. After all, it was likely the context in how the role was seen that first informed Jessica that she wasn't valued, which could have been avoided if the culture didn't view the receptionist role as less-than.

By calming the creature brain with a more understanding and appreciative approach, Jessica could soften, drop the passive aggressive indignation, and apply her energy toward being a more positive contributor.

Miriam can still communicate that Jessica can't order anything she wants from Amazon without approval — but imagine leading with recognizing Jessica, fulfilling her needs so that she can relax and not need to prove herself. Then Miriam can simply ask, "The next time, if you're making an order over [a certain amount], will you please let me know so that I'm aware there's a need and see what resources could best meet it?"

Approaching someone with dignity, gratitude, understanding, and, more specifically, soothing the triggered creature brain before delivering feedback isn't parenting or babysitting. *It is the most effective approach to getting the result you want.* You're not only fulfilling their needs, you're also better fulfilling your business' needs.

Honoring and working with the Hierarchy of Needs in the Workplace can unlock even your messiest employee issues. Often, they want to be seen, heard, recognized, valued, and have their contribution and competency recognized. Starting with these will calm the reactive creature brain, bring back employee receptivity and resourcefulness, and help you ditch uncomfortable confrontations in favor of productive conversations.

Integration Questions:

1. How important is it to you to be seen as contributing, competent, and important? Are these needs currently being fulfilled for you in your workplace?

2. How do you think your employees would answer the Needs Fulfillment Questions, summarized in the Key Take-Aways for convenience? Taking the time to do this exercise is a worthy use of time.

3. What do you think could be in the way of your employees having their needs fulfilled? Where are you most compelled to improve fulfilling your employee's needs? Note, more needs-fulfilling resources are to come in Chapter 14.

Key Take-Aways:

1. Humans engage in and make decisions based on what offers neurochemical incentive or reward (what *feels best*).

2. In the workplace, positive neurochemicals are primarily released when our needs of being seen as **contributing**, **competent**, and **important** are fulfilled, further providing incentive and reward.

3. The surest way to inspire accountability and engagement is by fulfilling these needs.

4. Needs Fulfillment Questions employees secretly ask themselves:

   - **Contributing:** How meaningful is the impact of my work to clients/customers/causes? What value am I creating?
   - **Competent:** How well am I meeting expectations?
   - **Important:** How much does my leader value my role? How much does my leader value what I personally and professionally bring to my role? How much do they care about my personal well-being?

5. Similar to when we are in an airplane and we're supposed to put our oxygen mask on first before a dependent's, we are best available for others *when our own needs are fulfilled*. Specifically in the workplace, employees are most available and willing to "put the company first" when they feel secure in their own need fulfillment.

6. Despite trying, employees can't satisfactorily fulfill their own workplace needs. They must be fulfilled by their leader, every employee's source of serotonin.

7. It is easier to ask for more money than ask to feel more appreciated. If an employee's needs are neglected or threatened, money will subconsciously be converted to a tool to obtain evidence that they are important to you.

CHAPTER 10

Proactive Accountability: The Employee Engagement and Experience Loop

"Enthusiasm is the mother of effort, and without
it nothing great was ever achieved."
—RALPH WALDO EMERSON

In this chapter, we'll be introducing the brain's secrets to employee engagement, covering:

- What "engagement" means and how to influence engagement components
- What signals employee engagement when coming into a new ask, task, or project
- The Employee Engagement and Experience Loop model
- How an employee's expectations, meaning, and beliefs affect engagement
- How leaders' beliefs limit employee engagement and performance
- The importance of clarity, confidence, and optimism

Inspiring Accountability's Approach to Employee Engagement

In a 2019 *Forbes* article on employee engagement, "10 Timely Statistics About the Connection Between Employee Engagement and Wellness," reporter Naz Beheshti digs into the details of how successful companies translate employee wellness into company value.

Beheshti writes, "The most successful organizations make employee engagement central to their business strategy. They give employees clear expectations and provide them with the tools and support to do their best work. Why are engaged teams more profitable? Those teams who score in the top 20% in engagement realize a 41% reduction in absenteeism, and 59% less turnover."

While companies with higher employee engagement have far more resources to outperform their competitors, the apathetic company that isn't proactive about engagement now gets pushed into a corner — or out of business.

According to *The Predictive Index*'s (*TPI*) 2017 article, "How to Calculate Employee Turnover Cost," average companies suffer 30% turnover, and each vacant spot that needs filling can cost the company up to five times that position's annual compensation. As *TPI* puts it, these costs are "largely avoidable."

Though *TPI* points to high turnover as a symptom of bad hiring practices, the blame cannot simply be placed on hiring mistakes. It's also about what an employer does with the workforce they have employed.

This is especially true regarding accountability. You want to develop employees with **proactive accountability**, helping them achieve Desired Results easier the first time around. With **responsive accountability**, too, you want to consider mistakes as a natural progression of learning. Poor employee engagement and development — not simply bad hires — are the most significant contributor to turnover.

Gallup's 2015 Q12 Survey observes, "Engaged employees are 59% less likely to seek out a new job or career in the next 12 months."

Consistent and high-quality engagement produces Desired

Results efficiently and effectively, and developing this potential is arguably any company's best path toward a competitive advantage.

So, what most affects an employee's engagement? The 2013 *Harvard Business Review* article, "Does Money Really Affect Motivation? A Review of the Research," offers a blunt answer: "The biggest organizational cause of disengagement is incompetent leadership."

Ouch, that was triggering.

Yet there's optimism in that line: it also means the greatest opportunity to *improve* engagement lies within *you*.

Inspiring Accountability asserts that leaders are 100% accountable for how they contribute to their employees' engagement. Engagement comes from what makes us human. It comes through our need to contribute, be competent, and feel important. Companies, leaders, and employees are all accountable for contributing to optimal engagement — but when employers task leaders with engaging their employees, this concept is often too elusive for leaders to have **actionable clarity** in *how* to do it.

To confidently contribute to engagement, it's necessary to understand it not as an abstract concept, but as a tangible process that can be influenced, inspired, and activated.

To do so, this chapter builds upon what you've learned in previous chapters about neurochemicals, our engagement and experience indicators, and the Hierarchy of Human Needs in the Workplace. Let's now explore the **Employee Engagement and Experience Loop**.

The Employee Engagement and Experience Loop: Defining Engagement

What does engagement mean to you?

Take a minute to think back to one of your own experiences of being engaged in a task. Was your feeling of being engaged activated by being busy? Working hard? Feeling enthusiastic while working? Think about what made that time of feeling engaged in your work different than times you didn't.

To truly understand how to support an employee's engagement, and your own, let's look at the first building blocks of Inspiring Accountability's Employee Engagement and Experience Loop model. Let's review how this loop is created, step-by-step.

INSPIRING ACCOUNTABILITY IN THE WORKPLACE

Employee Engagement and Experience Loop®

% Effort
toward Result

Feeling
during effort

www.inspiringaccountability.com
©Copyright Elaina Marie, 2018. Do not use, copy or duplicate without permission.

As shown in the above diagram, **engagement** is defined as the percentage of *effort* toward the Desired Result and the *feeling* experienced during that effort.

Feeling engaged is an active experience of exerting effort through action and feeling *good* during the effort and action. How closely does this relate to your personal example of being engaged?

Since effort is the only part of an employee's contribution toward results that is actually within their full control, *effort is the most solid component for which we can hold an employee accountable.* The Employee Engagement and Experience Loop model underscores the value of incentivizing and rewarding effort as the primary mechanism to get results.

But what determines the amount of effort we provide and what we feel during the effort?

The feeling we have *before* the effort (see diagram below).

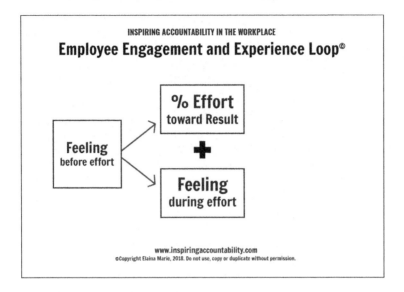

If we're feeling good and optimistic about the imminent task, project, or person with whom we will be working, we're likely to put more effort in and feel better doing it. If we're dreading a task, we'll be less motivated to put in full effort and likely continue feeling some dread throughout.

Think back to a specific project you worked on where you were truly engaged. How did you feel before you started? Do you see how that feeling affected your engagement, how much effort you applied, and how you felt during the task?

So, if engagement includes how we feel *during* effort, which is strongly influenced by how we feel before the effort, what determines how we feel *before* the effort?

This feeling is determined by how *we expect to feel after* or *how we remember feeling* when engaging in something similar in the past.

What lets us know if we feel positively or negatively about a task in the first place? What determines if our interest is positive (keeping us engaged, receptive, and resourceful) or negative (triggering us into disengagement, defensiveness, or complete shutdown)?

It could be none other than — drumroll — *neurochemicals!*

Usually dependent on the Hierarchy of Needs, neurochemicals incentivize and reward engagement, as well as create the interest, or expected or remembered feeling, to engage.

As if we are placed in front of a maze and expect cheese, we look forward to projects we remember as, or expect to be, neurochemically rewarding. We feel neurochemical benefits before the task, like Ralphie the Lab Rat got the feel-good dopamine at the beginning of the maze. That dopamine hit continues as we go along. It is the "cheese" we expect from last time that leads the brain to look forward to another round in our own workplace maze.

Our needs play a big role in creating this association. If we expect or remember positive feelings associated with being seen as contributing, competent, and important, the neurochemical reward becomes an incentive to repeat that experience.

And what is the primary source of an employee's neurochemical experience in the workplace? How do employees feel like they're being seen as contributing, competent, and important? Naturally, it is their leader's serotonin-rich acknowledgment. Now we can start to see the influence and opportunities you, as a leader, have in inspiring employee engagement.

As an example, meet Beth.

Beth is asked to write a prospectus that will outline a three-year plan for a large client her company is trying to acquire. Upon being assigned the task, she *subconsciously remembers* the last prospectus she wrote. Her work was integral to signing the company's largest client to date. For that hard work, she got meaningful acknowledgment from her managers and even received a bonus.

Remembering her previous success with a similar task generates positive feelings for the similar task that she is about to begin. She expects it to go well and coincide with a neurochemical reward. While this alone will not guarantee Beth's success on the current prospectus, it ensures she has the incentive to be highly engaged, boosting her overall odds of a successful result.

Let's learn why our brain loves these automated association loops, and how they apply to inspiring engagement.

Solidifying the Loop with Predictability

You may know the classic experiment on social conditioning: Pavlov's dog. Here's a quick refresher:

Russian physiologist Ivan Petrovich Pavlov started ringing a bell before he served his dog food. After a few rounds of bell ringing and food served, the dog's brain created a response loop of sensory input ("I hear a bell!"), meaning ("Food is coming!"), and expectation ("I get to eat now!"). Over time, the dog began salivating every time he heard the bell, even if the dog had not yet seen food. The anticipation created from past experience was enough to initiate this physical response and expectation. Pavlov's dog is the very same principle explored when Ralphie the Lab Rat associated the beginning of the maze with reward at the end.

What motivates the brain to create these associations that automate aspects of our experience? When it comes to the brain, safety is the top motivator, led by the creature brain, and these associations create a sense of safe predictability.

As discussed in previous chapters, the oldest part of our brain, the reactive creature brain, is highly protective when it senses perceived threats to our safety. The operative word here is "perceived," as the reactive creature brain doesn't clearly differentiate between physical and emotional safety or between real threats and imagined threats.

The creature brain's seniority means that our brains place extremely high value on keeping us safe from perceived threats, and the creature brain often becomes our brains' first responder.

To our creature brain, predictability is coded as safe, whereas uncertainty or not knowing what's next or what to expect is generally coded as less safe. This need for predictability makes it attractive for our brains to try to group familiar or similar sensory input into an automated input-response loop.

The brain creates a safe sense of predictability by connecting dots between situational experiences and ultimate outcomes. This data is then used to create a subconscious loop of association and expectation.

Let's recap what we've learned so far:

- Engagement is driven by feelings.
- Feelings start as neurochemicals.
- These feelings get triggered positively or negatively by how our needs are fulfilled or threatened.

Next, you'll learn how this loop comes full circle:

- We create meaning, beliefs, and expectations based on these needs.
- These beliefs and expectations become our experience.

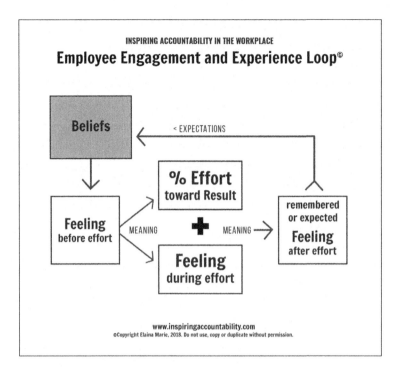

Employee Engagement and Experience Loop©

Beliefs

< EXPECTATIONS

Feeling before effort

MEANING

% Effort toward Result

➕

MEANING →

Feeling during effort

remembered or expected Feeling after effort

There's one more important step that solidifies the Engagement and Experience Loop: *How we create meaning, beliefs, and expectations.*

Meaning

Take a moment to consider differences between feeling nervous and feeling excited. Physiologically, there isn't much of a difference. Our heart beats faster, our breathing accelerates, and our palms get sweaty. *The difference is the **meaning** we attach to what we're experiencing or expecting to experience.*

Meaning is the explanation we create to make sense of a new experience, which usually determines our response (how we feel) before, during, or after the experience. Meaning is how we make sense of a moment. The details of what's happening remain the same, but the meaning we make creates different feelings about it and, therefore, completely different experiences.

If we expect the event will result in something positive for us, we will likely feel a sense of positive anticipation, excitement, and optimism. If, however, we expect a negative result may be looming, we'll feel nervous.

For instance, those who like public speaking probably anticipate they will do well, make a difference, and be seen as competent. Therefore, if they experience the above physiological symptoms, the meaning they make is to associate them with feeling excited. Conversely, for those who dislike public speaking, they are likely worried that it won't go well or that they may be seen as incompetent. The meaning of the physiological symptoms would instead be characterized as nervousness.

Humans are meaning-making machines! Whether we meet a new co-worker, get a new task, or try a new food, when we first recognize a new experience or sensory input (what we see, hear, etc.), our creature brain is eager to decide what it means (is it safe?) and our human brain is eager to decide how we feel about it (do we like it?). Broken down further, is this experience going to trigger avoidance-inducing negative neurochemicals or create incentivizing positive neurochemicals to engage more?

As a reference, we try to interpret what a given situation means by subconsciously looking for similar past examples.

For example, if we *feel* like we don't like someone whom we've just met, we'll probably start creating reasons to explain this feeling. But what came first, the feeling or the reasons? The initial feeling probably originated subconsciously from some reference point with a similar person we knew before. Especially since the subconscious processes an exorbitant amount more than our conscious mind can be aware of, our subconscious brain likely picked up on subtle cues to help us identify that we don't feel like we like this person, and then our conscious brain stepped in to create "rational" reasons to explain the feeling.

In the workplace, and when it comes to engagement, there are two types of meanings we make: **explanation meaning** and **needs impact meaning**.

Explanation Meaning

We first make an **explanation meaning** by using our conscious "thinking" brain. This is where we rationalize what's happening and create answers to questions like, "Why is this happening?" and "What is it about me, another person, group, situation, or environment that is making this happen?"

Let's use Jim, an employee, as an example. Jim is at his desk already when his supervisor Cameron arrives to work. Cameron uncharacteristically walks past Jim's desk without saying hello. In order to make sense of this uncommon occurrence, Jim can consider one of two different scenarios: 1. Perhaps Cameron is upset with him (negative); 2. Perhaps Cameron is very busy and focused this morning (positive). Each of these possible explanations for Cameron's behavior will leave Jim feeling completely different about the same experience.

Jim feels this interaction is positive or negative depending on past experiences that Jim's brain codes as similar, and what fits his current beliefs. If Jim believes Cameron genuinely likes him, and they have had positive experiences historically, he's more likely to make meaning that Cameron must be busy, and does not take it personally. However, if Jim is used to Cameron getting upset easily, he will be much more likely to make the meaning that Jim did something to upset Cameron to explain the brush off.

Needs Impact Meaning

After we make explanation meaning, we develop **needs impact meaning** in the *subconscious*. Needs impact meaning answers the question the creature brain needs to know: "How does this fulfill or threaten my needs?"

In the workplace, needs impact meaning can answer a question like, "How does this event impact my need to be seen as contributing, competent, and important?"

As for Jim, if he makes an explanation meaning that Cameron is busy, he may make a needs impact meaning that the brush off meant nothing and doesn't affect him. He's safe from criticism and judgment or other threatened needs because Cameron is not upset with him. Jim may even make a meaning that he could be useful and offer to see if Cameron needs help, adding to Jim's ability to contribute meaningfully, with the additional opportunity of positively impacting his needs.

If Jim instead makes the explanation meaning that Cameron is upset with him, Jim will likely subconsciously make a needs impact meaning that his competence or importance are damaged or under threat, perhaps going into a subtle self-protection mode against Cameron. He might internally get defensive and try to make Cameron wrong. This will be explored further in the next chapter on Trigger and Disengagement Loops.

After we create meanings, we start collecting, compiling, and compounding them into established beliefs.

Beliefs

Once we have collected enough evidence or similar meanings to solidify them as predictable — which doesn't take much — the brain integrates the sensory input and meaning together.

Our brains apply this association more generally to other moments. The meaning locks in as a belief, which in turn produces expectations. In an instant, that loop is locked in, and the brain no longer needs to put attention on re-evaluating similar sensory inputs and situations. For better or worse, a neurological shortcut has been established.

At its core, a **belief** is a generalization about our experience that helps anticipate and create future experiences to make life predictable and therefore safer for the creature brain. While meanings make sense of a moment, beliefs are generalized to make sense of related moments *forever,* and they are applied to every future moment with a similar context.

Thinking back to previous examples, we can see even more clearly how Ralphie and Pavlov's dog each created meaning which generalized into expectations (beliefs). When Ralphie noticed those same two corners, or Pavlov's dog heard his usual bell, their brains made the meaning that reward was imminent.

To make it even easier to process, these meanings generalized to become more abstract. We saw this when Ralphie began expecting reward when he remembered two corners, and soon the association generalized to simply seeing the maze. The expectation of reward becomes associated with more and more generalized sensory input.

So too, human brains adapted to help calm the protective creature brain by creating predictable expectations out of familiar sensory input. Beliefs solidify the Engagement and Experience Loop, automating what creates our incentive to engage and our feelings before, during, and after an experience.

As we saw with Beth, who was neurochemically rewarded at the end of the first prospectus, she now experiences a neurochemical reward as she thinks about beginning another, generalizing one prospectus to all. Reward becomes a neurochemical incentive and creates the expected or remembered feeling that indicates we "like" a task, project, or person. In short, beliefs and expectations give context to how we feel, which ultimately creates our experiences.

A simple example is having one or a few interactions with someone and deciding you don't like their behavior (meaning in the moment), which often becomes a generalized belief that you don't like that person (and probably never will). The same applies to tasks, departments, and essentially anything we would form an opinion about.

Once in place, beliefs shape all future-related decisions indefinitely until the belief is changed. Beliefs become a subconscious filter for what we consciously notice, directly informing our behavior and determining our decisions.

In the workplace, beliefs can do the following:

- Beliefs can be decisions about how things are and will be indefinitely, either explicitly or implicitly, using or implying words like "never" and "always." For example: "My manager *never...*" or "She *always...*" or "I can *never* rely on..."
- Beliefs are easily made about another person or team. For

example: "My manager is caring," or "My manager is clueless," or "That co-worker is difficult to work with."

- Beliefs can autopilot how we interpret actions and interactions. In other words, interactions are not evaluated and/or re-evaluated.
- Beliefs can stop us from being curious.
- Beliefs can include assumptions (which are also beliefs).
- Beliefs can reflect and/or create our experience because they shape what evidence our brains scan for and acknowledge. In other words, beliefs can become our filter.

Let's examine that last point a bit closer.

Do you have any beliefs that aren't true?

If you take a moment to contemplate this question, the answer is *no.* All of our beliefs are "true" to us, and our brain helps us continue to notice and code sensory input and behavior as evidence to reinforce our beliefs.

We then begin to subconsciously construct and create our experiences — and our very lives — to reflect our beliefs. Our experience is shaped by the evidence our brains subconsciously continue to notice. For example, if you see your manager as caring, you especially notice their caring behavior and disregard, ignore, or re-characterize behavior that another could consider uncaring.

How Beliefs Limit and Create Our Experience

The brain uses two powerful tools to help us create, stabilize, and repeat our experiences at work and in life: 1. The reticular activating system, and 2. inattentional blindness. Let's look at these in more detail.

Reticular Activating System

You may remember in Chapter 7 we discussed the importance of "Revisiting" Desired Results with your employees. Revisiting engages the reticular activating system (RAS), a small but significant part of the brain that acts as a "bouncer" for what subconscious information is allowed to come into conscious recognition. All of your senses, except smell, are wired directly to this bundle of neurons that's about the size of your little finger. Let's expand our knowledge of the RAS to apply to the Engagement and Experience Loop and beliefs.

To again cite Timothy Wilson's 2004 book, *Strangers to Ourselves: Discovering the Adaptive Unconscious,* Wilson explains that the conscious mind can only process 40 pieces of information per second while the subconscious can process 11 million pieces of information per second. Your subconscious notices, knows, and remembers a frustrating amount more than your conscious mind will ever allow you to "know."

The RAS is responsible for filtering the massive amounts of information your sensory organs are constantly throwing at it, and selecting what is most important for your conscious mind to pay attention. The RAS has a major impact in the sensory information that you are consciously aware of daily. And as we know, sensory input is what begins our engagement or disengagement loops. What we notice is what we then make meaning of, have feelings about, and eventually solidify beliefs and expectations around.

The RAS only allows that very small percentage of the most relevant information to come into consciousness.

How does the RAS decide what is relevant or irrelevant? How does it know what to bring to consciousness? The answers are found in topics that will be very familiar to you now. The RAS judges what's relevant primarily based on safety, beliefs, and attention.

Safety

The RAS filter's main priority is bringing to your consciousness anything that threatens your safety or the safety of your loved ones. This is why you can spot threats, large or small, in your day-to-day even when you're not looking for them. In the workplace, this will include physical safety, but more commonly in the workplace safety will be defined as threats to our top three needs, being seen as contributing, competent, and important.

Belief Validation

The RAS seeks information that validates your already established beliefs. It filters the world through the parameters you give it, and your beliefs inform those parameters.

Looking at how the RAS and the Employee Experience and Engagement Loop work together, the brain pays attention to and scans for what we expect and believe. When we create a belief like, "*This* is how it is," the RAS says, "Okay!" and ignores information that doesn't match this belief-based loop. Contradictory information becomes unnecessary and irrelevant.

If you believe your manager doesn't value your work, your brain will be searching for and bringing to consciousness evidence that supports this belief. If you believe you work efficiently, you will likely see evidence of how you are working efficiently. It doesn't mean that your manager never acknowledges your value or that your efficiency was unusually poor on your latest task. It means your brain won't pay precious attention to or prioritize evidence that doesn't fit your beliefs. The RAS helps you see what you want to see, and in doing so, influences your conscious experience.

The adage "seeing is believing" in this case is actually backward. More accurately, we see what we already believe.

Attention

Did you ever play "I Spy" on a road trip? Whether it was something yellow or a Volkswagen Bug, this focused attention helped you see these items more easily, letting less important visual input filter out.

Your attention and active interest in something communicates what else to bring to consciousness. The RAS's prioritization on attention is the reason that, for example, when you decide on a make and model of car to buy, you start seeing it everywhere. It's as if you said, "My attention is on a white Tesla, show me more!"

In this application, your RAS takes what you consciously want to focus on and creates a filter for it. It then sifts through the infinite sensory input in front of us, say 11 million pieces, and presents only the pieces that are important to you, whittling it down to the top 40. And that top 40 is *competitive*. All of this happens without you consciously noticing.

This is the final piece of context that supports the value of Revisiting, as we learned from **Accountability Attention** in Chapter 7. When an employee believes there will be revisiting on the completion and quality of a task, the brain warrants more attention to the task than something that won't seriously be followed up. It's protecting competency (marked important and worthy of attention) by keeping more focus on it and prioritizing it differently than if it was simply one more ask in a sea of sensory input.

What happens when our attention skews toward problems?

If your team culture is characterized by focusing on problems — incompetence, negligence, everyday frustrations — this focus will signal to the RAS to find evidence of problems and keep bringing them to consciousness.

Focusing on problems keeps people stuck in problems. By focusing on what's possible, though, you and your team can start seeing *possibilities*. This gives weight to the popular sayings "Perception is reality," and "You are what you think."

Further evidence of the power of attention can be found in the idea that where we direct attention can make us subconsciously blind to even the most obvious of conflicting evidence. This is a concept identified as **inattentional blindness**, and sometimes called **perceptual blindness**. The term inattentional blindness entered the psychology lexicon in the 1998 book *Inattentional Blindness*. The authors, psychologists Arien Mack, Ph.D., of the New School for Social Research, and the late Irvin Rock, Ph.D., of the University of California, Berkeley, described a series of experiments on the phenomenon.

In "Sights Unseen," a 2001 article for the *American Psychological Association's Monitor on Psychology* magazine, Dr. Mack said, "I came away from our studies convinced that there's no conscious perception without attention." The article goes on to say that the findings also led her to suspect that "the brain undertakes considerable perceptual processing outside of conscious awareness before attention is engaged and that objects or events that are personally meaningful are most likely to capture people's attention."

In summary, threats to safety, our beliefs, and where we direct our attention influence what's allowed into our consciousness, creating our experience and perceived reality.

In the workplace, these beliefs may apply to a colleague you trust, a manager you dislike, or an employee you are convinced is lazy. Your brain will keep finding evidence of these and ignoring conflicting evidence, strengthening the belief.

Once these beliefs are stabilized, there's only one more small step that solidifies the Engagement and Experience Loop: beliefs become baseline expectations.

Solidifying Baseline Expectations

Our beliefs become **expectations**, which are simply predictions about what will happen or be true whenever we experience familiar sensory input. Remember, our brains love predictability.

To that end, we hold expectations for almost everything, whether we realize it or not. Since predictability provides the brain a feeling of safety, we continually set expectations about the behaviors of other people, systems, cultures, and indeed the world itself to keep our experiences relatively stable.

When we are exposed to new information or a new experience, we eventually make enough meaning to figure out what we believe we can reliably expect. This creates a **baseline of expectations**. Ralphie the Lab Rat's eventual expectation baseline was that being put in front of a maze (sensory input) meant imminent cheese. Pavlov's dog? Food. Beth's prospectus? Ultimate success, and maybe even another bonus.

If, for example, every time we work on a project with Adam it goes smoothly and efficiently, we'll create a baseline of expectations that working with Adam will *always* go smoothly and efficiently. We'll expect that Adam's "good nature" and "integrity in his work" (explanation meaning) supports our need to be seen as contributing, competent, and important (needs impact meaning). As we know, this directly impacts our neurochemical experience.

We conclude that Adam is great to work with (belief) and when we are put on another project with Adam, we already feel good about it, *expecting* another imminent win ahead. Our brain keeps scanning for evidence of this belief, providing a better chance that we'll continue to see these attributes in Adam, keeping us feeling confident and optimistic during the effort and ready to celebrate neurochemically upon its successful completion. This is, in essence, the Engagement and Experience Loop.

How Can You Use the Employee Engagement and Experience Loop to Get Better Results?

Now that you understand how beliefs play an important role in employee success, how can you apply this knowledge to your team?

If an employee believes he or she will be successful, their brain will scan for evidence of competency and success, creating a much better chance of being successful. The reason that "success begets success" is because once you're successful at something, it creates a belief you can be successful again. Expecting success creates a belief that impacts what evidence we notice and where we put our attention, which helps us be more successful.

Which brings us to a core leadership concept: what we expect is usually what we get.

Although this is a useful generalization, now that you have this understanding of engagement, you might see it's actually one level deeper. Most leaders "expect" employees to perform very well but may not genuinely *believe* that their employees can or will meet expectations.

More accurately, *you get the results you believe your employees will actually get.*

Given that feeling confident going into a project determines engagement and likelihood of achievement, ask yourself if you are helping your employees believe they will be successful. Are you helping them expect a positive outcome with positive rewards, even if just a neurochemical acknowledgment?

Employees rarely exceed what they believe is possible for themselves to achieve, and *what you believe is possible becomes their possibility ceiling*. Note, what you believe is possible is not the same as what you want or expect. You can *want* your employees to be better or *expect* them to perform at a certain level, but if you don't genuinely *believe* in their potential to achieve results, it's likely they know it. It's unfortunately very easy to subconsciously, subtly, or overtly communicate and create an employee's personal **possibility ceiling**.

Leaders can also raise an employee's possibility ceiling by seeing more potential in the employee than the employee believes possible (also called **perceived capability**, highlighted in Chapter 14). We are inspired by those who see us as more capable or who help us believe we can be more than we are. Leaders that focus on cultivating employees' potential instead of pointing out their problems create a fulfilling and inspiring workplace experience. These are the leaders, in the workplace and in the world, that raise possibility ceilings.

If you help employees expect success, you will help them be more successful. If you doubt their abilities, you'll likely cause them to also doubt their abilities. Employees worried about being unsuccessful (a belief) will subconsciously scan for evidence of their own incompetency, leading to lower chances of success.

This also applies to you as a leader. If you believe your employee is inept or lazy, and therefore focus on these features, guess what evidence your brain will find and feed back to you? (You will learn more about combating this in the next chapter on breaking these sorts of disengagement loops.)

My two favorite phrases that capture the power of beliefs are: "What you focus on, expands," and "Where attention goes, energy flows." What do you want employees focusing on to expand? Do you want their attention and energy flowing to what's in the way or what's possible?

Some Thoughts on Positive Influence

The best way to contribute to an employee's engagement is to *help them have actionable clarity, feel confident, and be optimistic* coming into a task. The magic is in helping to create a positive feeling *before and after* the action, helping your employees expect to routinely feel great after a task or project. When employees enter into a task with actionable clarity (a.k.a. the "first action step" in the Results Model), they start feeling confident and optimistic going into the task. This helps them expect a positive result and therefore feel more positive during the task.

Any additional ways you build confidence in abilities, like perceived capability (covered in Chapter 14), will enhance the engagement loop. Additionally, creating a more optimistic team mindset and culture, one that expects good results are both *possible* and *probable*, promises neurochemical rewards that become engagement incentives.

Helping employees focus on what's possible instead of getting stuck in what's in the way is one way the Results Model positively contributes to positive engagement loops.

Before we go into more practical ways to help create positive engagement and experience loops, we first have to see what happens when this loop is instead linked to expecting negative outcomes. Instead of inspiring engagement, next we will battle disengagement.

Integration Questions:

1. How would you describe your current contribution to your employees' engagement?

2. How often do you expect positive outcomes for yourself? How about for your employees?

3. How might you improve clarity, confidence, and optimism for yourself? For your employees?

4. What is the difference, if any, between what you expect from employees and what you feel is likely for them to achieve?

5. Are you creating a limited possibility ceiling for any of your employees, and if yes, how can you start to shift that?

Key Take-Aways:

1. The Experience and Engagement Loop completes the following process:
   - Engagement is driven by feelings.
   - Feelings start as neurochemicals.
   - These feelings get triggered positively or negatively by how our needs are fulfilled or threatened.
   - We create meaning, beliefs, and expectations on these needs.
   - These beliefs and expectations become our experience.

2. Employees' feelings during tasks directly affect engagement, which affects future iterations of employee engagement with similar tasks.

3. Neurochemicals create the feeling of engagement, determining if we respond positively (keeping us engaged, receptive, and resourceful), or negatively (triggering us into disengagement, defensiveness, or complete shutdown).

4. Predictability is coded as safe, whereas uncertainty or not knowing what's next or what to expect is generally coded as less safe.

5. What a leader believes about an employee plays a significant role in the employee's engagement and performance. Inspiring Accountability methodology asserts that leaders are 100% accountable for contributing to how employees engage.

6. Helping employees focus on what's possible instead of getting stuck in what's in the way is one way the Results Model contributes to positive engagement loops.

7. Employees rarely exceed what they think is possible for themselves to achieve, and what you think is possible becomes their possibility ceiling.

8. Leaders can raise an employee's possibility ceiling by seeing more potential in the employee than the employee believes possible.

9. The most effective leaders help employees experience productive response loops by offering more positive sensory input, and creating a predictable environment where employees expect positive outcomes.

10. Consistent and quality engagement is our best bet for getting consistent and quality results from our team, strengthening proactive accountability.

11. High-quality engagement produces Desired Results efficiently and effectively, and it's arguably any company's best competitive advantage today.

12. The best way to contribute to an employee's engagement is to help them have clarity, feel confident, and be optimistic.

CHAPTER 11

Trigger and Disengagement Loops

"To avoid criticism say nothing, do nothing, be nothing."
—ELBERT HUBBARD, *LITTLE JOURNEYS TO THE HOMES OF THE GREAT VOL. 3: AMERICAN STATESMEN*

In this chapter, you'll learn about the brain's role in employees' disengagement and what to do about it, including topics like:

- Why and how the brain gets triggered and disengages
- Why it's against human nature to easily break Trigger and Disengagement Loops
- Tips to break Trigger and Disengagement Loops

The above quote by Elbert Hubbard illuminates the perplexing issue of engagement in the workplace: our safety-seeking brains are quick to shut down when criticized. We cope and compensate by saying less, doing less, and being less in an attempt to protect ourselves by limiting the behavior to criticize. Essentially, we disengage in life, or in this case, the workplace.

This type of shutting down can be both conscious and subconscious. Our brains often stifle engagement or get triggered into disengagement to avoid criticism or confirmation that we're not seen as contributing, competent, or important. Similar to engagement becoming an automated loop, disengagement also operates in this way. Disengagement is every leader's barrier to getting results.

Thankfully, similar to leaders having a significant impact on inspiring engagement, leaders can also learn about how **Trigger and Disengagement Loops** occur to better prevent threats to engagement.

How Engagement Loops Become Disengagement Loops

In the previous chapter, you learned how clarity, confidence, and optimism create sustainable engagement when one begins a task. You also learned how a leader's beliefs become possibility ceilings for employee effort and engagement.

We also know that positive expectations with a task, or the people associated with a task, create engagement loops. These loops incentivize us to put effort toward what feels neurochemically rewarding. Positive engagement loops add up to powerful, proactive accountability, which helps leaders get better results with employees faster, the first time, and prevents the need for responsive accountability.

But these powerful engagement loops can easily become associated with negative feelings. The **Employee Engagement and Experience Loop** can equally inform us on how and why disengagement happens.

Let's learn about this through the story of Amir and Cathy.

Amir just started as a customer service representative at a software company. He left his previous employer because he felt service representatives there were being treated like cogs in a wheel. In Amir's new position, he hopes everything he heard about this new company's friendly and appreciative culture is true.

Since Amir is coming into a fresh environment that he hopes (a form of expectation) will be friendly and appreciative, Amir will be looking for evidence to create new Engagement and Experience Loops, (subconsciously, of course), that will begin to solidify his beliefs, expectations, and experience of his new job.

After onboarding, Amir begins learning how the company manages customer service. Eager to begin his online training, Amir arrives in the morning, grabs some coffee, and gets ready to begin learning how to help customers.

His manager, Cathy, comes over to say hello. Smiling warmly, she asks how he's doing and if he needs anything to get started. Cathy sees a picture Amir put up of his golden retriever and asks the dog's name. The chat makes Amir feel welcome, valued, and cared about.

This kind of greeting from Cathy happens to Amir the next morning, the next, and the next. Sometimes Amir tells her a funny story about his family, or she tells him about her fun weekend plans.

Amir interprets Cathy's rapport and positive behavior to mean that she cares about Amir. Then, after multiple days of consistent evidence, he makes a generalized belief that Cathy is a caring person and a caring manager — just like he had hoped!

This meaning is now a belief, reflecting the way she "always" is, which advances to become an expectation that Cathy will always be a caring manager because *that's simply who she is.* His Engagement and Experience Loop around Cathy has been created. He has a positive experience with Cathy and likes engaging with her.

After a couple of weeks experiencing this positive loop, though, Amir starts to notice that Cathy still hasn't responded to three of his emails with questions that she said he could email her. At first, he gave Cathy the benefit of the doubt, in alignment with his positive beliefs about her. He's about to start interacting with customers, though, and feels worried he won't be prepared to contribute or feel competent without these answers.

During their morning chats, Amir reminds Cathy twice that it would be very helpful to have clarification around the points addressed in his emails to her, and each time she assures him that she will get back to him that day. Cathy, however, does not follow through as promised. Being new, Amir doesn't feel comfortable pressing her further for fear of being labeled "the difficult new guy."

To make matters worse, he starts noticing that after Cathy talks with him in the morning, she also goes and talks to Sharice. And Darryl. And Martin. And then he hears it. Walking past the break room, he hears Sharice and Darryl conversing quietly, and he hears the nickname "Chatty Cathy." Amir starts to believe that maybe Cathy *doesn't* actually care about him: she likes to talk to *anyone*. So, Amir starts making meaning that maybe he *isn't* as important as he has presumed. Not to mention his frustration about the unanswered emails is conflicting with — and challenging — his current belief about Cathy being a great manager.

Amir's loop is still malleable because it's new, and evidence is still being gathered for its solidification. Given that his ability to contribute and be competent is threatened by her not getting back to him, he stops kicking out the conflicting evidence that Cathy is a caring and great manager, and begins to *incorporate* this negative evidence.

The loop instantly shifts the meanings to match the new "evidence." It's now operating from the belief and expectation that Cathy would rather talk than work, Amir can't rely on her to get back to him, and she doesn't really care that much about him because she will talk to *anyone*.

Now, every time Cathy comes by to chat, Amir gets triggered because it's a sign that she's *not* getting back to him and that he's *not* actually special. She's taking his time away from contributing to the company's goals so that she can avoid contributing herself. He now releases hope that she is a caring manager and relies on his new loop, digging a deeper **trigger trench,** a trigger solidified and strengthened with each repetition. With every future chatty conversation and unanswered email, Amir's new loop is now a dreaded **Trigger and Disengagement Loop**.

Trigger and Disengagement Loops

In the example with Amir and "Chatty Cathy," we can see a great summary of how neurochemicals and the Hierarchy of Human Needs in the Workplace create our experience:

- **Engagement is driven by feelings**: Amir was feeling great and engaged, but now he's feeling discouraged, frustrated, and less engaged.

- **Feelings start as neurochemicals**: Amir was feeling serotonin and oxytocin when he was feeling important and hopeful he would be a strong contributor. Now he's feeling an absence of positive neurochemicals and is likely to experience adrenaline and cortisol when he gets frustrated.

- **These feelings get triggered positively or negatively by our needs:** Amir's frustration increases increase because he fears he won't be seen as important, competent, or contributing meaningfully.

- **We create meaning, beliefs, and expectations on these needs:** Amir made meaning of Cathy's chatty behavior and failure to get back to him. This meaning developed into a belief that she would rather talk than work and that he can't rely on her.

- **These beliefs and expectations become our experience:** Amir's once optimistic experience is discouraging, frustrating, triggering, and disengaging.

Through this example, we see how an Engagement and Experience Loop can seamlessly shift into a Trigger and Disengagement Loop if the experience turns negative. Unfortunately, our brains pay more attention to the negative threats to our threat-response system.

As reported by an article in *The New York Times* by Alina Tugend, "Praise Is Fleeting, but Brickbats We Recall" (2012), almost everyone remembers negative experiences more strongly and in more detail than positive ones. Negative feedback has more impact than positive feedback, and bad impressions and negative stereotypes are quicker to form and more resistant to disconfirmation than good ones.

Negative feedback and experiences are damaging in the moment and longer lasting in our memories. Tugend gives us two compelling neurological reasons for this:

1. The brain handles positive and negative information in different hemispheres. Negative emotions generally involve more thinking and are processed more thoroughly than positive ones. Thus, we tend to spend more time thinking about unpleasant events than happy ones.

2. "Survival," Tugend quotes, "requires urgent attention to possible bad outcomes but less urgent with regard to good ones." Back when survival was mostly escaping physical threats, those who were more attuned to threats were more likely to survive. These traits were passed from survivor to survivor, passing their superior survival instincts and extra-sensitive threat-response systems to later and later generations, whether through genetics or observable behaviors and mindsets. You and your employees come from a long line of survivors with sharpened safety system responses.

This confirms that it's easier to create negative disengagement loops than positive engagement loops. On the flip side, it's substantially more difficult to both break the disengagement loops and sustain the positive ones.

The problem with the brain's automated association-response feature, specifically in the workplace, is that while we save ourselves from exhaustively re-figuring out how to do every task or re-evaluating how to respond to every person, *automated loops kill our curiosity.*

Once we've *evaluated* sensory input as worth paying attention to, *interpreted* (created meaning) and consciously or subconsciously *decided* (created a belief and expectations) on what to do with this information, our brain stops being curious and runs the now established program instead.

What does this mean for employee engagement?

In the workplace, once we've made up our mind on how to do something, how we feel about someone, or how we feel about a project, we stop re-evaluating. We create patterns and loops that act as operational software, executing the program instead of remaining curious. If we expect a positive result from our effort, we are eager to engage. If we expect a negative result from our effort, we are less inspired to engage.

When an employee is in an established loop, it is challenging for them to remain curious, innovative, or even notice information that would challenge the beliefs that structure the loop. Changing an expected negative experience with a task, project, or person becomes much less likely.

Disengagement Loops in Ralphie the Lab Rat

Let's examine how this would affect our old friend Ralphie the Lab Rat.

When Ralphie proceeds through his maze expecting cheese, he eagerly expends effort, and feels good while doing so. Similarly, the power of prediction can create a negative trigger loop.

Let's imagine that Ralphie is initially sprayed with cold water at the end of the maze in lieu of cheese. Over and over and over — no cheese, just a cold dousing. Instead of being eager and feeling great going through the maze as he did expecting cheese, Ralphie would feel anxious, hesitant, and less enthused if he expects something negative around the corner.

Negative feelings and hesitancy — the latter of which we could interpret as "less effort — essentially define **disengagement**. We could expect that as soon as Ralphie is placed in front of the cold water maze, he would immediately feel disengaged. Additionally, he would experience negative feelings and be hesitant with his effort to proceed. When he gets close to the end — regardless if the splash zone is turned on or not this time — Ralphie would already be expecting and therefore experiencing the worse-case scenario. He's learned his lesson and has made the association that seeing the maze means getting hosed. The negative feelings and anxiousness would cue right up, even if there was no promise that the same negative experience would occur.

In the workplace, we easily get in these trigger and disengagement loops with tasks, projects, and people. Say you get teamed up to work on a project with Timothy. You interpret his attitude as poor and he frequently complains about what is in the way rather than looking for possibilities. This attitude makes the project unnecessarily tiresome. You worry his poor contribution is negatively affecting how you are seen as contributing and competent, and your brain generalizes these meanings into beliefs. Next time you're told to pair with Timothy, you jump right into your **Trigger and Disengagement Loop**, feeling negatively and hesitant about a task, project or person, resulting in less enthusiasm and effort during the action or interaction.

Before you even start the next project with Timothy — "Oh, no. Him again!" — you're already feeling frustrated, and consider Timothy a threat to your ability to contribute and enjoy doing so. These feelings will almost certainly continue throughout the project and scuttle any chance to break the disengagement loop.

This response is not limited to moments working with people we don't like: let's say you see a dreaded task that you've been avoiding has finally become inevitable on your to-do list. You're feeling like it will be boring and menial. Or worse, perhaps you don't know how to start or you don't feel confident you'll be able to execute competently. You will likely go into this task feeling bored, squirrelly, anxious, or not very engaged. Another disengagement trigger!

Before we learn how to break Trigger and Disengagement Loops, let's first look at what we are up against.

How We Get Stuck: Trigger Trenches

Donald Hebb, a Canadian neuropsychologist known for his work in the field of associative learning, coined the saying, "Neurons that fire together, wire together."

Hebb's axiom refers to how every experience of sensory input triggers thousands of neurons, which ultimately form a "neural network" of neurons that fire together in response to a single repeated trigger.

You might have noticed that once something triggers you, it seems easier and easier to get triggered by the same thing. Let's say your manager has been on your case about a project, and calls to check in or has you address new concerns multiple times a day. You begin feeling triggered when you see your manager's name on the caller ID. Now, every time you get a call from your manager, you're getting triggered, regardless what the call is about.

From here, it gets worse because your trigger becomes more and more generalized (like when forming beliefs), making it easier to become triggered by a diluted version of the original behavior. At this stage, every time the phone rings, before you've even seen who it is, you feel those triggering, negative neurochemicals flare up.

Extrapolating Hebb's theory to the experience of being triggered, repeated activation between the components of what triggers you, primarily the sensory input (getting a call from your manager), the meaning you make (he or she doesn't think I'm competent), and the feelings you have (negative), begin firing off together like their own trigger highway — except the more the highway is used, the faster you can go.

Every time you get triggered, you feel those negative neurochemicals faster and easier. This is because each time the highway is used, synaptic strength and efficacy between the associated neurons increases. So your triggered neurons that fire together when your manager calls are now "wired together," increasing the strength and efficiency of your response every time your phone rings. You are now digging a deeper and deeper **trigger trench**.

You can see this with tasks and projects where you're expecting a negative outcome (like failure or disappointment). You get triggered when you think about working on them, resulting in your creature brain desperately wanting to disengage while your rational human brain anxiously perseveres to complete them.

This trigger trench can be seen in Amir's issues with Cathy's failure to get back to him. Every time Amir sees a sliver of evidence of Cathy's managerial neglect, he feels triggered. He's knee-deep in his own trigger trench, digging deeper and deeper.

But what about the times that Cathy *did* get back to him? Did he notice those moments? Wouldn't conflicting evidence completely change the belief that Cathy is unreliable?

Unfortunately, there are some formidable brain patterns that make breaking Trigger and Disengagement Loops inconvenient and challenging.

Breaking Trigger and Disengagement Loops

Considering how inattentional blindness and our reticular activating system (introduced in the previous chapter) can powerfully filter out information, it can be really difficult to break trigger and disengagement loops.

These brain behaviors block us from consciously seeing or knowing what doesn't fit into our loop and its related beliefs. It will be difficult for the brain to register when, for example, Cathy *does* get back to Amir, or when Timothy *does* have a positive attitude when working with you on a project.

Before we explore breaking disengagement loops, let's learn common ways that employees become triggered.

The Classic "Triggering" Email

Melissa gets an email from her manager that says, "Please come see me in my office as soon as you get back."

What could this mean? What does it mean for her needs?

If she hasn't received an email from her manager like this before, red flags go up, but curiosity remains. Her brain identifies potentially triggering information and seeks to interpret the meaning.

Explanation Meanings start firing in Melissa's brain:

- Something must be wrong.
- I did something wrong!
- My manager is upset about the project I just submitted.
- Maybe she's upset with me because I spoke up too much at that meeting?
- I don't know how or why, but I am totally getting fired.

Then **Needs Impact Meanings** start to creep in:

- I must be in trouble (threatened importance).
- She must be upset with me (threatened importance).
- I must have messed up (threatened competence).

All this processing happens in an instant, and Melissa quickly heads to her manager's office.

"Melissa, I reviewed the document you worked on, and I'm very disappointed. Did you even put time or effort into it at all?"

The Explanation Meaning of getting the "come see me" email confirms itself as being, "My manager is upset with me."

The subconsciously-created Needs Impact Meaning gets registered as, "When I get emails like this, my importance, competence, and contribution are under threat." If this happens a few times in a row — or sometimes even only once — the belief and expectation become, "Every time my manager emails me to come see her right away, I can expect that I'm going to get chewed out for doing something wrong."

On some level, we have all probably come to expect that a stern tone and brief communications are indicators of a negative interaction.

So, next time a "come see me" email comes through, what happened before becomes the expectation for what will happen next time.

A great rule of thumb to prevent a trigger loop like this from solidifying for an employee is to include context in these types of emails or calls to employees. As you've learned, contribution context helps engage employees in the Results Model, and a little context also goes a long way to avoid triggering your employees. Don't let the threat-response system make up meaning if you can define it more usefully instead.

How can you add context to curt requests to help employees stay engaged, receptive, and resourceful? Try including contexts like, "We need to make some updates to the project," or "We need to brainstorm how to fix an issue right away," or "We have to revise this document right away." This simple and useful context will help the employee remain more ready, receptive, and resourceful for what's to follow. The creature brain, once triggered, can easily expect the worst, and we now know how powerfully expectations influence outcomes.

Given that so much of getting triggered is operating subconsciously, you can see why it's not easy to break these negative association loops. Although what's in the way is daunting, let's explore what *is* possible.

Breaking Trigger and Disengagement Loops: What's Possible

Did you know you're supposed to reapply sunscreen at least every two hours? Imagine you're doing a long weekend trip to your favorite sunny spot, and there's a new, innovative sunscreen on the market that provides all-day sun protection with no need to reapply. You eagerly grab a bottle of All-Day Sunscreen and head off to safely enjoy some Vitamin D.

The sun is great, but the sunscreen is *not*. Apparently, you're allergic to whatever is in the sunscreen. Your skin gets inflamed and itchy, and your face resembles a sun-dried tomato. Over time, the itch and inflammation go down, but your face is still noticeably red. Worse, you have to go back to work on Monday. The whole week back at work, you endure the inevitable looks, stares, and questions. You will never, *ever* use that sunscreen again. You experience maximum disengagement with this sunscreen.

One month later, you start hearing new advertising for All-Day Sunscreen *for Sensitive Skin* — the reformulated option for those with allergies to the original formula. You even have a couple friends who have tried it and had no reaction.

You're gearing up for a sunny summer weekend and cringe thinking about what happened last time.

Here's the question: how many ads or friends' testimonials would you have to hear to try the new and improved All-Day Sunscreen for Sensitive Skin?

Everyone has a different answer. Some say right away. Some say a few. Some recall that inflammation and embarrassment associated with the All-Day Sunscreen debacle and think, *not in a million years*. *When you're looking to break Trigger and Disengagement Loops, remember that the amount of time it takes to trust evidence that something (or someone) has truly changed is different for everyone.* Few people eagerly update their beliefs and engagement based on one conflicting piece of evidence. We not only need to *see* the new behavior, but we need enough consistent evidence to *trust* it will now be forever repeated, worthy of being replaced as the new predictable and safe expectation.

To get the brain to start seeing new and conflicting evidence, one has to overcome the engagement and experience loop, RAS filters, and inattentional blindness. These cognitive patterns have perfected their skills over millions of years, so having a little perseverance is the minimum requirement for battling a Trigger and Disengagement Loop.

It may be difficult, but it's not hopeless. Here are a few tips that will give you your best shot at breaking Trigger and Disengagement Loops, outlined here and then further explained:

Breaking your own Trigger and Disengagement Loops, or influencing employees' loops with tasks, projects, or people:
1. Put your attention on scanning for conflicting evidence
2. Reverse the generalization back to specifics
3. Focus on making new meaning

Breaking employee Trigger and Disengagement Loops they may have with you:
1. Be consistent
2. Acknowledge what you're working on
3. Be genuine
4. Don't expect change right away, but stay with it

Breaking Your Own Trigger and Disengagement Loops, or Influencing Employees' Loops

Requirement #1: Put your attention on scanning for conflicting evidence

Since what you put attention on is a priority for what the RAS allows through to your consciousness, you're going to have to put your attention on scanning for what you *would like* to see and believe.

Like search and rescue dogs, an effective search begins with a clear sample of exactly what to look for. This specific direction communicates where the attention goes.

If a search dog is out looking for the scent of a certain perfume, imagine the challenge if the dog didn't have a reference sample of what to scan or smell for. The dog would pay attention to every scent in the environment equally. The dog would be overwhelmed with options and would be slower and less likely to produce useful results. If you want to break a trigger loop, you have to choose a new reference sample your brain can start scanning for.

When we don't know what we're looking for yet — like in the first week of a new job — we're scanning everything. We're still curious. We're determining what's important. But once we start solidifying some loops, our brain's "scent dogs" stop spending so much energy to scan all sensory input, and instead begin to filter for what our newly established loops label as important. When scent dogs have one scent in mind, much like when we solidify a belief and expectation, the brain will scan and sort for that specific scent, easily filtering out anything else.

To break your own trigger and disengagement loops, you're going to have to update your scanning focus. Let's say you see one of your employees as generally incompetent. This means you've been scanning for examples of incompetence. To break this trigger loop and reclaim curiosity, you're going to have to start scanning for ways that employee *is* competent.

Or if you see your manager as uncaring, your brain scans for examples that they are, indeed, uncaring. You'll need to set the intention to scan for ways they *do* express care.

Which brings us to what happens when we begin noticing conflicting evidence. A solidified loop, complete with beliefs and expectations, allows only two responses to conflicting evidence:

1. You can kick it out and label it as a negligible exception, maintaining the loop and belief as-is (most common).
2. You can incorporate it and update the loop, creating a new belief and expectation.

Much like the previous sunscreen example, most of us will kick out initial conflicting evidence of a new formula quickly and easily because *we don't trust it yet.*

In cases where our employee showed some competence, or our manager had a moment we could interpret as caring, it's easy for the brain to write it off as simply an exception. It may have happened once, but it's not enough to change what we expect in the future. Changing beliefs into something more hopeful can be quite vulnerable, and the creature brain will eagerly stamp it as not worth the risk.

When influencing an employee to break a trigger with a task, project, or person, ask questions that help them put attention on the exceptions. Reframe their generalizations to more specific conflicting evidence. If the complaint is, "Alex always slows down projects," you could ask: "What about the time you and Alex completed the project perfectly and on time? Maybe this time you could look for ways to work together to get another perfect result!"

The effort to look for conflicting evidence, and the hesitancy for our creature brain to trust it, can make beliefs hard to change, which is why many of us stay in trigger trenches for a long, long time. But when you want change, here's the place to start.

Requirement #2: Reverse the generalization back to specifics

Remember how moments generalize more and more abstractly until a generalized belief is stabilized? To break trigger loops, we want to de-stabilize the belief by reversing the process that created it.

Move from a generalized belief about the person back to a specific behavior.

Using curiosity, challenge yourself or a triggered employee to narrow down to a more specific behavior so that it's easier to start noticing specific exceptions. You can ponder, "What does this person specifically do that most triggers me?" You can ask an employee something like, "What is the actual behavior you notice that you find most frustrating?"

It will make our third requirement easier because it's easier to focus on making a new meaning about a specific behavior than about a person in general.

Requirement #3: Focus on making new meaning

Another required step to breaking trigger and disengagement loops involves being intentionally curious to create a new meaning about what once triggered you.

Discovering new context can make a big difference. Say Lisa annoys you because she microwaves fish in the office kitchen. You've made a meaning that she doesn't care about anyone but herself when she microwaves fish, which generalized and solidified into a belief that she is self-centered and doesn't care about her co-workers. You've since disengaged as much as possible with her because you simply "don't like her."

What would happen if you suddenly learned that her husband has a terminal disease? Lisa is having a really hard time trying to take care of her husband while managing the rest of her life. Her husband once loved fishing, and she's coping with the caretaking by eating the rest of the trout they have in the freezer. Would you reconsider how caring Lisa is after learning this contextual information?

Whether or not you discover a more realistic meaning or fabricate your own, what matters is that *changing the meaning of the behavior changes how you feel about it.*

With an employee you're viewing unfavorably, you probably have many phrases that run through your mind when you see evidence of incompetence. If you want to break your trigger loop with this employee, you'll have to search for an alternate meaning about the behavior you see as incompetent.

Similarly, if you feel you have an uncaring manager, you would have to look for behavior to recode your beliefs about their ability to show kindness. Maybe it's not the style in which you interpret kindness, but you can get curious about how your manager shows it in his or her own way. Find evidence to support thinking, "That's how they show they care, even if it's not how I would show it." Change the meaning you make, and it changes the experience you have.

To loosen an employee's attachment to a meaning, you can help the employee reframe the situation. For example, you can say, "I understand that you feel Alex slows down projects. You are definitely high-achieving and fast-paced, and he probably has a different work-style that offers different strengths. What benefits could be helpful in being on a diverse team with someone who proceeds more cautiously?"

Above all, *focus on what's possible*. Since your brain scans for evidence of what you focus on, focus on discovering new ways to look at the situation or person to help loosen the grip of old negative Trigger and Disengagement Loops.

Breaking Employee Trigger and Disengagement Loops They May Have with You

With a little work, mitigating and breaking employees' Trigger and Disengagement Loops they may have with you is feasible. And let's be honest. Much like you likely get occasionally triggered by your boss, it's only natural your employees may sometimes have a similar experience. If you suspect an employee has an active trigger with you, or if you're just working on practicing a new leadership behavior, here are four effective strategies you can use to get employees to notice and trust your new approach:

1. Be consistent
The brain wants predictability and trusts consistency. Remember the face-reddening sunscreen example? Everyone needs a different

amount of time or "proof" before they're ready believe new evidence and allow the loop to update, and this simply requires consistency. You're earning your employee's trust that his or her brain can reliably expect this new behavior in the future. You're providing enough consistency that it's worth the risk to be hopeful about a new way of viewing the trigger. Consistency makes it more difficult to dismiss conflicting evidence as an exception.

2. Acknowledge what you're working on

If you are working on changing something in your leadership approach, acknowledging it can make a big difference. Sharing with your team that you are working on "asking more questions" or "checking in every morning" will make both your brain and their brains more primed to be receptive and attentive to this new behavior. This transparency can start to build curiosity, trust, and morale as you consistently follow through.

3. Be genuine

Our subconscious brains are human lie detectors. I'm guessing you can sense when someone isn't being sincere, and so can your employees.

If you're trying to break Trigger and Disengagement Loops with insincere "because I have to" effort, the employee might fawn to go along with it, but their highly-sensitive creature brain won't buy it. When we sense someone is not sincere, we kick the new behavior out of our loop as an untrustworthy exception. Without being rooted in genuine intention, even the greatest of changes are written-off.

4. Don't expect change right away, but stay with it

"Fool me once, shame on you. Fool me twice, shame on me." The creature brain must have been holding the pen when that old maxim was written.

We are all wired to not trust behavior that conflicts with our beliefs and expectations. Because of this, it's imperative that you don't expect changes you make or advocate for to immediately create loop changes in others. Patience is key.

This is not a one-and-done strategy. Similar to the sunscreen example, some people will gladly accept a revised product right away, while others will require more evidence of a genuine change.

Whether you're working with an employee on breaking a trigger loop with a difficult colleague, inspiring them to be more optimistic about a task they don't feel they're good at, or making an effort to improve your leadership approach, *give the creature brain some time to build trust.*

If you're making changes to support the employee experience, you might feel like employees should be impressed and grateful that you're extending the effort to try something new. But you may not get a visible response or verbal confirmation that it's landing with them right away. Don't be discouraged! Their creature brain may not be ready to lower its guard and create a new expectation until it trusts it won't end in being "fooled."

Your best bet is making the change for *you*, committing to a new way of being because it makes you feel good. Perhaps this new approach makes you feel like a better manager, or it simply makes your department run smoother overall. Because it can be a while before employees trust your new effort, fuel your commitment with internal "I did it!" dopamine instead of relying on external "You did it!" serotonin.

Consistent effort over time is the best way to ensure consistent results. This is true for your employees getting results and for you in improving your leadership approach. There might be a lag in the effects, but all consistent efforts to improve are progress. Be patient and allow the loop to get enough consistent and compelling evidence to incorporate instead of simply throwing in the towel before the method has a chance to be successful.

If an employee is slow to recognize your effort, it doesn't mean you are not making a difference. It simply means you're moving along the path for their brain to trust that this new way is here to stay.

Integration Questions:

1. What was your biggest *a-ha!* moment from this chapter? What are you most inspired to do with this new information?

2. What Disengagement or Trigger Loops can you notice that you have? Are there any you'd like to work on updating?

3. What opportunities do you see to improve your employees' experiences with being disengaged or triggered?

Key Take-Aways:

1. If we expect a positive result from our effort, we are eager to engage. If we expect a negative result from our effort, we are less inspired to engage.

2. Trigger and Disengagement Loops are easier to make (and harder to break) than Engagement and Experience Loops.

3. The reticular activating system judges what's relevant primarily based on safety, beliefs, and attention.

4. When you have what you code as a similar experience, the brain learns to trigger the same neurons each time, strengthening and solidifying the connection with every repetition. When considered a negative experience, this strengthening repetition creates a trigger trench.

5. Once we've evaluated something as important, interpreted it, and consciously or subconsciously decided on an action plan, the brain stops being curious and instead runs the now-established program.

6. To break Trigger and Disengagement Loops, you must:
    a. Put your attention on scanning for conflicting evidence
    b. Reverse the generalization back to specifics
    c. Focus on making new meaning

7. To help break an employee's Trigger and Disengagement Loop with you, you must:
    a. Be consistent
    b. Consider acknowledging what you're working on
    c. Be genuine
    d. Don't expect change right away, but stay with it

CHAPTER 12

Inspiring Optimal Effort

"Continuous effort — not strength or intelligence —
is the key to unlocking our potential."
—WINSTON CHURCHILL

In this chapter, we will examine five important "effort" concepts that affect engagement, including:

- What the best salespeople know about valuing effort over results that every leader needs to know
- How too much (and too little) challenge destroys engagement
- How to maintain "good-enoughness" and continuous growth to avoid Self-Protection Effort Withholding
- Solutions to get employees out of Anxious Effort and into Active Effort
- The value of helping employees predict a positive outcome

Employee effort is highlighted in the middle of the Results Model, between presenting a new Desired Result and Revisiting that Desired Result. You've used the **Accountability Anchor Conversion Checklist** to clarify the Desired Result, empowered with contribution, explored what's in the way, innovated with what's possible, and confirmed their first action step. You've set up your team for success. Now, it's time for your employees to take action and execute their efforts.

What could still get in the way and what's possible to maximize effort? Let's revisit one of our first distinctions between Inspiring Accountability and traditional accountability: focus on results, but reward effort.

Value Effort Over Results

Say you have two employees, Yiyun and Clarice, working on ad campaigns for two different clients. Yiyun's client loved the campaign, whereas Clarice's client wanted to see revisions.

Yiyun clearly achieved the best result. However, it turns out that Yiyun put in very little effort, the idea came easily and she used go-to formats for the ads, whereas Clarice stayed late, arrived early, and showed a great deal of effort on the project.

Do you reward Yiyun more than Clarice? Do you share disappointment with Clarice and heap praise on Yiyun? The answer lies in what behavior you want to incentivize and see more of in the future.

Of course, you want to acknowledge Yiyun for getting the result, but heavy praise loses its value when disproportionate to the effort it took to achieve it.

And what is the best acknowledgment strategy for Clarice? Even though she may not have fully met expectations, you want to continue incentivizing and rewarding *effort*. Acknowledging and celebrating Clarice's effort keeps her engagement and dedication high.

Have you ever been held accountable for a negative result out of your control, despite exerting your best effort?

If you have, then you know one of the most destructive experiences of accountability in the workplace is to be held accountable for something out of your control. Nothing will make an employee check job listings faster than being held accountable for not getting a result after putting in 100% effort.

If you punish an employee for circumstances out of his or her control, it's hard for an employee to ever feel motivated to provide 100% effort because of a concept called **Self-Protection Effort Withholding** covered later in this chapter.

If there's one thing we can predict to give us our best chance at consistent results, it's *effort*, so that is what we want to consistently reward and incentivize.

Salespeople Get It!

Seasoned salespeople know that sales is a so-called "long game." If they get paid a percentage of what they sell, they know that some months they'll do better than others.

They understand consistent effort is their best bet to close deals, which they also know can take months or years of effort depending on the industry.

To stay motivated, salespeople must value their effort over results, trusting that consistent effort is how they will get results. It's not surprising to hear salespeople talk about being satisfied if they get one yes out of 100 no's. Most non-salespeople don't have a mindset to withstand so much rejection prior to reward, but salespeople look at the no's as *progress*. The no's are the effort required to get closer to the yes.

Let's look at two employees, Tamela and Craig. They are part of an internship program teaching college graduates who have not been in sales to sell a product.

To sustain the many no's and often long waits for neurochemical rewards from closing deals, Tamela and Craig need some sources of reward to stay engaged and inspired along the way. If they didn't expect to face the amount of no's it can take to get to a yes, they'd be in a pretty rough state trying to feel like they're contributing, competent, or important, those three essential needs covered in Chapter 9.

Instead of waiting to reward employees for closed deals (Desired Result), inspiring leaders reward the effort, *marking out the effort as valuable contribution toward getting results*. This approach would feature a requirement such as requiring Tamela and Craig to each make 25 calls a day with prospects. In this case, 25 calls a day, not a closed deal, would become the Desired Result around which Results Conversations circle.

It is the effort toward the Desired Result that's in their control and for which they are accountable. This clear expectation is based on the behavior, effort, and action it takes to get the results, establishing a more powerful incentive from more frequent and fueling rewards.

Now having the Desired Result based on *effort*, Tamela and Craig have something to feel successful about *every day* instead of waiting for a deal to close. You're keeping the focus on the *result* (closing deals) yet rewarding *effort* (25 calls a day) toward it. Which strategy would inspire you to show up every day ready to work and leave feeling accomplished?

All employees need fuel to keep going, stay engaged, and persevere through setbacks. Frequent neurochemical rewards that come from valuing and rewarding dedicated effort provide that fuel.

The benefit of valuing effort isn't only for salespeople. Consistent Active Effort offers the best predictability at getting consistent, sustainable results in *all* roles.

Ask yourself: what are you incentivizing and rewarding your team with? How often do you want them to fuel up on neurochemicals? Give your employees more frequent and tangible effort-based achievements to ceremoniously celebrate and refuel.

How Too Much (and Too Little) Challenge Destroys Engagement

The Tale of Accountability, Effort, and the Right Amount of Challenge

The right amount of challenge incentivizes effort. The "right" amount requires enough effort to warrant meaningful reward while maintaining the employee's confidence that they can successfully meet expectations. Too little challenge and, like Yiyun's easy win, the reward isn't very meaningful. Too much challenge and one loses hope they can succeed, replacing engagement with discouragement.

Games are a relatable example of needing the right amount of challenge to engage. The brain loves doing things it's good at, putting in effort as an investment in something we think we can win (and getting the corresponding neurochemical reward).

For example, if you've always lost at a certain game, you will likely advocate to play a game that's "more fun" because it's difficult to feel defeated and engaged at the same time. We generally don't "like" games we don't expect to feel good playing, which is often influenced by the outcome from previous times playing that game.

As long as we have hope we can win, we generally enjoy playing and remain engaged. Sometimes, the reward comes from the experience of playing the game (though most people still prefer the neurochemical experience of winning). In the workplace, if optimism is low about the result, you can re-route the optimism toward valuing the development that comes with effort (the experience playing the game) more than result (winning). In doing so, you also re-route the opportunities for neurochemical reward because now the effort becomes the source.

So, what is it during the effort that can feel rewarding? We feel neurochemically good when we've felt appropriately challenged and have competently met that challenge because we're flexing our competency and contribution abilities. If these are appreciated before or despite the result being achieved, we can feel good and stay engaged even if the result we want is not achieved.

Leaders have to give employees a way to win. Since it can't be guaranteed they'll get the result every time, it's important to make the process of putting forth effort neurochemically rewarding enough to maintain the incentive to engage.

Conversely, winning games that feel "too easy" don't provide much dopamine reward because the sense of "I did it!" is diluted by the low level of effort we applied. If the "I did it!" is more like "I barely had to do anything," the impact of the reward is far less.

If we beat a level with "enough challenge" where effort and competency were flexed, we get a bigger dopamine reward because we actually *did* something—we applied effort successfully.

The right amount of challenge is essential to maintain engagement.

Too much and we shut down; too little and we don't feel we're contributing, resulting in feeling bored or disengaged.

Reward Effort, Not Results, to Prevent Self-Protection Effort Withholding

There's another important concept around effort that gets in the way of results: **Self-Protection Effort Withholding**, which is when we subconsciously limit our best effort to protect ourselves from our best effort not being good enough.

If an employee did her best, putting in 100% effort, and still didn't get the result, and she is punished for not meeting expectations (incompetence), the brain activates Self-Protection Effort Withholding to cope. It's an automated coping strategy that serves the creature brain: there's little worse in the workplace than giving our very best and not being good enough. This creates a feeling of hopelessness the creature brain will ferociously work to avoid.

In this moment and from here on out, this subconscious self-protection maneuver kicks in as if to say, "If my best isn't good enough, and I'm going to fail anyway, I may as well be able to blame it on not giving my full effort rather than accepting I'm hopelessly incompetent."

As a result, our brain subconsciously limits our effort on similar tasks so that the internal justification of being seen as incompetent is not because we're not good enough, but because we didn't fully try. This is simply safer for the creature brain that will use its seniority at any time to protect our top three needs: to be seen as contributing, competent, and important.

How do we prevent Self-Protection Effort Withholding?

The answer comes back, once again, to rewarding and celebrating effort more than results. Leaders must reward 100% effort as being "good enough" while maintaining a culture of continuous improvement, characterizing "failure" as learning and progress. When you reward effort and use the Results Model to continuously improve, you are preventing Self-Protection Effort Withholding.

Carol Dweck, world-renowned psychologist and author of *Mindset* (2007), has supportive evidence about praise and motivation. She found that children who are praised for being inherently "good" at something are less likely to take on new challenges than those who are praised for their approach and effort to the task. Being praised for being good at something that requires little effort doesn't incentivize any growth or future effort. It's barely meaningful, sometimes creating a trap of self-worth that subconsciously wonders, "What happens if all the sudden I am not good at that anymore? Then what will I have to be praised for?"

Julie Dirksen, author of *Design for How People Learn* (2015) shares a study that reveals a similar relationship between praising students and their future engagement, stating, "When the students tackled subsequent tasks, the students who had been praised for intelligence (something not in their control) did worse than they had done initially, and the students who had been praised for working hard (something they did control) did better overall."

When it comes to praising children, Dweck's advice is to "focus on the processes they used — their strategies, effort or choices."

For leaders praising employees for the sake of meaningful recognition that maintains "good enough-ness" while simultaneously encouraging growth, effort, and engagement, this strategy isn't any different. The most useful praise is specific to the employee's individual effort and approach — noticing it, acknowledging it, and sharing how the effort made a positive impact.

In addition, using the Results Model keeps the focus on continuous improvement and innovation toward results, while still creating opportunities to reward efforts that are seen as "good enough."

The Inspiring Accountability methodology aims to maintain "good enough-ness" and continuous growth simultaneously, encompassed in the mindset of, "We do great work while working to do better."

Solutions to Help Employees Out of Anxious Effort and Into Active Effort

Defining Anxious Effort and Active Effort

All effort does not equally contribute to results. The type of productive effort that effectively gets results is **Active Effort**. From an engagement standpoint, Active Effort feels more mentally stimulating than draining. When we are in Active Effort, we experience a feeling of excitement to contribute instead of feeling stuck, confused, or anxious about failing.

In Simon Sinek's 2009 book *Start with Why: How Great Leaders Inspire Everyone to Take Action*, he highlights a similar distinction: "Working hard for something we do not care about is called stress. Working hard for something we love is called passion."

Inspiring Accountability would add that working hard when expecting the worst is called stress. Working hard when expecting the best is called engagement. The effort we put toward "working hard" is the same in each instance, but how we feel during the work changes our experience of it.

Expecting the best begins with clarity, confidence, and optimism. When we know exactly what to do, this feels like a risk-free, guaranteed win followed by a neurochemical reward. Tasks that can be completed with actionable clarity result in a quicker hit of dopamine derived from feeling that we are contributing and competent. Imminent reward is far more enticing and incentivizing than tasks that confront us with uncertainty, threatening our competence.

When there's too much uncertainty or challenge associated with a task, our threat-response system gets anxious because we don't know if we'll be successful. The uncertainty of how to proceed, or the feeling of low-grade hopelessness that results from fear of not being competent enough, registers as a threat. With the threat-response system in a triggered state, we're now less resourceful to attempt the task successfully.

Inspiring Accountability calls this avoidant, unpleasant, and unproductive effort **Anxious Effort**. Anxious Effort is caused by too much uncertainty or too little optimism in approaching a task, usually when we expect the outcome might damage our ability to be seen as contributing, competent, or important. *A hesitancy of how to move forward creates hesitancy to move forward.* When we don't confidently know what to do and don't expect a positive outcome from our effort, our fight- freeze-flight response gets triggered and Anxious Effort ensues.

To escape this uncomfortable feeling, we tend to freeze or flee to another task with more actionable clarity: a task we know how to be successful at and one that promises reward for our brain.

This subconscious maneuver is often labeled "procrastination." At a tipping point, the brain chooses the "sure win" task with more immediate neurochemical reward, happily forgoing the task leaving us subconsciously questioning our competence and anxiously trying to avoid the corresponding negative neurochemicals. Tasks with more actionable clarity calm the creature brain.

When we can no longer "procrastinate" on one of these unclear tasks, we suffer through it in our foggy, triggered state, trying to keep the resourceful part of our brain active while our creature brain tries to pull us away. Persevering through this tug-of-war is *exhausting.* After all, as Carl Bucheit, Ph.D. and NLP Marin co-founder aptly points out, "When we're at war with ourselves, who wins?"

The activities to complete the task might not be different, but, as you learned in the Engagement and Experience Loop, how we feel going into an activity and what we expect after creates a dramatically different experience during the effort. Based on how we come into it, the same task can be energizing and engaging or a struggle of Anxious Effort.

Neurochemicals in a Culture of Stress

Working through Anxious Effort leads to stress and burnout. Stress feels like effort because it requires effort to operate rationally despite the flow of cortisol and adrenaline putting up road blocks to access the rational brain.

The physical symptoms of being triggered are meant to fade as an angry mammoth retreats or a pressing deadline passes. Unfortunately, many humans have become accustomed to operating under low-grade stress (constant cortisol).

In a company culture where everyone needs to be seen as working hard versus working well, operating in Anxious Effort practically becomes a company value. When every task is coded as confrontational without enough clear completion points to celebrate and refuel, the stressful cortisol release is reactivated before the previous spike is relieved.

Anxiety makes our bodies and brains work overtime, and we're not running from a woolly mammoth to burn it off. We're sitting in it, marinating, trying to stay calm, cool, and collected while anxious neurochemicals divert us away from the brain's best resource center for contribution.

In fact, according to Kronos.com, a human resources website, burnout is the primary reason 20-50% of people quit their jobs, and burnout is a primary symptom of working through preventable Anxious Effort.

Effort itself isn't inherently stressful. Effort is our most effective means to contribute meaningfully. It's not the effort or length of our task list that cues anxiousness. Anxiousness is sparked when we don't have the clarity, confidence, or optimism to believe there's a successful end to the task or a satiating reward to follow. When we don't know how to win, we don't enjoy playing.

Some Solutions to Avoid Anxious Effort

As you learned in the Engagement and Experience Loop, employees who work on an ask, task, or project with **clarity, confidence**, and **optimism** are more likely to maintain this experience during and after completion, completely avoiding Anxious Effort. For employees and leaders alike, the knowledge of how to win and remain neurochemically refueled is extremely important.

In exploring solutions to Anxious Effort, you'll notice the culmination of tools and strategies you are now familiar with. Here are the best ways to reduce Anxious Effort, so you can get better results:

Actionable Clarity:

- **Use the Accountability Anchor Conversion Checklist** to ensure each Desired Result is a clear expectation that has a concrete moment of achievement.
- **Clear what's in the way** during the Results Conversation.
- **Confirm the First or Next Action Step before closing a Results Conversation.** *Hesitancy on how to move forward creates hesitancy to move forward,* and it's inversely true that clarity on how to move forward creates incentive to move forward.

Confidence:

- **Maintain "good enough-ness" with continuous growth** by rewarding effort over results. Believe and encourage the idea that employees are *always* in progress toward meeting expectations, are *always* good enough, and are *always* continuously improving. Aspire toward adopting the mindset, "We do great work while working to do better."
- **Communicate that their engagement in the task will support their ability to be seen as contributing meaningfully, competent, and important.** You can help fulfill these needs by including contribution context and perceived capability (discussed in Chapter 14).

Optimism:

- **Help employees predict a positive outcome.** Predicting a positive outcome promises corresponding neurochemical rewards, incentivizing Active Effort. When employees expect to be successful, they can avoid Anxious Effort.
- **Get realistic with what's too much.** Help prioritize to give employees a way to win with each task completion. When everything is an urgent priority, neurochemical rewards can get buried, and the feeling of completion never truly feels like a win.

Neurochemically Refueled:

- **Celebrate with more "You did it!" neurochemicals.** Incentivize and reward effort with the fuel to persevere through challenges and keep showing up with excellence. Without neurochemical refueling along an endless road of to-do's, the only option is burnout.

- **Create clear completion points.** Create a clear beginning and end of an effort to provide evidence of meaningful progress and the opportunity for neurochemical reward. The clearer the moment of success, the more thoroughly it's rewarded neurochemically. If a completed task doesn't register as a fully fulfilled win, it doesn't refuel. Why not build in more refueling stations? Clarified Desired Results and Revisiting will also help here.

You can also have conversations that uncover Anxious Effort. Cultivate a culture where your employees will let you know when they've gotten stuck in Anxious Effort, and in using the tools above, you can turn Anxious Effort into engaged action.

Expanding: Help Employees Predict a Positive Outcome

While actionable clarity is always helpful, Anxious Effort doesn't arise simply from not knowing what to do. It's – surprise, surprise – about how we *feel* in that state of not knowing.

When we feel confident and optimistic that we can figure it out, exploring solutions can actually be one of the best ways for employees to feel engaged, contributing, and competent.

When in Active Effort, not knowing what to do becomes a serotonin-boosting problem-solving state. Employees can be energized by brainstorming and problem solving in a resourceful state and productively working toward the Desired Result without any triggered slow down. They may not have the answer yet, but they are optimistic, not anxious, about the process of discovering it.

If an employee is not confident or optimistic in their ability to successfully achieve the Desired Result, they'll move into Anxious Effort.

Help employees expect a positive outcome from their effort, and this confidence will keep them in Active Effort, excited to complete tasks with their competence intact.

With all the tools you've gained, you are ready to help employees avoid Anxious Effort and instead be engaged with Active Effort, reaping the neurochemical rewards and results that follow.

Integration Questions:

1. How often do you find yourself experiencing Anxious Effort? Thinking back on this chapter, what can you recognize as the cause? By understanding your own experience with Anxious Effort, you'll be able to better support your employees facing similar challenges.

2. How often do you think your employees experience Anxious Effort? From what you learned in this chapter, what are three clear actions you can commit to trying to move employees from Anxious to Active Effort?

3. How well do you maintain "good enough-ness" while expecting continuous improvement? Given what you learned about how important this is, what is the first action step you can take to improve your use of this stance?

4. How are you progressing at valuing effort over results? Have you improved in providing neurochemical boosts with celebratory recognition? How else can you improve at valuing and rewarding effort?

Key Take-Aways:

1. The right amount of challenge is essential to maintain engagement. Too much and we shut down; too little and we don't feel we're contributing, resulting in feeling bored or disengaged.

2. Rewarding effort in lieu of results keeps employees engaged, receptive, and resourceful.

3. Consistent Active Effort offers the best predictability at getting consistent, sustainable results in all roles. Rewarding consistent effort is how to create incentive to continue that effort.

4. Neurochemical incentive and reward lies in employees experiencing the right amount of challenge that allows them to maintain confidence and optimism that they can successfully meet expectations and receive the corresponding neurochemical reward.

5. The brain loves doing things it's good at, that is putting in effort that leads to a win, and getting the corresponding neurochemical reward. The more successful effort exerted, the bigger the "I did it!" dopamine and "You did it!" serotonin rewards.

6. Effort isn't inherently stressful. How confident, clear, and optimistic we feel during the effort determines our experience.

7. When we are uncertain about our ability to meet expectations, the quality of our effort decreases.

8. Solutions to avoid Anxious Effort:

  - **Actionable Clarity:**
    - Use the Accountability Anchor Conversion Checklist to offer clear Desired Results
    - Help clear what's in the way in Results Conversations
    - Confirm the First or Next Action Step before closing a Results Conversation

  - **Confidence:**
    - Maintain "good enough-ness" with continuous growth
    - Communicate that engagement in the task will support the ability to be seen as contributing meaningfully, competently, and importantly.

  - **Optimism:**
    - Help employees predict a positive outcome
    - Get realistic with what can be accomplished successfully

  - **Neurochemically Refueled:**
    - Celebrate with more "You did it!" neurochemicals
    - Create clear completion points

PART IV

INSPIRING LEADERSHIP IN ACTION: APPLYING CONCEPTS FOR BETTER RESULTS

CHAPTER 13

Engaging Leadership Language

"You get more bees with honey."

—AUTHOR'S PREVIOUS MANAGER

In this chapter, you'll discover tools and tips to improve your leadership approach, including:

- How to use the Four C's approach for accountability conversations to deliver feedback in a manner that maintains receptiveness
- How to use Engaging Leadership Language to:
    - Keep employees receptive and resourceful
    - Require engagement
    - Inspire possibility
    - Model accountability
    - Avoid triggering language
    - Listen for weak accountability language

While the traditional adage is actually, "You catch more flies with honey than vinegar," a previous manager once shared with me his own version of that line (seen as the chapter quote). At the time, I knew what it meant, and didn't question why someone would want more bees — *and don't bees make honey?* A larger point was being made, and it feels more valuable to me now than ever.

Since our goal is to inspire accountability, ditch the vinegar, the exhausting approach of exerting frustration to push for results that comes along with traditional accountability. It's in your best interest to use a more effective and appealing approach that will help you inspire your employees to give their best efforts every day so that you get the results you want.

Now that you have a strong foundation of how neurochemicals and human needs create engagement or trigger disengagement, let's look at practical applications of this knowledge to create a positive leadership approach that keeps your employees engaged, receptive, and resourceful.

Responsive Accountability – Approaching Issues with the Four C's

Whether you are "critiquing" an employee, offering "negative feedback," "developmental feedback," or "constructive criticism," if it feels negative to the employee, then it is a negative neurochemical experience regardless of what you name it.

Therefore, it is imperative to approach any conversation about an employee "issue" in a positive way. If you can induce positive neurochemicals, you can turn even the most difficult conversations into positive experiences. This allows the employee to expect a positive conversation that will lead to positive results.

Inspiring Accountability's goal is to help once-triggering feedback confrontations become engagement-driving development conversations. Development conversations reframe triggering criticisms into optimistic feedback in service of helping employees be better seen as contributing, competent, and important. Effective development conversations reroute the experience into something that supports success rather than diminishes dignity and productivity.

Your mindset plus your conscious and subconscious communication create your leadership approach. Approach these conversations by getting in a mindset that opens up more positive conscious and subconscious communication through words, tone, and body language.

Similar to the Engagement and Experience Loop, how you start a conversation has a huge impact on how it goes and how it ends. The **Four C's** approach will help you establish a positive and productive mindset for approaching historically uncomfortable accountability conversations, allowing for a better experience during and at completion. The Four C's approach includes being **caring, curious, careful**, and **comfortable**. You'll find with your neurochemical and Hierarchy of Human Needs knowledge, the Four C's will have deeper context and meaning to you than they would have before.

Caring

If you care about results, you must also care about the people getting the results. A caring approach is about supporting an employee's development as the primary means of achieving better results.

Remember: employees who feel great get great results. And employees who feel seen as contributing, competent, and important are more available, more resourceful, and better able to provide their best efforts toward results. A caring approach, one that focuses on their development and need fulfillment, will keep employees connected to how it's in their best interests to make the changes because doing so ensures they will be seen as even stronger contributors, more competent, and more important.

People welcome change when it improves their lives, but they don't like being changed to comply with someone else's agenda. If you want employees to be inspired and engaged in the change, you want it to connect with what's in their best interest, not just to appease a personal preference.

To initiate this approach, ask yourself:

- How can I provide feedback with my employees' best interests in mind?
- How can I maintain a caring tone that indicates that I value them and will be here to support their workplace needs?

Approaching these questions in a caring, empathetic, and supportive way will help your employees be more open to hear what you have to say.

The purpose of feedback is to let an employee know what to improve and be inspired to do so. You're there to help employees better contribute, grow their competency, and therefore grow their importance.

To paraphrase Ed Catmull from his book *Creativity Inc.* (2014), feedback should always leave the recipient inspired to improve. Delivering feedback in a manner that leaves an employee feeling discouraged is equivalent to taking one step forward and two steps back; no one benefits.

As a leader, when the purpose of feedback is to be framed as in service of employees, the nervousness that naturally comes with feedback conversations subsides. You're no longer the bad cop. You're their supportive ally, courageously addressing the issue so that they can be more successful, which in turn is success for you.

Think of yourself as a bowling bumper that is the push back they need to get the lucky strike instead of defeating gutter balls. Eventually, you'll help them develop the skills, default patterns, and optimistic brain programming to empower them to knock down pins every time without the need for your "bumper" feedback.

Feedback conversations where employees sense genuine helpfulness and caring from their leader can be radically more positive and productive. That is, after all, the goal of feedback: to create new avenues of productivity for an employee.

Let's say Sheila, an employee, uncharacteristically flared up at a meeting, raising her voice and cutting off a colleague. Do you have grounds to call her out and demand changed behavior? Yes. But will that get you the best possible results in keeping her engaged, receptive, and resourceful? Unlikely.

A more effective approach is to get into the caring mindset by asking yourself:

- How can I provide feedback to help Sheila be inspired to handle these situations better in the future?
- How can I maintain a caring tone that indicates she needs to change her behavior in meetings to be seen as a strong contributor?
- How can I help her work more effectively with her colleagues by supporting her development on this issue?

By applying this caring approach, your feedback is now in service of development, not simply a critique, helping you more easily inspire better results.

Curious

George Loewenstein, a professor of economics and psychology at Carnegie Mellon University, cited a useful definition of curiosity in his classic 1994 paper, "The Psychology of Curiosity."

Curiosity arises, Loewenstein writes, "when attention becomes focused on a gap in one's knowledge. Such information gaps produce the feeling of deprivation labeled curiosity. The curious individual is motivated to obtain the missing information to reduce or eliminate the feeling of deprivation."

Inspiring Accountability's methodology would specify further, highlighting that only when one feels confident in one's capability and optimistic about the possibility of closing that gap does curiosity feel good and engaging instead of discouraging and disengaging.

The 4C's application of curiosity combines the Results Model questions and your knowledge of the Hierarchy of Human Needs. Since you know employees are instinctually driven to be seen as contributing, competent, and important, then there must be something of note in the way employees *aren't* aligning their mindset or action with these human needs. Therefore, when your employee isn't performing at a specific level of expectation, be curious about *what's in the way.*

Additionally, you want to maintain a supportive and curious stance of *what's possible* for their growth as an employee, since all feedback is in support of their development and greater fulfillment of needs (in addition to you getting better results).

When you are curious about what's in the way, and confidently supporting your employee toward their success, you'll create a safer and less accusatory environment. This allows you to unearth what's in the way and what's possible. Generally, issues that require this type of feedback will go into the Results Model for Revisiting, but this also works as a leadership stance in more casual feedback conversations.

Consider the example of Sheila having an outburst in a meeting. Instead of being frustrated with her behavior, get curious by asking yourself questions like:

- I wonder what was going on for that to have happened?
- I wonder what was in the way of her remaining more calm and resourceful?
- I wonder what could help her stay resourceful in situations like these?

Approaching the conversation with this curious mindset will make your leadership more effective by helping your employees remain engaged in the conversation, receptive to the feedback, and resourceful toward solutions.

Careful

This mindset component is about being careful to not discourage the positive behavior that may have been hidden by the negative behavior.

Often, an employee's intent is good but would be more productive with different execution. The questions you can ask yourself are:

- What could have been the positive intent of their behavior?
- Despite the negative execution, what positive behaviors or mindsets were they utilizing that I still want them to continue?

In the case of Sheila's outburst in the meeting, what is the positive behavior you can extrapolate from her behavior? Perhaps she feels passionate about the issue and highly engaged in the project's success. You want to maintain, if not acknowledge and reward, her passion and engagement while adjusting to a more professional execution.

You can use this careful approach to then offer, "I know you are really passionate about this project, and I want you to stay just as engaged in it. Where we need to adjust is in you raising your voice and cutting off colleagues." From there, you can start asking questions around her experience: what got in the way of maintaining a more respectful approach? What's possible for her to better contribute in the future?

Without acknowledging the *positive* in her behavior, a leader may have thrown the baby out with the bath water — or, in other words, thrown the good behavior out with the bad.

If you went straight for attacking the behavior, it would have been easy for Sheila's threat-response system to create thoughts like, "If you don't want me to be passionate about this issue, then fine. I just won't participate next time. Why should I care if it fails if you don't want me participating?"

By acknowledging the positive and productive aspects of her behavior and mindset, you'll help the employee stay more receptive to being accountable for the execution versus justifying her intent.

Comfortable

If you start the conversation being uncomfortable, you can bet your employee will also be uncomfortable, and the threat-response system will probably start interfering. Self-protection kicks in when we get confronted with anything resembling the classic "we need to talk" phrase.

But what triggers us?

For starters, the manager's tone and body language: the shifty eyes aimed toward the floor, the nervous discomfort that precedes the conversation. These cues alert the employee that something uncomfortable is happening, resulting in mirroring the leader's discomfort.

The best way to inspire an employee to be receptive is by being comfortable *yourself.* When I hear someone say, "I'm so uncomfortable with confrontation," I'm surprised for two reasons: for starters, this is expressed as if feeling this way is an uncommon experience when, in fact, it's very common. Secondly, it qualifies a lot of interaction as "confrontation."

Very few people are naturally comfortable confronting another.

Confrontation raises adrenaline and cortisol levels, prepping for a threat, which can easily be interpreted as nervousness or discomfort, especially if the outcome is uncertain or feared to be negative.

It's completely natural to be uncomfortable with confrontation because it is a triggering experience. We want to move from labeling our interactions as *confrontations* and instead have *conversations.* Check out the difference from these Google definitions:

con·fron·ta·tion: *(noun)* 1. a hostile or argumentative meeting or situation between opposing parties.
synonyms: conflict, clash, brush, fight, battle, contest, encounter, head-to-head, face-off, engagement, tangle, skirmish, collision, meeting, duel, incident, high noon

con·ver·sa·tion: *(noun)* 1. a talk, especially an informal one, between two or more people, in which news and ideas are exchanged.
synonyms: discussion, talk, chat, gossip, tête-à-tête, heart-to-heart, head-to-head, exchange, dialogue, parley, consultation, conference

With our caring mindset intent to help an employee develop, it's time to stop having confrontations and start having conversations.

Do you have an issue with an employee you'd like to address but have been holding back? How would you need to think differently about addressing that issue to de-escalate the confrontation to a conversation? How can you keep it less formal and create space for new ideas to be exchanged as you explore what's in the way and what's possible?

When you come to a meeting serious and heavy-handed, the employee's brain will likely register a threat and go into self-protection mode, zapping receptiveness. This approach tries to teach employees a lesson, but instead it teaches them to shut down. By shifting from confrontation to conversation, you can talk freely about issues in a more approachable way that doesn't trigger the safety system.

You can lighten your approach while staying committed to resolving the issue. You don't have to use seriousness, anger, or frustration to hold an employee accountable when you have trusted accountability tools.

In the case of Sheila's outburst, you can ask yourself:

- What do I need to think or ask myself to feel more comfortable having this conversation?
- How can I focus on being curious to share ideas in a *conversation* instead of it being a one-sided hostile *confrontation*?
- How can I connect to how I'm being of service by helping her better contribute?
- How can I pair my Inspiring Accountability tools with a lighter, more curious tone, instead of unnecessarily using my tone to communicate the importance of this issue?

Employees *need* your honesty and courage to aid in their professional development. Let the caring and curious mindset help you learn to be more comfortable with these conversations.

Now that you have your approach setting the stage for a successful conversation, let's add some specific language tools that will help you get better results from these conversations.

Engaging Leadership Language

In this section, we will learn how to use **Engaging Leadership Language** to guide conversations that get more engagement and useful responses. Designed for you to use with your employees, you can also adapt to influence more productive conversations with your manager.

Inviting vs. Engaging Questions

One of the best ways to inspire engagement and accountability is to move from **inviting questions** (that only invite the brain to passively respond) to **engaging questions** (that *require* the brain's full participation in the conversation). Questions must engage employees' brains if we want employees thinking and exploring, not passively responding.

Think about a time you had to ask for something repeatedly, and it wasn't happening. Perhaps, after all that frustration, what needed to be adjusted was simply how you were asking questions.

If we want employees participating and problem-solving to create useful responses, we must intentionally ask questions that engage employees' brains.

When the brain process inviting questions, it produces a simple answer, usually yes or no. These "closed-ended" questions often start with *is, are, can,* or *do.* These may *imply* a more thorough response is needed but don't actually require it by the nature of the question. For instance, the questions, "Are we all on the same page?" and "Are there any questions before we end this meeting?" actually as for a yes or no response, even though they imply you want to know what someone may not understand or agree with.

The brain first processes the yes or no of the answer, and it's usually easier for employees to respond with the answer they know their manager wants to hear. In this case, a manager doesn't get authentic answers and employees' brains are not required to engage in coming up with those authentic, useful answers.

Inviting questions *sound like expectations*, but they're simply *invitations* to think or contribute thoughtfully.

In contrast, engaging questions *require* thought, attention, and a participatory response. These "open-ended" questions usually start with *what* or *how*, and require the brain to formulate a unique answer. This is where you get a real response, instead of a rhetorical one. If instead you ask, "What areas do you disagree with?" and "What questions are still lingering?" now the brain is scanning for unique content. You're engaging employees' brains and getting the real answers you want.

Inviting questions are very effective at getting *an* answer, but not as effective at engaging the brain to produce a *meaningful* answer. They also don't create accountability.

Compare the following questions and answers:

Q: "Can you get this to me this week?"
A: (Thinking avoided) "Yes, sure."

Q: "What might be in the way of getting this to me by Friday at noon? What can we do to ensure this is possible?"
A: (Thinking initiated) "Well, we finished up this other project, and I have an open slot to work on that. There's nothing that will get in the way right now, and I'll ensure it gets to you on time."

When we ask, "Can you get this to me by Friday?" the employee's answer may be automated without much thought because it's easy for the brain to rhetorically respond. Employees know what answer their manager wants to hear, and they'd rather not get into a triggering conversation if the manager isn't actually open to discuss the feasibility of delivering Friday. An employee might respond yes and do their best, but Friday may not have been truly possible and the leader wouldn't know until the deadline is missed.

You can use engaging questions to contribute to employees engaging in the answer and the accountability that comes with it. Here are some additional examples. Notice the quality of answers in response to each approach.

Inviting: "Do you have any ideas to share?" (Yes or No.)
Engaging: "What ideas do you have?" (Requires thinking and participation.)

Inviting: "Do you have any questions?" (Yes or No.)
Engaging: "What questions do you have?" (Thinking and Scanning for possible questions.)

Inviting: "Can everyone on the team think about how you can better demonstrate our values this week?" (This is an invitation to think about values "if there's time," which there never is. Without revisiting, it won't get done.)

Engaging: "At our weekly meetings, we'll all be sharing one way we demonstrated a company value, one way we could have done a better job, and one way we plan to in the coming week. What do you need to do to ensure you come to the next meeting prepared with this share?" (Engagement is enacted with the clear expectation with Revisiting. Employee has to think proactively about showing up with this new information and is now accountable if he or she does not show up to the meeting prepared.)

Also, watch for statements that only invite engagement and accountability instead of require it:

Inviting: "Here's how I think you did." (One-way conversation, not curious, doesn't require engaging brain or participation. Not expecting the employee to be self-aware, think or participate.)
Engaging: "How do you think you did?" "What went well?" "What could have been better?" (Two-way conversation, requires engaging the brain, answers, and expects full participation.)

Inviting: "It's really important you do this." (Okay, Yes, I know.)
Engaging: "We'll be checking in next week to see how this is progressing." (Utilizes Revisiting to show this is a non-negotiable expectation that requires attention.)

Many times, a leader will respond with, "*Obviously*, employees are *expected* to do what I've asked, regardless of how I asked it. That's what we pay them for." But workplace cultures with poor accountability practices are only *inviting* employees to be accountable and not *engaging* them in an active practice of inspiring accountability.

A compliant "yes" ensures nothing without a clear "how." A

fool-proof way to ask engaging language is to challenge yourself to begin questions with *what* or *how*. Here's a handy phrase to keep your language engaging: Avoid inviting with *is* or *can*, and get what you want with *what* and *how*.

Balancing Praise and Accountability

Many leaders are afraid too much praise will create complacency, but this is only true when you don't have trusted accountability measures in place. As one leader shared, "I want to offer more praise in this email to get my employee feeling confident about her skills, but she already lacks a sense of urgency. I'm worried she won't be motivated to take action on this project if she's already getting a pat on the back before she even starts. There have been unexpected obstacles to completing this project this week, and I'm worried that if I acknowledge them, I'm handing her an excuse not to get things done. How do I show I'm supporting her and increase her sense of agency on this project?"

The answer? Pair your praise with Engaging Questions to provide neurochemical incentivization while maintaining accountability for taking action.

In reviewing her email, the leader discovered that each question related to action or commitment was an Inviting Question or just a statement. In one example, "Are you able to work on these today?" became "Given this week's extra busy schedule and our approaching deadline, when do you expect to be able to complete these components?" followed by "What tasks seem doable for you to work on today?" The Engaging questions required a thoughtful response and a commitment.

She also customized the Results Model question of "Given what is in the way, what's possible?" to acknowledge the challenges without sacrificing accountability. With this foundation, she could productively offer a dose of inspiration and appreciation, closing with, "I know this is even harder now due to our busy week, but we totally got this! Thank you for your dedication and perseverance on this project."

Being direct doesn't have to degrade another's dignity. Often, using direct, Engaging Questions means you'll get direct, engaged responses. Because the leader changed her language and asked a specific, open-ended question, her employee responded with an estimated date for completion and which tasks she would be focusing on that day. The employee closed with an energized, "I'll go to the Google doc now and get to work!" The leader got the commitment and accountability, and the employee received the encouragement.

Practice and Integration

An easy way to practice asking Engaging Questions is to review questions you've included in emails before you click send. Here is a helpful prompt to upgrade Inviting Questions to Engaging Questions in your emails:

1. Start by asking yourself: What do I *really* want from this employee?
2. Notice where you've softened the ask to an Inviting Question. Look for *is, are, can,* or *do* questions.
3. Craft an Engaging Question, starting with *how, what,* or sometimes *when,* that will respectfully and directly address what you want to know or have done.
4. Close with authentic praise, encouragement, or perceived capability to establish a positive tone, activate engagement, and maintain accountability.

As you practice this exercise, you will be able to expand it proactively and reflectively to all forms of communication. Watch as Engaging Questions elevate your leadership effectiveness and inspire employees to be engaged, receptive, and resourceful.

Asking to Develop

When I see leaders who want employees to take more initiative, I wonder if they are using inviting or engaging questions.

The initiative and accountability that leaders want to see in their employees originates from having to think for oneself.

For example, a leader wants their employee to stop taking over meetings and leave space for other ideas. The leader states, "You should allow others to talk more in meetings," which functions as a closed-ended order that does not ask the employee to develop. This statement is unlikely to create the space to explore what behavior would need to be different so that it's primed and waiting to go at the next meeting. Without the employee discovering what they need to do differently for themselves, which the Results Model is designed to include, the employee will resort to default patterns.

Instead, ask a question like, "We want participation in meetings (Desired Result), and it's great that you are so willing to participate (acknowledging needs and being careful to maintain the positive behavior). What do you think we could do to allow others to participate more?" This engaging language requires the employee to think about how they will contribute to the solution without using triggering language.

A great "Asking to Develop" strategy is to challenge yourself to ask at least three questions before you answer with an idea, not in the spirit of being difficult, but with the intent to let the employee discover ideas for themselves.

Kubra Sait said it best in a 2018 interview with *Outlook India* about her controversial role in Netflix India's first original show, "Asking questions is the first way to begin change." Although Sait was referring to social cultural change, this idea applies just as much to a leader's ability to inspire change in employees and create a new workplace culture.

When an employee comes to you with a question like, "What should I do?" see how many times you can respond with an engaging question before providing what you think is best. When you do it *for* them, you take accountability *from* them. Let them be accountable for the origination so they will be more accountable for their contributions.

This approach will help teach your employees to think for themselves, to lower reliance on you, and to create solutions for which they'll be more committed to engage.

A leader's competency is better revealed by the questions they ask than the solutions they offer.

Perception Language

Perception language is another essential component of Engaging Leadership Language.

Perception language involves both sharing your own perception and inquiring about other perceptions instead of talking about events and experiences as fixed facts.

Since everyone on your team experiences events through a different lens filtered by their perspectives, history, beliefs, and feelings, engaging with employees through perception language helps to more productively explore issues. Instead of the creature brain digging its heels in to defend a position of how a situation "just is," we can explore how a situation is experienced by the employee and everyone else involved.

This is primarily done using four key concepts:

- **Noticing or Appearing**: "It looked like/I noticed [there was a lot of tension in that meeting]."
- **Thinking**: "What did you think about [that meeting]?"
- **Feeling**: "How do you feel about [that meeting]?"
- **Experiencing**: "What was your experience [in that meeting]?"

By exploring employees' perceptions of what happened, we learn about their experience (which is real for them) and leave room for others to have a different perception of what happened. This allows leaders to listen, validating an employee's experience without having to agree with the "facts" of what happened, keeping the employee more receptive. Perception language is an important linguistic tool to keep interactions curious and conversational.

In the example of Sheila's outburst at the meeting, you can ask what she noticed, thought, felt, or experienced in the meeting, starting with your own perception in an "It looked like," or "I noticed," statement. For example, "I noticed you got really upset in that meeting. What was going on for you?" From here, you can understand her perception of what happened and also leave room for your perception and those of other colleagues who were also impacted.

Perception language doesn't damage competence because it isn't criticizing or placing judgment on what happened — it's simply exploring what happened. It allows each affected party to have their individual experiences, allowing curiosity, conversation, and exploration.

Asking "Why" Creates Defensiveness

If you're plagued with defensive employees, it might be worth assessing if the language that you use promotes defensiveness.

To answer a "why" question usually requires responding with a justification for why something occurred. Much like the definition of traditional accountability, being "required or expected to justify actions or decisions," asking "why" has the same tenor. "Why" is past-focused, problem-focused, and often infers guilt or incompetence. Referencing again Chris Voss' book, *Never Split the Difference: Negotiating as if Your Life Depended on It* (2017), Voss confirms the volatile nature of "why" by saying, "why is always an accusation, in any language."

On a neurological level, too, there's a subtle difference in how the brain responds to "why" versus less confrontational questions. See if you notice the difference in the following examples:

- **Why didn't you get this done?** *(Confrontational and triggering)*
- **What got in the way of getting this done?**
  (Rational, impersonal exploration)

- **Why did this happen?** *(Asking for a defense)*
- **What's possible to ensure this doesn't happen again?**
  (Focused on solutions. We don't need to know why if we have a better solution.)

You might've noticed the non-why questions explore possibilities from a rational, exploratory purview, whereas "why" invites a defense. Imagine you took a few wrong turns on a route home you thought you could easily maneuver. To get back on track, you load your navigational app and enter your destination. Imagine, instead of quickly getting the next step to the most direct route home, the route pauses to load while you get berated with questions like: "Why did you make so many wrong turns? Why aren't you at your destination yet? Have you thought about how much time you've lost due to the mistake you made?"

It's easy to see that these questions are unnecessary, a waste of time, and likely triggering. All that matters is getting back on track as efficiently as possible. The only priority for both a navigational system and an inspiring leader is to assist employees in getting from where they are to where you want them to be as efficiently as possible. Asking triggering "why" questions unnecessarily delays getting to the Desired Result.

Engaging Leadership Language: A Quick Language Guide

We've learned some ways language reveals major distinctions between a traditional accountability manager and an Inspiring Accountability leader. By being intentional with your language, you'll see these open up greater opportunities to empower and engage (for improved proactive accountability) and contribute to reducing triggering experiences for your employees (for improved responsive accountability).

Here's a quick reference guide that reviews and expands on additional components of Engaging Leadership Language.

Require Engagement

Inviting (not requiring engagement) vs. Engaging Questions (requiring brain engagement and participation): Expect and require a thoughtful answer versus inviting a yes or no response, avoiding *is, are, can,* or *do,* and use *what* or *how* instead.

- *"What ideas do you have?"* instead of *"Do you have any ideas?"*

Asking to Develop: Empower employees to develop their problem-solving skill set. Ask three engaging questions before sharing your opinion, even when they ask you for yours first.

- *"What do you think is the best response?"* instead of telling them what you think the best response is first.

Inspire Possibility

Imagining and Envisioning:
- "What do you imagine is possible...?"
- *What do you envision for...?"*

Obstacles:
- *"What got in the way?"*

Solutions:
- *"What's possible?"* and, *"Given what's in the way, what's possible?"*

Trying a new behavior for a period of time:
- *"What do you think of **trying** this out for [an amount of time]?"*

When vs. If:
- *"**When** you [successfully practice a new behavior, achieve result, etc.]"* vs. *"**If** you [successfully practice a new behavior, etc.]."*

Preventing Feeling Overwhelmed:
- *"Where can you start?"*

Perception Language

Noticing and Appearing: Shares an experience through your perception with room for their perception, versus an accusation.
- "I noticed you were upset in that meeting."
- Similarly: *"It seemed like..."* or *"It looked like..."*

Thinking and Feeling: "Thinking" and "feeling" give context to the recipient that you're on their side and won't shut them down if they speak candidly.
- "What did you think about...?" "How would you feel about...?"

Wondering: By staying light and curious, you're showing there's room for other opinions.
- *"I'm **wondering** if you..."*

Model Accountability

Acknowledging your own contribution first:
- *"I realized I could have..."* or *"I'm sorry."* or *"I wish I would have..."*

Avoid Triggering Language

Talking About "We" Instead of "You" or "I": Using "we" is less triggering than "you," even if you rhetorically mean "you."
- Hear the difference in *"What can **you** do about it?"* versus *"What can **we** do about this?"*

Remove the Personal Reference: Sometimes it's better to leave the "we" out and keep it neutral. For example, asking *"What got in the way?"* instead of *"What's wrong with you?"*
- *"What can be done about this?"* instead of *"What can you do about this?"*

Asking: Asking instead of telling is vastly more empowering for an employee. Ultimately, it's better for engagement and receptivity, as many people are triggered being told what to do. Asking is more respectful, and in applicable circumstances, telling reduces empowerment and accountability because whoever generates the idea has the most inherent accountability for the idea.

- *"Could you/Can you...?"* instead of *"I want you to..."* or *"Do this..."*

Acknowledging the Positive to Soften the Negative: Genuine positive acknowledgment builds some neurochemical currency, and at a minimum, softens the negative feedback.

- "I saw that you _____, which is great. I am curious about [this other thing that's a part of it...], though? Could you speak to that a bit?"

But:

- **Avoid:** *"You're doing great, but you could improve here."*
- **Instead:** use "and" instead. "But" cancels out the acknowledgment.

Should:

- **Every "should" can be a question with "could"**
- **Avoid:** *"You should have done this."*
- **Instead:** *"What could you have done to get a different result?"*

Why:

- **Avoid:** *"Why did this happen?"*
- **Instead:** use the less confrontational, *"What got in the way?"*
- You'll get the same answer with better results.

Dealing with People: We deal with problems, not people. It's much better to use phrasing such as: talk with, have a conversation with, address, work on, brainstorm, work on a solution with, etc.

- **Avoid:** *"I have to go deal with Paul."*

- **Instead:** *"I need to have a conversation with Paul."*
- **Avoid:** *"I'm dealing with the marketing department."*
- **Instead:** *"I'm working with the marketing department to resolve..."*

Weak Accountability Language from Employees

They/Them:

- *"They — the higher ups — don't let me do..."*

"Trying" to avoid committing: Trying to do better next time without clear action steps won't effectively activate Accountability Attention to break old patterns. It's equal to, "I'll try to remember to do this differently," but the brain doesn't work this way. The brain doesn't "try" to do things differently, it just runs established response patterns and programs. You have to update the program before you need to use it so it will activate and run as you'd like in the future. An intention to *try* to remember won't change anything without a plan for *how* to remember.

- *"I'll try to do better."*

Idea vs. Commitment:

- *"I could do..."* versus *"I will do ..."*

There are myriad ways to use Engaging Leadership Language to get better results from your team in positive and productive ways. Keep employees engaged, receptive, and resourceful, provide more room for employees to be accountable for solutions, and inspire stronger employee contribution.

Integration Questions:

1. Where is the first place you'd like to start developing your 4C's to be more caring, curious, careful, and comfortable in your approach to providing feedback?
2. How can you start using Engaging Questions instead of Inviting Questions?
3. How can you practice increasing your perception language?
4. What other Engaging Leadership Language tips do you see bringing you better results from your team? Which three would you like to start actively practicing?

Key Take-Aways:

1. How you approach a conversation greatly impacts how it ends. Using a positive approach for negative feedback helps the employee expect a conversation that will end positively, contributing to their engagement, receptiveness, and resourcefulness throughout the conversation.
2. The **Four C's** approach for accountability conversations will help you establish a positive and productive mindset for approaching uncomfortable accountability conversations. The Four C's establish you as **caring, curious, careful,** and **comfortable**.
3. When your employee isn't performing to expectations, be curious about *what's in the way* of them meeting their needs and *what's possible* for their growth as an employee.
4. If you care about results, you must also care about the people getting the results.
5. Employees who feel great get great results. Employees who feel seen as contributing, competent, and important provide their best effort toward results. A caring approach, even when providing negative feedback, can keep their needs and dignity intact.
6. Feedback should always leave the recipient inspired to improve.
7. When an employee feels you genuinely want to support their development, you can have radically more positive and productive conversations.

8. If you start the conversation being uncomfortable, you can bet the employee will also get uncomfortable.

9. Allow feedback to be a conversation, not a confrontation.

10. Avoid asking Inviting Questions that start with *is*, *are*, *can*, or *do*; these only invite engagement and accountability. Instead, use Engaging Questions that begin with *what* or *how* to require a thoughtful answer, engagement, and accountability.

11. Everyone on your team experiences events through their own lens, and perception language leaves room for these different possibilities. This involves both sharing your perception and inquiring about other perceptions.

12. Asking "why" creates a defensive need to justify. Instead ask questions that open up a conversation, focus on the future, and explore solutions.

Find a reference guide of all
Engaging Leadership Language tips on pages 249-252.

CHAPTER 14

How to Infuse Positive Neurochemicals into the Workplace

"Can't forget, we only get what we give."
—NEW RADICALS

In this chapter, we'll be covering best practices for how to acknowledge needs and intentionally infuse engaging, incentivizing, and rewarding neurochemicals into your employees' day-to-day experiences, including:

- Contribution context
- Perceived capability
- The importance of meetings
- Serotonin-boosting recognition best practices
- The value of neurochemically refueling regularly

Employees who feel great, get great results. And great results make employees feel great. This is the results-getting loop you want to create by infusing positive neurochemicals into your workplace. Aligning with the New Radicals' 1998 upbeat one-hit-wonder, "You Get What

You Give," when you give neurochemical incentives and rewards for employees to feel great, you get employees who do great work.

Using your foundational knowledge of neurochemicals and the Hierarchy of Human Needs in the Workplace from earlier chapters, let's look at the best proactive accountability strategies you can apply to help your employees get the results you want the first time, saving you from having to address it with responsive accountability after-the-fact.

A blog from *Undercover Recruiter* titled, "How Workplace Happiness Affects Your Paycheck," CEO Ken Sundheim writes, "Countless studies have shown that our brains are literally hardwired to perform at their best when they are in a positive mindset. When we feel optimistic about our future, dopamine and serotonin are released in our brains. In conjunction with providing a heightened sense of well-being, dopamine and serotonin allow us to more rapidly organize new information and become more skilled at complex analysis and problem solving."

Sundheim highlights how we can be more engaged and resourceful by feeling optimistic about our future — and the reverse is also true. Perseverating on problems exhausts most of our capacity for attention, draining energy as well as performance levels. Sundheim later writes about one University of Toronto study, which researched how one's mood can change what he or she can consciously see. "When shown pictures with multiple images, those in negative moods could not process as much as those registered as in a positive mood." The evidence indicates that our moods greatly impact our performance, and neurochemicals are primary mood creators.

Now we'll learn about how you and all leaders can infuse positive neurochemicals in the workplace, giving you tremendous influence to contribute to employees feeling positive, naturally allowing them to be more engaged, productive, and resourceful.

Proactively Fulfill Needs

For employees in self-protection mode, it feels very risky to make decisions to support and protect the company vision when it may reflect negatively on themselves. An employee whose baseline needs are fulfilled feels more secure in their position and can safely leave self-protection mode to do what's best for the company.

To illuminate this idea, let's talk about Freddie. Freddie works for a software company in an e-commerce department. He realized that he had made a mistake that cost this large company more than $30,000. If Freddie was worried that he'd be judged as a poor contributor, incompetent, or unimportant, he would not bring his mistake to his manager, Sara's, attention.

Because Sara doesn't rely on blame and shame and values keeping dignity intact, Freddie did reveal the mistake to her. Sara quickly jumped from what was wrong to "What's possible?" to prevent this error from happening in the future. There was no need for punishment, as Freddie already felt horrible. Sara knows productivity is at its best when her employees feel confident about their work and secure in their importance. Instead of using the mistake to blame, shame, or punish, Sara instead explored what's possible to make this mistake unlikely to happen again in the future, maintaining Freddie's dignity, confidence, and engagement.

If Freddie hadn't come forward, the company would have missed the opportunity for the dual brainstorm on how to prevent problems like this. Had Freddie not had his baseline needs met, he would be stuck in self-protection mode. His attention would've been situated more on covering up the mistake than admitting it and imagining how to prevent it.

In addition to single mistakes, when there's a consistent foundation of fulfilled needs, employees don't spend time trying to protect or fulfill their own needs as much. This means employees comfortably and consistently put their attention to fulfilling other needs, like those of your company and customers. In the *Harvard Business Review* (2011) article, "The Only Thing That Really Matters," author Tony Schwartz says: "The more our value feels at risk, the more preoccupied we become with defending and restoring it, and the less value we're capable of creating in the world."

Similar to when we are in an airplane and we're supposed to put our oxygen mask on first before a dependent's, we are more available for others *when our own needs are fulfilled*. Specifically in the workplace, employees are most available and willing to "put the company first" when they feel secure in their own need fulfillment. If you allow employees to be human, and fulfill their workplace needs, you will more effortlessly watch your organization's needs get happily and eagerly fulfilled.

This chapter offers tools and strategies to address practical and impactful ways to easily fulfill needs and get the correlated positive neurochemicals to fuel your employees' engagement. Let's start with the number one tool to help fulfill an employee's need to be seen as contributing meaningfully.

Fulfilling the Need to Contribute with Contribution Context

How do we keep employees inspired when the going gets tough? To Friedrich Nietzsche: "He who has a *why* to live can bear with almost any *how*."

When your employees know the value of their effort, they can stay engaged and feel like they're contributing, even when the task is boring or not flexing their competency.

On the other hand, tasks that diminish dignity or feel menial are major morale and engagement diffusers. When we don't think what we're doing matters, it threatens our need to contribute meaningfully, as well as our ability to share our competency. *It's hard to imagine that we will be seen as important if we don't think what we are doing is important.* This is why it's difficult to engage in or enjoy tasks that seem to prove we're *not* contributing, competent, or important.

This is disengagement at its finest, and in cases like these, detrimental effects *only* exist because of an insufficient **contribution context**.

The difference in feeling like our work is valued or not is the communicated context. **Contribution context**, as you learned to include in using the **Accountability Anchor Conversion Checklist**, is intentionally and proactively communicating why an ask, task, or project is meaningful. It highlights why what an employee is doing would qualify as a meaningful contribution, creating more neurochemical incentive to do it.

Instead of reserving contribution context for active Desired Results, we can apply it to any request. Let's see in more detail how contribution context makes all the difference with engagement and our experience of menial tasks.

Imagine you're volunteering for your favorite non-profit. You care about their mission and those they serve, and you give your time because it helps you contribute to something that matters to you.

You come in to do a few hours of volunteering, and they bring you to a desk piled with an overwhelming number of envelopes and a large stack of Forever stamps.

The volunteer coordinator motions for you to sit down. "Today, you'll be stuffing and stamping these envelopes. There are about 1,200, so get done what you can. Thanks." You put your headphones in and start stuffing, thinking about what email you're missing, where you're shuffling your kids next, the grocery list, or that car you've been wanting. You may be putting in the effort, but you're not *feeling* very engaged. The job gets done, but you wouldn't recommend this gig to a friend unless they have a great podcast to binge. You get bored. Fast. You consider looking at other volunteer opportunities that might make more of a difference.

Imagine the difference if the experience was this instead:

The volunteer coordinator greets you, "Hey, it's so great to see you! Thank you for being here. Today, you'll be helping us with our biggest mailing fundraiser of the year, and the donations we get from this mailing you're helping with are the primary funding for [that program that really inspired you to volunteer in the first place]! By stuffing and stamping all of these envelopes, you're helping us make that program possible. I know it looks like menial work, but it is actually really important, and we're so grateful you're here to help. Our clients and donors thank you!"

Which version has you *feeling* more engaged? More inspired? Feeling good about the menial work ahead?

Interest, inspiration, and engagement can be generated by contribution context. The intentional usage of it for this purpose doesn't make it less real or meaningful. It means you can choose to activate an improved experience for your employees simply with your word choices.

In 2013, Deloitte Insights produced *Unlocking the Passion of the Explorer,* a report that states over 87% of America's workforce feels they are not able to contribute to their full potential because they don't have passion for their work. As we saw with the envelopes, the task might not change, but the meaning of the task can be highlighted. This is enough to convert a menial experience to a meaningful one.

How to Provide Contribution Context

A general framework for providing contribution context might look like this: "By doing [this task], you will be improving/contributing to [this important thing], helping make an impact [in this way]."

The "important thing" could include:

- Mission, vision and mini-vision statements
- Clients and customers
- Other departments, co-workers
- Culture (values and principles)
- Goals (company, department, or individual)
- Anything else you can think of that could matter to the employee or anyone positively impacted by their work

You can also refer to the following questions to help you identify contribution context, first introduced in Chapter 5:

☑ Why does the ask matter beyond personal preference? What is important about the task? To whom or what does it meaningfully contribute?

☑ What is the negative impact of not doing the task? To whom, what, when, how, or where does it negatively contribute?

☑ What is the expected positive impact of completing the task? To whom, what, when, how, or where will it positively contribute?

☑ How will completing this task help the employee meet his/her need to be seen as contributing, competent, and important?

In daily work life, this can be as little as one extra sentence. The goal is to establish *why* the ask is meaningful instead of menial. You want to make engaging with the task compelling.

Let's see how this looks in a simple scenario.

Meet Henry. Henry is knee-deep in some serious work. He hears a ping and sees a message from his manager, Shelly: "Henry, can you get me some water?"

This is not exactly Henry's job.

How would you respond if you are Henry? It depends on the meaning you make and already established beliefs. If Henry feels like Shelly sees Henry as beneath her, he could easily respond indignantly, thinking to himself, "What am I, your servant? I have actual *work* I'm doing. Did your legs suddenly stop working?" This could leave Henry feeling like he's not seen as important *simply because context is not included*.

Perhaps Shelly could have better presented it as the necessity it was all along? "Henry, are you able to get me some water? I've been on hold with this client for 15 minutes and I really need to take some headache medicine. I'd really appreciate it!" Contribution context greatly improves upon this request because it shows that it's not because Shelly sees Henry as beneath her. Elucidation goes a long way.

Contribution context keeps Henry's dignity intact and will probably make him feel *good* (a far cry from indignant) because he is contributing and helping his manager's threatened well-being. What was once a menial task is now an act of generosity with the promise of gratitude, already getting the serotonin flowing. The same ask without contribution context would likely trigger negative neurochemicals.

This is the same with email, text, or, quite honestly, any communication. It also works great in personal relationships or as a universal tool to inspire action in others.

Here are some additional, general examples of contribution context. Use this foundation to see what's possible for you:

- "You stuffing these envelopes might seem like menial work, but it's helping us add that personal touch for our guests. We do everything by email, so getting this hand-stuffed invitation will create such a fun surprise for our clients!"
- "This report you're doing will help accounting determine our best timing for launching our new product, which is sure to increase our business by 10%!"
- "You fixing this will help us restore efficiency, so customers get the products they love on time."
- "You researching this will help us pitch to marketing why we need a new brochure, so customers understand how to get the most from our new product line."
- "When you improve your ability to provide feedback more positively and effectively, you will be better demonstrating our company value of respect, and you'll be contributing to a more positive company culture. You'll also be an example for the managers that report to you, helping them be better leaders."

Contribution context is most important when work seems repetitive, unchallenging, menial, or doesn't seem to offer much opportunity to show competence or earn importance. To help, you can acknowledge the above with a "might seem" phrase: "I know this might seem like boring and menial work, but [here's why it really matters]."

You can also add, "This is important because…" and "You are so good at…" for extra neurochemical *oomph*, of course, only when it's authentic.

Remember the reticular activating system (RAS) and Account-ability Attention, how the subconscious brain marks a Desired Result as important and then applies more attention and effort toward it? Contribution context can help the brain mark the ask, task, or project as "important," earning a spot in being worthy of prioritized effort and attention. Why not make it easier for your employees (and their brains) to be more successful, especially when it's so easy?

The return-on-investment for adding contribution context is *massive*. The specificity of the context provides even more reward through need fulfillment. Similar to vague Desired Results getting vague results, vague or absent contribution context creates vague or absent incentive to engage.

Usually, one sentence added on to each ask is enough to change the neurochemically-bland day-to-day to an engaging job that fulfills one's need to contribute. If you're not thinking about how the ask, task, or project is meaningful, your employees aren't either. Don't wait for them to make it up — they won't. Intentionally infuse contribution context so they have no choice but to realize their value.

Be Genuine

Have you ever felt too inspired to work on a task? Have you ever felt too important to your company? Or felt too appreciated for your work? I didn't think so!

Genuine recognition never gets old. Even if contribution context initially feels like overkill, or even if employees know you're doing it intentionally, *they won't get tired of knowing how valuable their work is.* It doesn't matter if it feels forced or awkward at first. What matters is that it's *useful*.

Daniel M. Cable's (2018) findings in *Alive at Work: The Neuro-science of Helping Your People Love What They Do,* confirms the same benefits: "Leaders' investments into personalizing purpose make the difference." Further on, he adds: "Both philosophy and empirical research suggest that the higher our level of interpretation or con-strual, the more we will stick with it when the going gets hard." This means that the higher level and stronger meaning of your offered contribution context creates more inspiration to keep engaging, regardless of how difficult or boring a task might be.

It should be noted that there is an important distinction between authentic inspirational and inauthentic manipulative contribution context. *Keep the context genuine and simple when needed.* Don't do it to con your way into an employee being engaged with inflated value because your employee's careful creature brain will sense it, distrust it, and you'll be worse off than before.

If a task is worth doing, then there's genuine contribution context worth communicating.

How Often Do I Provide Contribution Context?

Your employees won't get tired of hearing how the work they do matters. They key is to keep it simple, authentic, and frequent, ideally accompanying each new ask.

No matter what the role, you can also tie client testimonials back to the work of each department or employee, verbally connecting this success back to the work they are doing. Thank your employees for making success possible — and be specific to their work, effort, and contribution. This could be the difference between an unappreciated job seeker and a satisfied employee who "knows" the value of their contribution.

Every role has the opportunity for greater contribution context. Make it impossible for employees to question if their work and contributions matter. By doing this, you'll have a highly engaged team of fulfilled employees. It's an effortless way to produce exponential engagement rewards.

Now that you know the number one contribution tool, contribution context, let's examine the top tool to support an employee being seen as competent: perceived capability.

Fulfilling Perceived Capability

Best-selling motivational author and speaker, Denis Waitley says, "If you believe you can, you probably can. If you believe you won't, you most assuredly won't. Belief is the ignition switch that gets you off the launching pad." How can leaders help create positive beliefs in their employees to ignite engagement?

Leaders have a super power to impact how much effort and capability employees offer: it's called **perceived capability**. Perceived capability is expressing genuine belief in another's abilities in a way that raises their perception of what's possible. Inspiring leaders use perceived capability to inspire employees to see more capability than previously believed possible.

In her book, *Counter Clockwise: Mindful Health and the Power of Possibility* (2015), long-time researcher Ellen Langer shares an experiment she conducted to explore the connection between one's perception of aging and its actual effect on aging.

Langer and her colleague Judith Rodin divided elderly residents in a nursing home into two randomly selected groups. They encouraged the first group of participants to find ways to make more decisions for themselves. At this age and stage of life, these were not what most would consider stressors on one's abilities.

The first group was allowed to choose where to receive visitors, and if and when to watch the movies that were shown at the home. Each resident also chose a houseplant to care for, and they were asked to decide where to place the plant in their room, as well as when and how much to water it.

Langer states, "Our intent was to make the nursing home residents more mindful, to help them engage with the world and live their lives more fully."

The second control group received none of the above instructions to make their own decisions. They were given houseplants, but told that the nursing staff would care for them. None were asked to make choices on where to receive visitors or when to watch movies.

But how much do choices matter when we're talking about taking care of plants, greeting visitors, and watching movies? According to Langer's study, what seemed like a negligible nudge toward self-empowerment made the difference between life and death.

Here are the results reported by Langer: "A year and a half later, we found that members of the first group were more cheerful, active, and alert, based on a variety of tests we had administered both before and after the experiment. Allowing for the fact that they were all elderly and quite frail at the start, we were pleased that they were also much healthier: we were surprised, however, *that less than half as many of the more engaged group had died* than had those in the control group."

Not to get morbid, but this is a shocking correlation between being seen as capable and empowered to make decisions and life and death.

How do we take this substantial association and relate it to what works in the workplace? In addition to Langer's interesting findings, this study also reveals the power of perceived capability.

When the residents were broken up into groups, there wasn't a distinction between each groups' abilities. *Once entrusted and believed to be more capable, the individuals in the first group naturally utilized more capability.* The actual ability wasn't different; what made the difference was that someone else believed in the additional capability of the participants and empowered them to use it.

In the workplace, employees often perform at the level of perceived capability their managers believe and express. In other words, the leader sets the limit on an employee's **possibility ceiling**, defined as the limit on what one believes is possible, especially in relation to an employee's potential, abilities, and competence. For better or for worse, possibility ceilings generally become performance ceilings.

As Stephen R. Covey says in his 2004 book, *7 Habits of Highly Effective People: Powerful Lessons in Personal Change*, "Treat a man as he is and he will remain as he is. Treat a man as he can and should be and he will become as he can and should be." When read with more gender-inclusive pronouns, it remains as true today.

When leaders believe and communicate the belief that an employee has more potential than the employee believes possible, the employee eventually engages in this belief, raising their possibility ceiling.

Of course, the opposite is true. How many times have you been shocked and pleased when employees exceeded expectations? Not as often, I'm guessing, as you've been disappointed when they didn't. If an employee doesn't feel you believe they are capable, the chance of them raising the bar to surprise you is very low. You can imagine that it's not likely for an employee to go above and beyond for a manager who doesn't see much potential in them. Eventually, the employee gets exhausted trying to prove them wrong and lets the manager be right.

How to Express Perceived Capability

Perceived capability can be overtly expressed in simple and more frequent statements like, "I know you can do this." Even simple statements, when genuine, organically offer effective "you did it" serotonin boosts with the proactive and still rewarding, "you can do this."

Usefully, it is more easily believed when you can tie what you've noticed from the past to what's needed now, as in, "I saw how well you completed this project, and I completely believe you demonstrated the skills needed to complete this next project with excellence, as well."

At times, you can reference your own trust in them, as in, "I see you have what it takes or I wouldn't be asking this of you."

More broadly, there are times you can offer a more generalized approach, as in "I see so much potential in you, and I want to help you get there."

Part of building competence is also holding back from competence-crushing statements, often rampant in traditional accountability's focus on problems, blame, and shame. If an employee didn't meet a result, you can instead look at the difference between the achieved result and Desired Result as an opportunity rather than lack of capability.

As with all Inspiring Accountability tools, the creature brain can sense when you're being inauthentic. Don't overdo it; be authentic and sincere. If you set the possibility ceiling so high, you'll cross the **impossible expectation threshold,** when what's expected feels more impossible than inspiring. This can also occur when an employee feels they are trying to focus on too many behavioral changes at once. Once the threshold is crossed, employees respond as more hopeless and worried about disappointing you than inspired to make you proud.

Lastly, perceived capability can't do the impossible. There isn't enough perceived capability in the world to allow an employee to do the equivalent of running a marathon in 30 minutes. While it can unlock a surprising amount of capability, expectations that feel completely unachievable will trigger shut down. *Use perceived capability as a tool to create possibility, not to ask the impossible.*

In short, confident workers access greater capability, producing more competent results that meet expectations more often.

Fulfilling Importance with the Neurochemical Value of Meetings

Meetings were scorned as waste of time with the popularity of Tim Ferris' 2007 hit, *The Four Hour Work Week*, but meetings can be an excellent use of time to support proactive and responsive accountability when designed with neurochemical production in mind.

When operated thoughtfully and intentionally, meetings with team brainstorming and achievement celebration can enhance connection, collaboration, transparency and trust, thereby enhancing the chance for oxytocin release. Meetings can also be a dedicated space to offer recognition, which produces serotonin. And when meetings offer the ability to self-report successes, they offer dopamine boosts.

When you check in on a project, you provide an opportunity to learn about how your employee already successfully contributed. Simply because this is pointed out and discussed creates an opportunity for them to celebrate an "I did it!" success milestone, and for you to offer your recognition of an equivalent to "You did it!"

The act of providing feedback delivered with the caring tone (of the previous chapter's 4 C's) and intent to help an employee increase their contribution, competence, and importance also fulfills the "importance need." *Feedback is an investment in the importance of someone.* Your time and attention helping employees improve requires you to see them, to notice what they're doing well, how they could improve, and empowering them to do so with your feedback. This comes with the serotonin boost of feeling important, along with the ability to increase contribution in the future, promising more neuro-chemicals down the road.

Regular check-ins offer better opportunities for employees to stay on-track, making success with each item they're working on much more likely. When they meet expectations, they get even more dopa-mine and serotonin.

Additionally, connecting and conversing with your employee offers oxytocin, with opportunities to build trust, loyalty, and more inspiration to offer extra effort to make you proud. If check-ins are infrequent, they leave employees short on neurochemical fuel and less frequently meeting expectations because there isn't enough calibration and feedback to drive development.

Recognition and Reward Best Practices

Learning from Ralphie the Lab Rat: Positive surprises are the best (and negative surprises are the worst!)

Let's think back to Ralphie the Lab Rat from Chapter 2. His journey illuminated a major recognition best practice: positive surprises are the best bang for your recognition buck.

The first round through the maze was powerful for Ralphie because *he didn't have any expectation of cheese,* and then — BOOM — he got a huge surprise with the reward. This reveals that positive sur-prises are your most powerful reward in the workplace, whether it's a bonus or simply unexpected recognition.

It's the little things that we don't expect that give us the biggest neurochemical reward instantaneously. Yes, we may look forward to Friday Free Lunches or baseball game team-building, but it's the little token of appreciation sitting on our desk that we didn't expect that provides the bonus boost. It's the surprise recognition of a job well done when it would be easy to take it for granted and move on to the next. It's the surprise perk that really moves the needle on fulfilling needs, creating boosts of dopamine and serotonin for your employees. The best part is that surprise small-scale recognition is often easy, inexpensive, or free. Leaving a simple Post-It on an employee's desk with a line like, "You are awesome! I'm so glad you're part of our team!" or "Great work on that project yesterday!" is still a hit of serotonin, regardless if you know it's headed into a desk drawer or the recycle bin. The reward has been delivered and the engagement tank has been refueled.

Regularly offered appreciation celebrations become *perks*. Once regular and expected, these lose some neurochemical benefit because they become a baseline. If Ralphie enjoyed cheese with every meal, he would get more neurochemical reward from something more unique and special. Leaving a note everyday will lose its boost as the brain comes to expect it, but occasional surprise notes and tokens of appreciation are one of many ways to help employees enjoy more positive neurochemicals.

This doesn't mean to stop doing regular perks employees expect and look forward to (but sometimes take for granted). You still need enough baseline rewards and recognition to keep a baseline of contentment. Perks help employees share why they work for you or help a candidate consider why they should. Few employees stay loyal for catered lunches or annual company events, but they will cite these as important perks when asked if they like their job or how well they feel taken care of by the company.

Employee retention lies in an employee's day-to-day experience, which is largely defined through the neurochemicals we experience. Offering a mix of expected recognition, positive perks, and occasional appreciative surprises will enhance an employee's day-to-day experience, making you an unforgettable leader, and making your company a place where people want to work.

But similar to how positive surprises are the best, negative surprises are the *worst*.

When Ralphie expected cheese, and it wasn't there, that was far worse than if he never expected cheese in the first place. For you, this looks like an employee expecting a reward or recognition and not getting it or not expecting negative feedback and being surprised with it. As Ralphie experienced, neurochemically plummeting below baseline expectations feels terrible and discourages engagement. You also do not want to have a team of employees who expect nothing, because their engagement will be as lackluster as their neutral expectations.

The Results Model helps you create dedicated time and structure for your employees to expect feedback delivered in a productive, un-triggering way, significantly reducing your need to deliver surprise negative feedback.

To reiterate what we can learn from Ralphie's experience with the new knowledge you have now:

- You want enough workplace perks and recognition (baseline) to retain employees and get potential hires interested.
- You want the future to be predictable (safe) and positive (optimistic for reward).
- You want occasional surprise perks and recognition to get the extra positive neurochemical boost.
- You want to minimize negative surprises.

Neurochemicals prove why celebrating small wins are so important. Creating opportunities for you and your employees to get boosts of positive neurochemicals makes the difference between the daily, "This is just what I do," (no upticks in neurochemicals because there's nothing unusual) and a feeling of, "I'm feeling great doing what I do," (highlighting the wins we often take for granted to create more good-feeling neurochemical boosts).

The workplace should be like a treasure hunt for neurochemicals. Your employees are hunting for these golden rewards that make the journey engaging and exciting. If you're not finding a way to make the mundane magical, you're missing meaningful opportunities to infuse neurochemicals into employees' daily experiences.

You have to add neurochemical fuel to continue driving forward

Essentially, you are on a road trip with your employees. Like any road trip, you don't fuel up once and go on forever. At some point, you'd be running on fumes and then peter out. You have to refuel your employees' neurochemical tanks to keep them moving forward. And in today's fast-paced workplaces, it's easy to forget to stop for fuel. It feels like we can endlessly keep going at a rapid pace, but this is where we experience **burnout**, running on neurochemical fumes or at full-on depletion.

As you learned in the Anxious Effort chapter, effort is not inherently stressful. It can be active or anxious. Employees want to work because it is the means to contribute meaningfully, but they need to be neurochemically refueled to keep going and persevere through today's overwhelming workplace demands.

The Revisiting step of the Results Model becomes an opportunity to ask about how your employees contributed successfully to the Desired Result, and, more importantly, gives you specific effort to recognize, reward, and celebrate! Don't miss this crucial stop to refuel with rewarding and incentivizing neurochemicals, helping them be more engaged in their most productive **Active Effort** next time.

The simple shift of rewarding effort (like rewarding the number of sales calls per day instead of closed deals) often doesn't change the daily activities required for success, but it does provide more frequent moments to neurochemically celebrate progress and accomplishment. These more frequent fuel-ups proactively keep employees feeling more fulfilled, confident, and optimistic while on their long road-trip driving results for your company.

Our day-to-day tasks may be relatively the same, but our experience putting effort toward those tasks can improve significantly simply by being rewarded for smaller wins more frequently. This shift, and almost every other tool in this book, is designed to help you keep employees engaged, fulfilled, and neurochemically fueled to prevent burnout.

Recognition, Rewards, and Celebration

This chapter wouldn't be complete without some final tips to boost neurochemicals. Here are some quick tips to help employees experience more dopamine, serotonin, and oxytocin rewards:

- **Record and celebrate small accomplishments:** To-do lists are classic dopamine-producers. It's why you feel better crossing something off a list instead of just remembering and completing it. By requiring formats that provide opportunities to cross off or ceremoniously celebrate, the more dopamine your employee will experience. This supports breaking up larger goals into smaller tasks that can be completed on a more rapid timeline.
- **Create celebration space:** Use bulletin boards, department or company emails, internal recognition platforms, or social media to share successes by employees, offer peer recognition, and even to allow employees to self-share successes. How much space can you create to celebrate wins? Do you want a culture of employees scanning for what people are doing wrong or what they are doing well?
- **Make meetings meaningful:** In addition to getting business done, ensure your one-on-one meetings and team meetings include opportunities to share, recognize, and celebrate successes.
- **Offer opportunities for peer recognition:** When we provide acknowledgment for others in a way that makes us feel good, we get an increase of dopamine, they receive serotonin, and the collaborative nature boosts oxytocin.

Tips for Serotonin Boosts

Since serotonin is the leadership neurochemical, here are some tips for how to fulfill employees' needs and proactively infuse serotonin.

Providing Acknowledgment and Recognition
- Affirm and acknowledge an employee's direct contribution, competence, and importance

- Offer encouragement
- Offer gratitude

Providing Care
- Acts of generosity
- Active listening

Asking Questions to Highlight Importance
- Ask what the employee would do rather than telling them what you want them to do
- Care about employees' personal interests. Ask questions to get to know more about what's important to them

Expect Success
- See employees as able to achieve success
- Offer perceived capability

Congratulations! You're almost done filling your Inspiring Accountability toolbox! Hopefully, you are seeing how everything you've learned is coming together to help empower you to get more from your team through a more positive and productive approach.

Up next, you'll use the foundation you now have to learn how to hold employees accountable for their attitudes, mindsets, and behaviors, or as most company's call these, company values.

Integration Questions:

1. How can you build in more refueling rest stops to celebrate effort and success to keep you and your employees fueled?
2. How can you begin offering more contribution context and perceived capability? What will you have to do to remember to include these more often?
3. What other tips resonated with you? What else would you like to start practicing more intentionally?

Key Take-Aways:

1. When you give opportunities for employees to feel great, you get employees that do great work.

2. Our moods greatly impact our performance, and neurochemicals are primary mood creators.

3. If you fulfill employees' workplace needs, you will more effortlessly watch your organization's needs be happily and eagerly fulfilled.

4. Genuine recognition never gets old. Even if contribution context initially feels like overkill, or even if employees know you're including it intentionally, *they still won't get tired of knowing how valuable their contribution is.*

5. If a task is worth doing, then there's contribution context worth communicating.

6. Vague or absent contribution context creates vague or absent incentive to engage.

7. You want enough workplace perks and recognition (baseline) to retain employees and be compelling to potential hires.

8. Employees often perform at the level of perceived capability their managers believe and express, setting an employee's possibility ceiling. Possibility ceilings generally become performance ceilings.

9. Use perceived capability as a tool to create possibility, not to ask the impossible.

10. Positive surprises are the magic. Negative surprises are the worst.

11. Make meetings neurochemically meaningful. When operated thoughtfully and intentionally, meetings with team brainstorming and celebration can enhance connection, collaboration, transparency, and trust, thereby enhancing oxytocin. Meetings can also be a dedicated space to offer recognition, which produces serotonin. And when meetings offer the ability to self-share successes, they offer dopamine boosts.

CHAPTER 15

Accountable for Attitude, Mindset, and Behavior (Values)

"In order to carry a positive action, we must develop here a positive vision."

—DALAI LAMA

In this chapter, you'll learn how to productively hold employees accountable for attitude, mindset, and behavior, usually known as company culture values, including:

- How values can be upgraded to effective accountability tools
- Best practices for Revisiting values (essential for Inspiring Accountability)
- How holding employees accountable toward values offers new neurochemical rewards

Previous chapters outlined the importance of creating positive engagement loops and to help employees see where they're going with clear expectations qualified through the **Accountability**

Anchor Conversion Checklist. But when it comes to trying to hold employees accountable for their attitude, mindset, and behavior, there's often something missing in the way leaders dispense their managerial strategies.

Quite simply, it's often the case that companies aren't upgrading values, and the expectations that come with those values, into clear enough **accountability anchors**. It's also common for values to be visible in many formats, like on the walls or at company-wide meetings, but it's less common to have effective Revisiting of the values.

Many companies think their effort to make values visible should be enough to mandate compliance. Since *accountability always requires revisiting*, what's often missing is effective Revisiting that initiates and inspires the desired accountability.

To hold employees accountable for attitude, mindset and behaviors, the easiest way is to use values upgraded to effective accountability tools to provide the clear expectation to work toward and calibrate against during progress.

Regardless of whether you have formal values or not, employees require a clear vision of success and regular Revisiting to calibrate toward that success. Clarity in expectation becomes clarity in demonstration, allowing you to offer "You did it!" serotonin rewards, which become incentives to continue demonstrating the desired attitude, mindset, and behavior.

How do you upgrade values to effective accountability tools to reap these benefits? Let's find out.

Accountable for Demonstrating Values

Company values, team values, and leadership principles are designed with good intentions to provide guidance and accountability. Once in writing or on the walls, it is assumed these values are strong enough expectations to guide behavior.

You know enough about accountability now to know that simply making expectations visible is not enough to effectively direct employees toward certain behaviors. There was thought put into creating the values, and so too should there be thought on how to practically demonstrate them.

Without company values or leadership principles explicitly crafted and executed as clear accountability anchors, they remain to be seen as only ineffective *invitations* instead of Revisited *expectations*. Most values are stated too generally to be useful, and *undefined values get undefined demonstration.*

It's easy for employees to see values in the workplace as fairly useless "nice to haves." They can be seen as "marketing fluff," or worse, cause resentment because there can be hypocrisy and exceptions. These are symptoms of possibly effective values without effective accountability.

Since we can't talk about accountability without talking about holding employees accountable for values or related attitudes, mindsets, and behavior, we will now explore how the Inspiring Accountability methodology makes this possible.

Why Traditional Accountability Values Don't Work

In the workplace, **values** are words or short phrases that describe how employees are "expected" to consistently act, interact, and prioritize.

Values help provide company culture structure and standards — emotional safety expectations that the creature brain appreciates — and can be upgraded to clear Desired Results that leaders confidently point to when behavior or attitude improvement is needed.

Values drive behavior, decisions, who you hire and fire, and what products you pursue or cut. They indicate what you reward and what you adjust.

Your mission statement is your *what,* your vision statement is your *why,* and your values are your *how.* Again, undefined values get undefined demonstration because the *how* is left too vague.

Once you upgrade values to their own form of accountability anchors, you can more easily and effectively hold employees accountable for how they act, interact, and prioritize.

Traditional values stop at a general definition, often just a word or short phrase, with far too much room for personal interpretation to provide actionable clarity. It's also fairly unrealistic to think any human's default in the middle of a stressful encounter would be to pause, evaluate the company values that could be used in the situation, *figure out what they mean*, and then resume action. *Employees need to know exactly how to demonstrate the value before the situation occurs that requires it.*

There are also companies with well-versed values that haven't figured out how to effectively revisit them with employees, leaving values as generic mentions on a traditional annual performance review for the manager to subjectively rate. This subjectivity rewards favoritism more than it inspires accountability, favoring those who naturally demonstrate values in a way each leader prefers.

Additionally, once a year is not nearly frequent enough Revisiting to drive development. Much like any other Desired Result without Revisiting, values that are seldom referenced are seldom *thoughtfully* employed. The brain won't offer Accountability Attention toward changing current behavior patterns, and so we *don't*. We stick with our default programming and get lucky if our leader agrees with our default demonstration.

Values can make excellent accountability anchors that statistically improve results. As reported by the *SHRM/Globoforce* survey, "Employee Recognition Report" (2018): "Values-based recognition programs — where employees are recognized and rewarded for behavior that exemplifies a company's core values — continue to be more highly adopted (70%) than recognition programs not tied to a company's core values (30%). Programs tied to values are also more than two times as likely to be focused on reinforcing and driving business goals."

Given the results-getting power of recognizing and rewarding behavior through values, we can see the opportunity to drive proactive accountability, using this recognition to fuel engagement. We can also see opportunity to drive responsive accountability through providing development feedback tied to these values to create a productive and aligned culture.

Upgrading Values to Clear, Revisitable Expectations

When values stop at "respect" or "committed to excellence," they are too broad to be useful. What if one of your employees grew up showing respect through teasing? And another showed respect by not asking questions once a decision was made? This won't be helpful if you're pushing a different definition of respect where you don't want employees teasing each other and you do want them participating in innovation by asking more questions.

If your employees aren't demonstrating your company values, it could be because:

- Low Revisiting frequency leaves values as invitations instead of expectations.
- So many others in the workplace are out of compliance that an employee rising up to demonstrate values would violate belonging in the *actual* current and default culture. Adherence becomes suspicious and alienating.
- Or, quite simply, employees don't know how they're supposed to do it.

Remember that a lack of clarity on how to move forward creates a hesitancy to move forward. An employee's uncertainty on how to personally demonstrate values, and a leader's uncertainty on how to hold an employee accountable for behavior, leaves everybody stuck in Anxious Effort and unable to change the culture.

Encouragement to demonstrate values without actionable clarity and Revisiting is perceived by our brains as an invitation.

Note the accountability differences in the (slightly) exaggerated example of presenting values to employees:

Inviting Engagement and Accountability: "Here are our values. Please ensure you are living these every day."

Requiring Engagement and Accountability: "Here are our values. How will you personally demonstrate these in the workplace day-to-day? Each month, we will all focus on better demonstrating one value. Once a month at our meetings, we will carve out ten minutes to share how each of us demonstrated it well, a missed opportunity where we could have demonstrated it better, and one way we can better demonstrate it next week. What questions do you have? What will you need to do to remember to practice this value?"

If you want to hold employees accountable for behavior and attitude, you must update the expectations to their own form of accountability anchors, present them as Desired Results, and offer regular Revisiting until demonstrated satisfactorily. Before I show you how to do this by creating company **Culture Values and Action Steps** (CVAS), let me first share where the inspiration came from in taking values to the next level.

Clif Bar — The Inspiration

My inspiration to take values to an accountable level was inspired by Clif Bar. Clif Bar has five company values called "Aspirations," and five internal culture values they call "Ingredients."

The Ingredients reflect the desired internal behaviors. Each offers a brief descriptor line followed by about seven descriptors that expand upon the meaning of their values through the company lens. For example, their fifth "Ingredient."

BE YOURSELF: Bring your best self to work each day
- Don't check your values or your personality at the door.
- Develop a level of self-awareness, recognizing both strengths and self-development areas.
- Demonstrate humility and know there is always more to learn.
- Respect one another's values.
- Respond appropriately.
- Balance work with fun and the spirit of play.
- Take yourself lightly and your work seriously.
- Keep it real.

Don't you get a great feel as to what Clif Bar means by "be your-self," which would otherwise be open to many interpretations? I was inspired to see how usefully this feeling was captured and how transparently these expectations were boldly shared on their website. If you want to be a Clifster, you have a significantly better understanding of what attitude, mindset, and behavior it takes to do so successfully.

When I interviewed Jen Freitas, Director of People Learning and Engagement at Clif Bar, I learned that they really walk the talk. Clif Bar put their own flavor on integrating values, establishing themselves as an inspiring example of how to incorporate values into their day-to-day work environment.

Freitas shared, "People come alive when they see their work aligned with our values. They feel good about what we're trying to do with this company." It's clear, at Clifbar, demonstrating values has become a source of "feel good" neurochemicals. She went on to share, "Employees take pride in contributing to something bigger." Values are also providing the means to increase a sense of contribution, becoming yet another tool to fulfill workplace needs, boost neurochemicals, and drive engagement.

You don't get these bonus benefits without a reliable integration and revisiting practice. So, how does Clif Bar do it? Clif Bar integrates the values into essentially every aspect of the employee experience, including email communication, personal and professional development, goal setting, career pathing, working through challenges, performance review conversations, and peer recognition.

"We want Clifsters to have a real, tactical sense of our Aspirations and Ingredients," she said, hinting at the value of bringing actionable clarity to once vague concepts. "We want employees not just to think about them, but to consistently reflect on how they can show up and navigate situations better through them." As we'll see later in the chapter, reflecting how each employee can demonstrate values in their unique role brings personalized clarity that enables powerful action and application.

Freitas shared that they designed their company culture Ingredients to:

- Provide people a North Star for how to show up.
- Answer: "How are we getting things done?"
- Describe the "ways we work together."
- Help us feel good about the day to day.
- Speak to "what we do," and also the spirit of "how we do it."
- Inform context and goal setting for individual goals and Key Performance Indicators (KPIs).

Freitas told me about Clif Bar's founder, Gary Erickson. "[Gary has a] real love for the planet and a real love for people. Gary wanted to create a place where people can play, have fun, and be who they are."

The values started with Erickson's vision for the culture, and continued by unearthing the experiences that employees already most enjoyed about working at Clif Bar. The Ingredients started to take form after a grassroots process that involved having conversations with employees across the company to understand what was important to them and what was already working in the culture.

Pretty inspiring, isn't it? No doubt dopamine, serotonin, and oxytocin are flowing steadily in a company as dedicated to its people and culture as Clif Bar.

With the additional descriptors that paint a clearer picture of what it means to successfully demonstrate the Ingredients, paired with strong, ubiquitous, and thoughtful integration, Cliftsers are set up to succeed in meeting expectations for their attitude, mindset, and behaviors.

Inspiring Accountability takes this inspiring foundation and adds another layer of actionable clarity to help your employees apply values to their day-to-day work life and help you increase employees' accountability toward those values. Let's see how it's done.

Defining Company Values with Actionable Clarity

You want company values not only noticed on the wall but noticed in the work.

How to demonstrate company values is not obvious by default. Often employees have a sense of "what we do," but the "how we do it" remains subjective to each individual's default patterns, interpretations, and preferences.

We interpret what values mean through our own experience, beliefs, our family's inherent values, and a plethora of cultural influences. Those create our personal defaults for our attitude, mindset, and behavior, whereas *company culture values should reflect a clear, unified definition of the company's standards.*

If "respect" is one of your core values and your company isn't guiding clarity on how to demonstrate this value, employees will use their personal definitions, which, as previously mentioned, can be very different than how a company wants respect to be demonstrated in the workplace.

When we accept a job offer, we are opting-in to a new culture with a new set of values and principles that we agree to be part of when we step "on campus."

We generally don't mind adjusting our behaviors to align with company values, but we *do* need to know what to adjust to successfully meet expectations.

In addition to guiding current employees, without clear cultural values and accountability to support them, you won't attract new employees that align and opt in. You'll be hiring whomever and hoping they'll be a good cultural fit. Optimism is important, but hope is not a strategy. You want a diverse workforce that is opting in to demonstrate values the way your company has defined them.

Actionable clarity is crucial here. The clearer your attitude, mindset, and behavioral expectations are in a job posting, job description, interview process, and even in onboarding, the more likely you'll hire employees willing to behave in alignment with your company culture and core values.

Now, let's examine how to add this actionably clarity.

Converting Values to Accountability Anchors

There are four types of values and principles that will help you create a company culture that gets results:

1. **Culture Values**: How employees are consistently expected to act, interact, and prioritize internally in day-to-day work.

2. **Customer Service Values**: How customer service is consistently provided to the customer base.

3. **Company/Organization Values**: How decisions are made interacting with the outside world, and how values reflect company priorities, what a company stands for, and how it does business.

4. **Leadership Principles**: What consistent attitudes, mindsets, and behaviors define being a leader at a company.

To inspire accountability, all of these would need to be clarified into clearer Desired Results. One of my favorite exercises to facilitate for companies and leaders through the Inspiring Accountability methodology is upgrading Culture Values to **Culture Values and Action Steps (CVAS)** and Leadership Principles to **Leadership Principles and Action Steps (LPAS)**.

Both CVAS and LPAS are upgraded to offer the actionably clarity needed to create a strong company culture when paired with Revisiting.

Leaders most commonly struggle to hold employees accountable for attitudes, mindsets, and behaviors, so we'll focus on Culture Values for the rest of the chapter.

Inspiring Accountability upgrades values to Culture Values and Action Steps (CVAS) by including three components:

1. **Value:** Word, brief phrase, or both

2. **"We" Descriptors:** 1-6 sentences that provide expanded context and definitions
   - Usually starting with we, in the format *"we [verb][context]"*

3. **Personalized "I" Action Steps**: 6-8 bullets of action steps

custom to how each employee in their individual roles can successfully demonstrate each value in their day-to-day

- Usually starting with I, in the format *"I [verb][context]"*
- A set personalized to the individual role
- Can also be expanded to have a set for the team

Here are the CVAS components in more detail:

1. **(Culture) Values:** What do you want every employee demonstrating consistently to define your culture and work experience? How do you want them to act, interact, and prioritize? You can use one word, a short phrase, or a word and a phrase to describe it.

   If your company is fun, these can be fun! If your company is more serious, don't jazz them up if it doesn't match your culture. It is most useful for a value to be clearly understood and reflect the authentic tone of the culture.

2. **"We" Descriptors:** 5-8 statements that answer, "What does this value mean at our company?" in the format "We [verb] [context]." These should outline general behaviors and demonstrable actions that clarify the expectations aligned with the company's interpretation. For example, if a value is Integrity, then some descriptors could be:

   - We follow-through on every deliverable or communicate a change as soon as we're aware.
   - We share honest opinions without making different opinions wrong.
   - When we recognize we are out of alignment with our values, we acknowledge it and work toward improvement.

3. **Personalized "I" Action Steps:** Answers "How specifically can I demonstrate this value and its descriptors in my role and in my day-to-day work life?" These generally start with "I [do

this]" for individuals, and you can use "we [do this]" for teams. I recommend 6-8 action steps for each value.

- For example, using, "We share honest opinions without making different opinions wrong," could be personalized to: "I participate in department meetings with my ideas, and I don't shoot down others until I've considered and acknowledged how another's idea could be helpful."

You want your employees and teams to brainstorm these examples. Since self-creation increases interest and accountability, leaders should offer their ideas only after employees and teams have exhausted their own. Plus, employees know their day-to-day work the best. If you want them engaged in demonstrating values, start by engaging them in creating their own action steps.

Accountability with a New Focus on Values

Start fresh. Don't try to hold an employee accountable for past behavior out of alignment with poorly-defined values unsupported by ineffective accountability measures.

Instead, acknowledge you are revamping values and the attention on them. Share how you are going to set up your team for success by helping each individual understand with actionable clarity how to successfully demonstrate them, and that you will support their effort and development with regular Revisiting.

Only now can you begin to offer value-related accountability anchors, give your employees opportunities to practice the new behaviors, and then begin effective Results Model-style accountability that keeps them engaged, confident, and optimistic about these new change requests.

Focus on One Value a Month

To effectively integrate, I recommend everyone in the company (or on your team) focus on one selected value each month. Each employee selects between one and three actions steps to focus on that demonstrate that "value of the month." These are Revisited at each meeting as part of the Results Model conversations, team meetings, or, at a minimum, other regularly scheduled meetings.

Imagine the power of every person in your company collectively focusing on one value, and sharing different ways to demonstrate the value regularly. It will be impossible not to see improvement in the visibility of that value in day-to-day work.

This ever-present and ongoing reflection on one value at a time creates an *expectation that demonstrating values is a required contribution for all.* This activates and inspires accountability because everyone is sharing in the experience, bringing transparency and Accountability Attention to the effort. It creates opportunities for your employees to get recognized and celebrated for their contribution to your culture.

Accountability Still Requires Revisiting

To effectively hold employees accountable for values, you'll need to regularly Revisit, calibrate, and adjust the demonstration of these. The Results Model is the perfect Revisiting solution for values.

In using the Results Model, you may have to adjust the contribution question slightly. Instead of asking, "How did you successfully contribute [to the result]?" you might ask, "How did you successfully demonstrate this value?" Then you can still follow with, "What got in the way?" and, "What's possible?"

Team meetings can also be a good option to keep values top of mind. If everyone is working on the same value at the same time, in their own unique application, Revisiting can be self-reflective, including a quick check-in sharing:

- One way I demonstrated this value well (since last meeting)
- One missed opportunity where I could have demonstrated it better
- One way I envision being able to demonstrate this value in the coming week

Employees at all levels need to know exactly how to demonstrate the value *before* a situation requires it. By thinking proactively about future ways to demonstrate values, the brain becomes primed to use this new pre-planned behavior.

Address Exceptions

There are many exceptions to values that can create confusion and resentment among your team members.

- Does a value of authenticity mean you *always* say exactly what you think?
- Does a value of trust mean you *never* doubt another or check an employee's work?
- Does a value of consistency mean you *never* make exceptions?
- Does a value of accountability mean that it is or isn't okay to say, "That's not my job."?

Oftentimes, it's not overtly apparent how much interpretation and (in worst case scenarios) how much hypocrisy can live in values. That's why describing them with actionable clarity is key. To prevent confusion or resentment, it's important to identify exceptions and ensure your descriptors include them.

If "authenticity" is a value, it's easy to question if this gives free reign to self-expression. You may want to acknowledge exceptions with descriptors like:

- ☑ "I share my opinions honestly in service of improving the quality of work and experience at work."
- ☑ "I share my opinions without judgment or criticism about different opinions."
- ☑ "I appreciate the similarities and differences I have with my colleagues."

Deconstructing your values in this way creates clear expectations for your employees while leaving room for their individual expressions of those values.

Recognizing Values — Time for a Neurochemical Boost

Leader Recognition

Now that employees have their attention on demonstrating values, you have plenty of opportunities to boost neurochemicals. With the clarity that comes with upgrading values to effective accountability anchors with action steps, you now can spot new opportunities for recognition.

When you Revisit, you'll learn how they have successfully demonstrated values so you can recognize their successful effort, boosting serotonin while also boosting culture and morale.

Peer Recognition

Another fun way to use this tool is to have employees recognize others in their department for demonstrating values. Some companies have online platforms or dedicated Slack channels for peer recognition.

Companies like Clif Bar have peer recognition sticky notes readily available. With a large "I appreciate" heading at the top and small logos representing each of their Ingredients (Culture Values) on the side, they make peer recognition easy, as well as keeping values top of mind as a great lens for acknowledgment.

If you don't already have a system for peer recognition, find ways that work in your team and company so you don't neglect opportunities for "You did it!" serotonin, team-building oxytocin, and the incentive these rewards create.

Negative Feedback Made Easy

Some of the trickiest negative feedback, or development feedback, is when you need to see behavior and attitude improvements. Without values as clearly defined demonstrable actions, you're likely asserting *preferences*, which are more effective at inspiring resentment than inspiring improvement.

In the event of behavior contradicting a value, assuming you can wait until your next meeting to address it, you can now add a behavior, mindset, or attitude challenge to the employee's Results List, although you will need to ensure it is presented as a clear action step or qualified through the Accountability Anchor Conversion Checklist. With values, you can have the employee explore their own behavior and create the anchor, or, if more appropriate, you can provide it for them.

To introduce it, you might lead with perception language: "I noticed you have been slow to respond to requests from Linda. Since our value of Integrity outlines responding to emails within three days, can we explore what might be making this challenging?" Go from there to discover what's possible, and consider if it's a good candidate to be added to the Results List for focused Revisiting until aligned again.

Or, if a behavior arises that must be addressed right away, you can still use an informal version of the Results Model combined with Engaging Leadership Language. You might say, "It seemed like you were pretty sarcastic with Betty in that meeting. It looked like she didn't respond well. How do you think your approach could better align with our value of Respect?" You can then use, "What got in the way?" and "What's possible?" as needed.

If everyone in the company is focusing on the same value, conversations using the Results Model for behavior improvement have more inherent context and therefore less potential to trigger the defensive creature brain.

Know that you don't have to do it all at once. Trying to focus on too many behavioral changes will either dilute the effort or trigger the employee's **impossible expectation threshold**. They will then lose confidence and optimism in their ability to meet expectations, and you now know how this negatively affects engagement, effort, and the potential for results.

When working on demonstrating values or behaviors, it's best to only focus on one behavior adjustment at a time. However, you can apply it to different areas. Perhaps this same action step can be demonstrated in one-on-one meetings, with customers, and in team interactions.

Let your employees keep their focus narrow and specific to make noticeable progress. Let them have the capacity to win, adapt, and be celebrated before moving attention onto another requested improvement.

Accountable Without Values

Until your team or company has created a culture of accountability for values, address attitude, mindset, and behavior requests like you would address any Desired Result using the Results Model.

Let's say you are having trouble between two of your employees. You could say, "It seemed like there was some tension between you and Betty in that meeting. What do you think you could do to help improve your dynamic with her?" From here, shape a behavior-specific Desired Result, qualified as an accountability anchor, and Revisit with the Results Model. Reference Part II for a refresher as needed.

Upgrade Job Descriptions to Effectively Include Values

As you upgrade Culture Values with Action Steps for each role, you can add these action steps, which are personalized to each role, to job descriptions, creating clearer accountability anchors for the current employee, as well as anyone who holds the role in the future.

When you notice performance not meeting expectations, you now have a clear accountability anchor to calibrate against as you add it to the Results List and begin using the Results Model consistently.

Because job description overhauls can be a large project if done by Human Resources, I recommend updating job descriptions over time with your team. You can even ask each team member to update their own job descriptions with action steps and clearer expectations as you move through the Inspiring Accountability process.

Implementing with Help or On Your Own

In addition to helping companies and teams bring actionable clarity and accountability to their values, another favorite process I facilitate is creating Leadership Principles and Action Steps (LPAS), leadership values that encompass what it means to be a leader at a given company defined with actionable clarity.

As much as I enjoy helping clients create useful CVAS and LPAS, this step can also be done internally if the right resources are available. I facilitate this process with clients starting wherever they are, whether they don't have values, have weakly defined values, or have well-defined values without an effective accountability process. You, too, can start anywhere.

You don't have to wait if your company isn't ready to implement these steps company-wide, or if your company values aren't created yet. You can initiate CVAS within your team, beginning with a brainstorm to create team values, collectively imagining value descriptors, and facilitating time for each employee to determine their individual action steps.

Should a moment happen where you need to address something specific with one person, and you don't yet have values or CVAS established, simply clarify the behavior, mindset or attitude with the Accountability Anchor Conversion Checklist. You can then take this new Desired Result, add it to their Results List to actively work on, and use the Results Model to Revisit until the Desired Result is demonstrated satisfactorily.

Whatever approach you start with, you can now create clear expectations to point to and revisit whenever attitude, mindset, or behavioral concerns arise.

Integration Questions:

1. If your company or team has values, what ways are those company values demonstrated or not demonstrated by your team? How well are your current values acting as accountability anchors?
2. How can you start to upgrade your values to CVAS?
3. If your company or team doesn't have values, where would you like to start?
4. Which attitude, mindset, or behavioral challenges do you have on your team that you'd like to see improved? How can you tie those directly to company values or convert to accountability anchors?

Key Take-Aways:

1. When it comes to holding employees accountable for their attitude, mindset, and behaviors, most leaders and companies have not upgraded these expectations to clear accountability anchors and action steps.
2. In the workplace, "values" are words or short phrases that describe how employees are "expected" to consistently act, interact, and prioritize.
3. Values and principles are not inherently clear expectations. They are often far too vague to offer actionable clarity to be effective accountability tools. Similar to how vague Desired Results get vague results, undefined values get undefined demonstration of those values.
4. Employees need to know how exactly to demonstrate the value *before* a situation occurs that requires it.
5. When a part of your culture is seen as a non-negotiable expectation, the brain resists change less than if it's an "unrevisited" invitation.
6. If you want to hold employees accountable for attitudes, mindsets, or behaviors, you must define them with actionable clarity, present them as Desired Results, and offer Revisiting.
7. You want company values not only noticed on the wall but noticed in the work.

8. Inspiring Accountability upgrades values to Culture Values and Action Steps (CVAS) by including three components:
   - **Value:** Word, brief phrase, or both
   - **"We" Descriptors:** 1-6 sentences that provide expanded context and definitions; usually in the format: "we [verb][context]."
   - **Personalized "I" Action Steps:** 6-8 bullets of action steps custom to how each employee in their individual role can successfully demonstrate each value in their day-to-day work; usually in the format "I [verb][context]."

9. To effectively hold employees accountable for values, you'll need to regularly revisit, calibrate, and adjust the demonstration of them. The Results Model is the perfect Revisiting solution for values.

10. Oftentimes, it's not apparent how much interpretation and, at times, hypocrisy can live in values when they're not explored, defined, and described with actionable clarity. It's important to identify these resentment-causing exceptions and ensure your descriptors include them.

11. Without values proactively defined with action steps, you're likely asserting *preferences*, which are more effective at inspiring resentment than inspiring improvement.

12. When working on demonstrating values or behaviors, it's best to only focus on one behavior adjustment at a time so employees can fully win before moving on to the next change request.

13. Trying to focus on too many behavioral changes will either dilute the effort or cross the impossible expectation threshold, triggering a loss of confidence and optimism in one's ability to meet expectations.

14. As you upgrade Culture Values with Action Steps for each role, you can add these action steps to job descriptions, creating clearer accountability anchors for the person in the role, as well as anyone who holds the role in the future.

CHAPTER 16

Additional Internal Accountability Tools

"You cannot mandate productivity, you must provide
the tools to let people become their best."
—STEVE JOBS

**This chapter introduces you to the top four internal tools that
you can upgrade using what you've learned from Inspiring
Accountability. These tools include:**

- Performance reviews and contribution conversations
- Compensation success criteria
- Innovation and Efficiency Meetings
- Proactive Accountability Measures (PAM's)

Performance Reviews and Contribution Conversations

Although an entire alternate book could be written on effective performance reviews and correlated compensation, and there are many great ones already published, here is a quick overview of Inspiring Accountability's stance on these important accountability topics. In the next two segments, you won't find the same prescriptive how-to's as in previous chapters, but you will find relevant information to guide opportunities to improve these two important areas.

Why You Don't Need Performance Reviews Anymore

It's no secret. Employees and leaders don't enjoy the traditional performance review process. It's triggering for employees, it's impossible for leaders to validly remember a year's worth of performance, and studies have shown that these reviews do nothing for productivity.

Writer Mark Murphy reports in his 2012 HR.com article, "The 3 Reasons Employees Hate Performance Reviews" about the widespread belief of their ineffective nature. In a survey of 48,000 CEOs, managers, and employees, only 13% of managers and employees and a mere 6% of CEOs thought their year-end reviews were effective.

Equally frustrating, the evaluation aspect of the performance review itself is heavily biased. Mario Buckingham offers an unsettling fact in his 2015 article for *Harvard Business Review*, "Most HR Data is Bad Data." His research shows approximately 60% of any given performance rating actually has to do with the traits of the person conducting the evaluation and *not the person being evaluated*, a bias known as the "idiosyncratic rater effect."

Perhaps most troubling of all, according to the 2011 *Psychology Today* article, "Why CEO's Need to Scrap Employee Reviews," it's reported that at least 30% of performance reviews result in *decreased* employee performance.

Isn't the purpose of performance reviews is to *improve* performance, get better results, and offer feedback and accountability to drive these improvements?

You've already learned an effective way to do what performance reviews have been failing to do for decades. Using the Results Model regularly will meet these *exact objectives* without the ineffectiveness of reviewing a year's worth of work through a triggering experience that statistically (and neurochemically) *decreases* performance.

The Results Model already covers this need to improve performance regularly with a mutual understanding of proactive accountability, responsive accountability, and the Results Model. So, if we're covering this need through frequent Revisiting, what is left to address that the classic performance review once offered?

The answer? Long-term goal setting, career pathing, and compensation changes.

When you clarify Desired Results with the **Accountability Anchor Conversion Checklist**, you are moving toward something more specific and actionable, and away from vague and broad goals. But bigger, long-term goals are still important. Employees are inspired to contribute toward bigger aspirations, and they want to know where they're going so they can keep their contribution in alignment with this long-term path. Let's examine how to accomplish each of these remaining objectives in more detail.

Contribution Conversations for Goal Setting

Taking more inspiration from the approach Torani leaders use in their performance reviews (as described in Chapter 1), you can utilize **contribution conversations** to cover some of what performance reviews once covered.

The contribution conversation approach leaves the employee reaching to contribute instead of the manager pulling for it. Employees will determine how they contribute, explore how their efforts can best be utilized, and ask for what they need to be successful.

One effective framework is to have employees create individual annual goals that support company goals (instead of being told what to do). We are most inspired to initiate ideas we originate, and employees are naturally more inspired to be accountable for goals they create.

Here's how this would look:

- **Present the annual company goals to your employees.**
  This can be in a team or individual meeting. Be available to answer questions.

- **Give employees time consider how they can individually contribute to the goals this year.** Two to four weeks is a good amount of time before reconvening.
- **Schedule individual meetings.** In this meeting, employees share how they want to contribute toward the company goals this year and what resources or development they may need to do so successfully. In this meeting, explore what could get in the way and what's possible. Leave with clear contribution goals.
- **Align Desired Results with Big Picture Goals.** Use the goals to guide what employees are working on as active Desired Results. Distill goals into accountability anchors to serve as success milestones, neurochemical reward opportunities, and to guide progress. Review the big picture goals quarterly to inform what progress milestones would make worthy accountability anchors.

If you want to add or re-route an employee's ideas for their goals, do so mindfully, keeping them as empowered as possible. Ask questions instead of directing them what to do because when you do it *for* them, you take accountability *from* them. The Engaging Leadership Language segment in Chapter 13 is a great resource for you in conversations like these.

Explore your own version of using the concept of Contribution Conversations for goal setting, revisiting, and calibrating, and then adjust using the Results Model.

You may find contribution conversations helpful or unnecessary in determining when an employee is eligible for a raise, but don't assume raises must be tied to annual evaluations of goal achievement. Ideal context to provide raises and bonuses is covered later in this chapter.

Development Goals and Career Pathing

Since the Results Model is not focused on general or long-term results, we need a designated time to get out of the weeds of daily tasks to look at the horizon to inspire an expanded purview. From there, we can come back to the Accountability Anchor Conversion Checklist to clarify specific steps toward that horizon.

This goal setting starts with what employees want for themselves. These general goals are what you, as their leader, support in finding what's in the way and what's possible for them to reach their goals. They may want to talk about their career path or projects to which they wish to contribute. They may talk about skills they want to learn to improve their contribution. Help uncover what is important to them and how you can productively and realistically support them.

Broader goal setting is best done every three, six, or twelve months, depending on the company and role.

Not everyone wants to keep upping their title (which isn't always possible), but most want to know they're growing their contribution at a pace that feels right for them. Even those who don't readily express this sentiment still benefit from the positive neurochemicals and additional engagement by growing their capability when it's recognized and rewarded.

Then, there are those employees that *do* want to move up in title fast. This step will help create realistic expectations and steps to feel in progress toward those goals. Help these ambitious employees see a path toward the result they want. Help them take practical steps toward developing the skills and experience necessary, and most importantly, stay engaged from the feeling of progress toward it.

Compensation Success Criteria

Often, companies use performance reviews to evaluate which employees are "worthy" of a raise. Given performance reviews' implicit bias, this process becomes subjective and rewards luck and favoritism instead of effort and contribution.

Inspiring Accountability asserts four compensation tenets:

1. Employees should always know exactly what is required to make the salary they want.

2. Raises should not be subjective, based on bias or preference, and certainly not on a leader's ability to remember and judge a year's worth of effort.

3. A bump in salary should relate to a bump in job level (not necessarily position but pre-determined performance levels within a job).

4. Rating employees on meeting expectations should not be incentivized with annual raises.

Let's explore these tenets through Inspiring Accountability's approach to compensation.

Drop the Rating Scales

If you want people to "exceed expectations," then increase your expectations.

The idea that "meeting expectations" is like getting a "C" in school may work for some, but being labeled as "average" can be very discouraging and disincentivizing for others. Clarify the expectation you want met and hold employees accountable to perform at that standard. Meeting expectations should be an "A." It should reflect the *full* fulfillment of expectations to get the full neurochemical reward.

The Results Model will ensure that all employees are fulfilling expectations or are actively and transparently working toward them. Anything less produces a lackluster neurochemical reward, if any, for your employees.

Inspiring Accountability's tools and strategies can eliminate the need for summary performance ratings, but if deemed necessary, the evaluation choices would only identify that an employee is either:

☑ "Successfully meeting expectations," or
☑ "In progress toward meeting expectations."

If an employee is performing above expectations, then either: 1.) They should be promoted to the next level within their position in pay, title, or both, or 2.) Previous expectations were too low.

If an employee is performing below expectations, they should be actively "in progress" with these areas as active Desired Results, clarified through the Accountability Anchor Conversion Checklist, and Revisited effectively.

Only when an employee fails to improve after, say, three months of weekly Results Model Revisiting, does it make sense to identify an employee as in the wrong position. After three months, if the weekly check-ins around "What's in the way?" and "What's possible?" haven't uncovered a practical path of meeting expectations, the impasse likely exceeds any performance review rating.

Employees should know how to fulfill expectations and the level of compensation associated with that performance. How can you contribute to this transparency more frequently and effectively?

Raises and Bonuses

So why and when do we give raises and bonuses? Let's look at some diagnostic questions:

- What does the structure of how you compensate employees communicate about what's *invited* and what's *expected*?
- How often are employees rated as exceeding expectations? Are your expectations set to a perfect fulfillment point to allow maximum neurochemical reward?
- Are you incentivizing over-working or punishing those doing exactly what is expected?

Up next are three areas that, when clearly defined, can be used to determine a fair and transparent pay structure that maintains performance accountability: competency levels, cost of living increases, and bonuses.

Competency Level

If an employee wants a raise, they should know exactly what demonstrated competency is required to get it.

When someone has outgrown the competency and contribution expectations that came with their job description, it's time for a merit increase or bonus. How do you know who deserves it?

Your job descriptions should offer enough actionable clarity in the stated expectations to give clear indications of what performance qualifies for which position.

Some jobs already have this breakdown, like many customer service position levels where there is a Level 1, Level 2, Level 3, and so on. What if you identify skill levels that already exist within each position? Instead of needing to "exceed expectations" to get a raise, what if employees needed to demonstrate specific skills and behaviors to earn it?

If employees are motivated to stay by expected annual increases, wouldn't it be more practical and better serve accountability to provide increases at new competency levels that you calibrate with them? You'd be incentivizing them to work toward specific performance goals, not waiting for the obligatory review time at the end of the year.

Cost of Living Increases

Cost of living increases are usually provided annually, but too often they are co-mingled with performance evaluations. To have a competitive salary that allows employees to maintain the same relative value of their salary year-to-year, cost of living increases need to align with the reality of the location's rental landscape. It's useful for companies to be clear on their cost of living increase policy, and keep it separate from performance since it isn't performance related.

Bonuses

Bonuses are tricky. Their distribution can be biased and difficult to fairly discern, but as we learn from Ralphie's neurochemical party when he was first surprised with cheese, surprise bonuses are a major engagement and neurochemical boost. So, when is the optimal time to reward with bonuses?

Bonuses should be given as surprise recognition or for temporary exceptional effort beyond what was "contracted for." In alignment with a fundamental Inspiring Accountability tenet, bonuses create better accountability when they're used to acknowledge or reward effort, not results.

For surprise recognition, you provide a bonus when you see effort or behavior you want to incentivize to continue. This could include an employee demonstrating a value they've been working to improve for three months. If an employee is naturally good at something, this is not what you want to reward. You want to reward when an employee extends *effort* toward improvement. It could be something as small as a gift card or as large as a cash bonus.

I recommend having a budget for each employee so that, in the end, everyone receives a chance at a fairly distributed bonus. What you get to decide is the individual timing and distribution associated with each employee's efforts. Bonuses should function as ways to say, "Thank you for this effort. I want this behavior to continue!" Or, in the case of someone staying late over a few months on a big project, the bonus might actually be more of a salary compensation for the un-logged "overtime."

What's the neurochemical reward difference between getting a bonus for completing an arduous six-month project versus getting a surprise bonus because a leader noticed her employee asking more open-ended questions, an active Desired Result he's been working on? Because of the surprise, specificity, and timeliness of the bonus that's tied to the employee's effort of asking more questions, the brain will be neurochemically motivated to keep the employee's attention on continuing that behavior. Providing a bonus for six months of overtime is not a reward – it's compensation for exorbitant overtime.

An exception to rewarding specific effort is for those employers who offer company-wide annual performance bonuses. Although this structure is not specific enough to effectively inspire individual accountability, it is an excellent employee retention *perk* and does neurochemical and engagement wonders when distributed and celebrated. It simply doesn't incentivize specific behavior to help drive development toward that result being achieved again.

Our next internal accountability tool will help you engage employees in their productivity and help proactively clear what's in the way of greater performance.

Innovation and Efficiency Meetings

Innovation and Efficiency Meetings are regular team meetings held every one to three months to unearth what's in the way of innovation and efficiency. Once brought to light, you can move to brainstorming what's possible.

Each team member brings one to three ideas that, if implemented, they believe will positively contribute to their day-to-day (or their teams') efforts. Because everyone will need to come up with at least one idea to improve innovation and efficiency, employees' brains will be scanning for these opportunities much more than if this "search and rescue" scent hadn't been supplied.

In addition to the obvious benefits of hearing from your "boots on the ground" employees in how to improve, these meetings can open up the conversation for types of feedback that are not readily available.

For example, Pietro is having trouble focusing at work because his cubicle is across from his manager's.

"If I could just have some blocks of uninterrupted work time, I could be so much more productive," Pietro confessed to me one day. "My manager interrupts me so many times throughout the day, and although I understand that's her style of working, it is so difficult for me to get my work done with frequent interruptions."

Pietro didn't see a way to productively bring up this issue, and instead remained at his manager's service and preferred work style. Productivity and therefore contribution suffered because there wasn't a space for this "ask" to be made.

If Pietro's team had a regular Innovation and Efficiency meeting, Pietro would have the context and opportunity to share what he feels would contribute to his efficiency, perhaps asking about blocking off four hours of un-interrupted time each day.

From here, Pietro's manager can decide if this idea is practical for her own needs and those of the team, and a productive *conversation* (instead of a *confrontation*) has begun.

Our final internal accountability tool will help you utilize the brain's built-in proclivities to make desired results more easily and naturally achievable.

Proactive Accountability Measures (PAM's)

If a phone manufacturer knows humans tend to drop their phones, should the manufacturer argue that customers should be more careful with their expensive devices? Or should the manufacturer innovate around this common issue, taking considerable time and resources to accommodate, and design phones to be shatterproof?

As a person who has cracked many phone screens, the answer seems clear to me. Sure, I'm accountable for dropping my phone, and no amount of care will ensure I won't drop it again. Like me, you probably also want a phone manufacturer that feels some accountability in the longevity of your phone, despite that it's your fault if you drop it.

Yet, it's harder as a manager to be as empathetic to common human mistakes, not to mention applying time and resources to make it easier to avoid the negative effects.

Inspiring leaders, similar to companies that lead the cell phone markets, don't rely on righteously imposing the virtue of accountability *without making it as easy as possible for common problems to be avoided in the first place.*

When you make it easier to meet expectations, everyone wins. You've learned to make employee success easier by improving actionable clarity and clearing what's in the way, and here's another excellent and easy proactive accountability tool to add to your leadership toolbox.

Since not achieving the Desired Result is a loss for your employee, a loss for you, and a loss for the company, how can we help improve the chance for an all-around win?

Proactive Accountability Measures (PAM's) include any proactive tools and methods that make it easier for an employee to meet expectations.

The power of PAM's can come from an increase in:

- **Accessibility or visibility of success criteria**: Humans simply perform better when they know exactly what's expected and can easily reference it. Success criteria that is more accessible or visible keeps it top-of-mind and makes it easier to adhere.

  Examples: Accessible Actionably Clear Expectations and Specs (ACES) or other completed checklists to turn in with work, job aids, reminder signage of what's important, reminder post-its, visible values (ideally with descriptors), or real-time statistics about safety, errors, accidents, or accomplishments.

  Every day example: A soft-pretzel company with outlines of the pretzel size on baking sheets to easily ensure pretzels are all crafted to the perfect size.

- **Visibility of one's work, behavior, and effort:** Humans simply perform better and with more compliance when we know someone is paying attention. Some of these PAM's offer proactive transparency, somewhat of an "in-the-moment" expected revisiting.

  Examples: Working next to your manager, having security cameras, sharing commitments at meetings, displaying individual, team, or company commitments in the workspace.

  Every day example: Known security cameras that capture cash-handling activities.

- **More frequent expected feedback**: Humans simply perform better when they know they'll receive direct feedback on their effort. Additionally, the more humans know how they're doing, the more they can calibrate and adjust to align with expectations. Increase the opportunity for expected feedback, especially from sources other than you, like customers or relevant statistics.

Examples: More frequent progress reports or statistics, real-time statistics or feedback, or known customer service surveys at the end of calls and online chats. If the surveys are *not* known to the customer service representative, while you may get an excellent understanding of how the representative is doing, you won't be proactively inspiring improved behavior.

Every day example: Ride-sharing app ratings for both drivers and passengers, creating more natural accountability for both.

In addition, these Proactive Accountability Measures are conveniently built into the Results Model and Inspiring Accountability methodology, as highlighted here:

- More frequent scheduled Revisiting to review and provide feedback on effort and results
- Providing accountability anchors or inarguably clear expectations, making it easier to meet the expectation the first time
- Promised or scheduled Revisiting, offering calibration and more frequent opportunities to adjust
- Expected feedback in each round of the Results Model, making it safer to stay receptive to feedback and resourceful toward improvement

The goal is to make failure impossible by *making it easier* for the human brain to perform well and naturally be accountable. We're working with the brain's default inclinations to do better when the previously mentioned factors are in play.

Let's look at an expanded example of a Proactive Accountability Measure created to inspire accountability in employees that arguably have one of the least inspiring jobs: cleaning airport bathrooms.

Built-in Feedback

In this example, you'll see how the proactive part of PAM's don't trigger defensiveness because they're a known, expected, and non-negotiable aspect that becomes part of day-to-day work.

The SEATAC airport in Washington State has a simple kiosk in their bathrooms with "How satisfied were you with the cleanliness of this restroom?" There are three buttons from which you can select your feedback: a happy face, a neutral face, or a dissatisfied face.

Outside of my personal sanitation concerns of the buttons, since there is no foolproof accountability measure for washing hands in sight, this is a wonderful Proactive Accountability Measure. Those that clean the bathroom know each customer has the opportunity to provide immediate feedback.

But the magic of this PAM is not actually about how many patrons participate in giving feedback. The accountability is created for those who clean the bathroom simply by *knowing* there's Revisiting, patrons paying attention, and an expectation of feedback. Humans perform better when they know each customer, in this case, could provide immediate feedback on their direct effort and contribution. There's no escaping the need to do excellent work that meets "happy face" expectations.

Creating Accountability, Not Just Evaluating Feedback

The accountability power of an immediate customer feedback PAM is much like the instinct to press down the brake pedal when one sees a cop. Both the renewed willingness to apply the brake pedal to slow to the speed limit and the willingness to apply one's best effort into a task *is much more about the existence and visibility of the PAM than about using its feedback.* Highway Patrol accomplishes "inspiring" drivers to drive more safely without even handing out tickets to every speedy driver. Having the knowledge that that feedback is always available — whether old, new, or in the moment — has its own value that shapes behavior. Yet not all feedback, like in our airport bathroom example, is easily translated to productive direction on what to improve.

Let's assume a worker received a series of sad faces during a shift. Was it the worker's neglect to refill paper towels or did a boisterous kid pull them all out right after the bathroom was cleaned? Additionally, given that this feedback happens to be anonymous, can we trust that as many satisfied people will hit the happy button as those dissatisfied being compelled to hit the unhappy button? Was a kid mashing at the red button for fun? The variables of *how* that feedback is generated is something that needs to be taken into consideration, as it can be particularly destructive to accountability to use vague and unreliable feedback punitively.

With vague feedback, like simple positive or negative ratings, you want to look at inarguable trends and explore what could be in the way of receiving better ratings. You want to stick with holding employees accountable for *effort*, not results, especially because this type of feedback doesn't indicate the actual problem (most of the time). Instead, get curious and conversational with the employee about what might be in the way of receiving better ratings, and from there, see what's possible.

In alignment with Engaging Leadership Language, you could ask, "I noticed there was an exceptional amount of dissatisfied feedback yesterday in the 11 a.m. hour. What do you think might have contributed to this?"

There are many reasons that this string of dissatisfied responses may have come in, and you don't want to discourage an employee who was doing a great job whose performance was compromised by a button-pushing kid. What affects accountability the most is that the employee is aware that feedback can happen any time and will be discussed. The feedback provided is secondary to the act of offering a Proactive Accountability Measure.

This is the same with companies that say there will be a customer satisfaction survey at the end of your customer service call or chat. Employees know that every customer they speak with will be prompted to rate their experience, so their brain engages more accountability regardless of how many callers engage in the option.

Creating PAM's

Here are questions to help you create PAM's that, with good intentions, can help support your employees in meeting expectations the first time, inspiring proactive accountability:

Identifying a concern that will benefit from a PAM:

- What's not working, and what do I want to see instead?
- Where do I want to see improved results?
- What is the result I want?
- What gets in the way of getting the result now? Given what's gotten in the way, what can be done to make it impossible to fail?
- What's being missed or forgotten?
- What needs to be improved?
- What needs to be done differently or included for the employee to improve?

After identifying and exploring the concern, ask *yourself* these questions:

- How could feedback on effort be obtained more immediately or easily?
- How could visibility of effort be increased (in a way that supports dignity)?
- How could visibility to commitments be increased (in a way that supports dignity)?
- How can I offer more revisiting?

Then, if useful, *ask your employee* the most relevant of these questions to uncover and solidify PAM's that could be beneficial:

- What would make it impossible to fail, forget, or not get it right?
- What would help you remember?
- What barriers are keeping you from succeeding?
- What would make the success criteria or completion requirements more accessible, visible, or easily referenced?
- What would make doing this new process convenient?
- What would make it easier to meet expectations exactly and every time?
- How can we improve the current process to make it easier?
- Are there resources that would make getting the result successfully easier?
- How can we add more actionable clarity?

Use your discretion to determine if PAM's should be brainstormed within your team or if you should develop the PAM's yourself. For example, installing surveillance cameras. In many cases, employees won't be excited about coming up with PAM's that feel childish or surveillance-y. Honor the employee's dignity in the process. Pulling from the 4C's approach you learned in the Engaging Leadership Language chapter, we want to have a caring mindset, helping your team be the best contributors they can be, and not to be a leader that is confrontational, controlling, or untrusting.

Installing New PAM's

Although PAM's don't negatively trigger employees once established, creating new PAM's can. Creating PAMs may make employees feel like they're not trusted or not doing a good job. Employees that feel like they're not trusted can have their morale sapped. And bad morale is contagious.

Preventing bad morale is directly linked to how you introduce these new concepts into the workplace, and how much you can maintain employees' dignity, confidence, and optimism about a PAM's impact.

Say you institute one of the most triggering of all PAM's: surveillance cameras. Here's an option if you're doing a rather contentious PAM install: "As you know, we have a 98% accurate stock rate. We know you really care about your work, and because we trust your integrity, we never want you to worry about the security of your job. If we discover we hired someone who doesn't have the same integrity you do, we don't want you wrongfully blamed. To continue to have our same success rate, we're installing warehouse security cameras, an industry standard that we've been behind on. We know with our trusted workforce today that these will only highlight your already impeccable standards and set us up to grow with ease. I understand this is still a new change, and I want you to feel comfortable with it. What do you think about this new tool? What questions can I answer?"

Can you spot the Hierarchy of Needs' acknowledgment, perceived capability, and Engaging Leadership Language? Can you sense the care in crafting a message that intentionally creates more safety for the reactive creature brain to reduce triggering? Do you notice the lean toward including the desired outcome that's stated in the positive to guide employees toward what you want, not what you don't want (criterion from the Accountability Anchor Conversion Checklist)? When delivered sincerely, which can absolutely be done with the above example, you can create traditionally triggering PAM's in non-triggering ways.

To reiterate, PAM's are not about expecting you can't trust people — because you might get that if that's what you expect. PAM's are about working with what makes it easy for the human brain to be naturally accountable, therefore making it impossible for employees to fail. Your effort toward including more productive Proactive Accountability Measures are in service to your employees' success, and therefore your own and the company's.

Integration Questions:

1. Given what you've learned in this chapter, what possibilities do you see to update why and how you measure performance?

2. Reviewing your current pay structure, what are your salary, raise, and bonus structures incentivizing? What does the structure of how you compensate employees communicate about what's invited and what's expected? Is there a way to re-structure these more usefully to incentivize effort and reward the exact competency level you expect?

3. What challenges does your team face that could benefit from a Proactive Accountability Measure? Make a list and choose one to brainstorm, using this section's included questions to unearth opportunities.

Key Take-Aways:

1. Using the Results Model regularly meets the performance objectives of traditional performance reviews without the ineffectiveness of reviewing a year's worth of work through a triggering experience that statistically (and neurochemically) *decreases* performance.

2. The arenas that are not included in the Results Model process that still need attention are longer-term goal setting, career pathing, and compensation.

3. Contribution conversations work well for longer-term goals.

4. Employees should always know exactly what is required to make the salary they want.

5. Raises should not be subjective, biased, and certainly not reliant on a leader's ability to remember and judge a year's worth of effort.

6. There are three areas that, when clearly defined, can be used to determine a fair and transparent pay structure that maintains performance accountability: competency level, cost of living increases, and bonuses.

7. Rating employees on meeting expectations should not be incentivized with annual raises.

8. The only two performance ratings approved by Inspiring Accountability methodology are "Successfully meeting expectations" or "In progress toward meeting expectations." If employees only win when they "exceed expectations," then increase your baseline expectations.

9. Innovation and Efficiency meetings held regularly will help unearth what's in the way of greater innovation and efficiency, asking each employee to present one to three ideas.

10. The goal of PAM's is to make failure impossible by making it easier for the human brain to perform well and be accountable. We're working with the brain's natural inclinations to do better when there are proactive incentives to motivate or proactive pitfalls to avoid.

11. The power of PAM's can come from increased:
    - Accessibility or visibility of success criteria
    - Visibility of one's work, behavior, and effort
    - Revisiting, and therefore increased Accountability Attention
    - Expected feedback

12. The most important goal of customer feedback-related Proactive Accountability Measures (PAM's) is creating Proactive Accountability, *not* evaluating or utilizing the content of the feedback, which can often be biased.

13. In can be destructive to accountability to use vague customer feedback to be punitive. With vague feedback, like simple good or bad ratings, you want to look at inarguable trends and explore what could be in the way of receiving better ratings.

CHAPTER 17

A Final Note: Leaders Need Neurochemical Boosts, Too

"Most of us go through life...waiting for the 'time to be right' to start doing something worthwhile. Do not wait. The time will never be 'just right.' Start where you stand, and work with whatever tools you may have at your command, and better tools will be found as you go along."

—NAPOLEON HILL

Your leadership toolbox is now full of strategies and tools to inspire accountability among your employees and within your company. As you build the next version of your leadership approach, set your sights on your **Desired Results** and focus your **effort** toward them.

Reward yourself along the way, because *you* also need **neurochemical fuel**. Allow yourself to set **clear moments of achievement** and savor in the dopamine reward. Celebrate more with your team, and notice how recognizing your employees' successes helps refuel you, too.

If you notice you are feeling overwhelmed, check-in with yourself and assess if you are in **Anxious Effort**. Ask yourself if you need more **clarity**, to feel more **confident**, or be more **optimistic** about getting results. Evaluate your own **Experience and Engagement**

Loops, finding new ways to expect success, and therefore experience more of it.

Find yourself no longer needing to rely on triggering **traditional accountability**. You now **inspire accountability**, approaching challenges by exploring *what's in the way* and quickly moving to *what's possible*, watching blame and shame dissolve as solutions appear. Unearth new challenges that once remained excuses but now are seen as concrete opportunities to craft a practical path to success for your employees.

See yourself transform your team's accountability culture with new **proactive** and **responsive accountability** tools, equipped with best practices to ensure the result is met the first time and respond if the result is not met to get the result in the future.

Offer effective **Desired Results** derived from the **Accountability Anchor Conversion Checklist** to efficiently and effectively focus and calibrate employee effort. Empower your employees with this **actionable clarity** to **confidently** take action and know exactly what it looks like to be successful, maintaining their **optimism**.

Have more **conversations** and less **confrontations**. Use the **Four C's** approach for accountability conversations to deliver feedback in a manner that maintains receptiveness, upping your stance of being **caring, curious, careful,** and **comfortable**.

Remember that being a leader is about helping employees feel great, so they get great results. Honor their dignity by seeing them as **contributing, competent,** and **important**, fulfilling the **Hierarchy of Human Needs in the Workplace**.

Help employees avoid **Anxious Effort** by confirming the first or next action step. Maintain that their best effort is good enough while helping them discover ways to continuously improve and anticipate positive outcomes. Be realistic with what's too much, being mindful not to cross the **impossible expectation threshold**.

Improve engagement one line at a time with **contribution context** and **perceived capability**.

Reap the rewards of **regular Results Model Revisiting** with your team, helping employees better understand the impact of their contribution, as you lead them in calibrating, adjusting, and continuously improving. Rebuild trust in their work while they begin to realize that achieving the Desired Result, under your inspiring leadership, is possible, probable, and eventually inevitable.

Watch employees feel more engaged and empowered when you value and reward effort over results, creating effective incentive to persevere. Make the most of the brain's secrets to employee engagement, helping employees expect success and feel good in the process.

Notice all the ways you can now contribute to your employees being **engaged** in their work, **receptive** to feedback, improvement, and accountability, and **resourceful** toward solutions. Inspire them to create **positive beliefs** and reward adequately to maintain them. Help employees have **clarity, confidence,** and **optimism** to expect and experience success. This will provide you with neurochemical boosts as well.

In addition to asking more questions that inspire engagement and accountability, use your **Engaging Leadership Language** to begin having more effective conversations with both your employees and your manager. Perhaps you can now ask for more of what you need to stay engaged. Notice that you are asking questions that *require* engagement, rather than inviting it.

Refuel your employees' neurochemical tanks along this journey together. Create more success milestones to celebrate their effort with positive **neurochemicals** while avoiding **disengagement triggers**. Spot more and more opportunities to infuse these valuable **engagement and experience indicators** into your employees' day-to-day work experience.

Establish a productive way to hold employees accountable for their attitude, mindset, and behaviors by upgrading values to **Culture Values and Action Steps.**

Use Inspiring Accountability methodology to modernize your **performance reviews, compensation approach,** and **job descriptions**, noticing which outdated structures can be updated to better reward the effort you want to incentivize and provide strong **accountability anchors** to reference and calibrate against.

Create **Proactive Accountability Measures** to make it nearly impossible for employees to fail.

Leave the problem-focused traditional accountability in the past, and let the Results Model evolve your team to be curious, solution-seeking, and initiative-taking contributors. As you utilize **Possibility Thinking**, ask, "What's in the way?" and "What's possible?" so employees begin to think this way themselves, relieving you of the frustrating and now outdated method of pressuring, pushing, and pulling for results.

While all of these steps are in service to your employees, they will serve you as well —exponentially — as you continue to inspire the best from your employees.

Above all, make it work for you. Sometimes you will need to fire an employee. Or if you've offered rounds of Revisiting, sometimes you need to directly ask an employee what's going on without using Inspiring Accountability language. Now that you have the foundation, you can improvise what works best for you and your team.

For unanswered questions, explore for yourself how to fill in the blanks. Visit inspiringaccountability.com for more resources and services. Hire me to help you implement a culture of accountability through training, coaching, and consulting. Or be your own best resource and schedule a personal revisiting with this book and its concepts to continuously improve your leadership effectiveness.

As Napoleon Hill says, "Start where you stand, and work with whatever tools you may have at your command." From here, anything is possible.

For engagement and accountability consulting, leadership coaching, and training consultations, or to access additional resources, please visit www.inspiringaccountability.com.

Glossary

Accountability Anchor: A clearly defined Desired Result that an employee works toward and by which a leader calibrates the employee's success. With an Accountability Anchor, a leader can effectively "anchor" the employee to a clear expectation, closing the distance between the actual result and Desired Result. Primarily created using the Accountability Anchor Conversion Checklist.

Accountability Anchor Conversion Checklist: A series of criteria to convert an expectation to an effective accountability tool. The output is a clear Desired Result qualified by Inspiring Accountability methodology that can be productively Revisited using the Results Model.

Accountability Attention: The extra attention our brains provide to efforts and their corresponding Desired Results simply because there is expected and non-negotiable Revisiting.

Actionable Clarity: Knowing exact steps, tools, and strategies to take action to get the results needed, and a crystal-clear concept of what success looks like when expectations are fulfilled.

Actionably Clear Expectations and Specifications (ACES): ACES provide a clear reference sheet for exact requirements needed to achieve the Desired Result. ACES take into account the details, format, and specifications required to successfully meet expectations. Leaders can maintain an ACES checklist to have in meetings to quickly evaluate what details could possibly be included, especially if important specs are forgotten from time to time.

Active Effort: Effort with productive action, usually in an energized state of engagement. Opposite of Anxious Effort.

Adjusting: The Results Model process of Revising any aspect that will help an employee better meet expectations. These can include adjusting the Desired Result, the effort toward the result, an aspect in the way, or expanding on what's possible.

Adrenaline: A hormone secreted by the adrenal glands, especially in conditions of stress. Increases rates of blood circulation, breathing, and carbohydrate metabolism, and prepares muscles for exertion. Also called Epinephrine.

Agile Project Management Methodology: A popular format of managing projects from an almost real-time calibration of what's possible.

Anxious Effort: Avoidant, unpleasant, and unproductive effort caused by too much uncertainty or too little optimism in approaching a task, usually when we expect the outcome might damage our ability to be seen as contributing, competent, or important. The antidote is having actionable clarity, feeling confident (perceived capability), feeling the task is important (contribution context), and being optimistic about the outcome.

Assumptions: Subconscious or hidden beliefs.

Baseline of Expectations: When we are exposed to new information or a new experience, we eventually make enough meaning to figure out what we believe we can reliably expect from a co-worker, a manager, and the world in general.

Belief: A decided generalization about our experience that helps predict and create future experiences to make life predictable and therefore safer. Beliefs then become the filter for what we see and hear, directly informing our behavior and determining our decisions. Meanings make sense of a moment, but beliefs are generalized to make sense of related moments *forever,* and are applied to every future moment of similar context, solidifying the loop.

Brain: See Creature Brain or Human Brain.

Burnout: When employees are running on neurochemical fumes or at full-on depletion, sometimes associated with long-term Anxious Effort. Employees want to work because it is the means to contribute meaningfully, but they need to be neurochemically refueled to persevere through today's overwhelming workplace demands.

Calibration: The act of comparing what was achieved with the Desired Result, determining how precisely an employee met expectations.

Capability: One's abilities and the current capacity to access and demonstrate these abilities. Humans have more ability than capacity to utilize it.

Careful: As a component of the Four C's approach for accountability conversations, the stance of being conscientious to acknowledge the part of the behavior or intent that was positive and that leaders want to continue seeing, despite the other requested changes in execution.

Caring: As a component of the Four C's approach for accountability conversations, providing feedback is in service of employee development, not simply as a means of preference or critique.

Closed-Ended Questions: Questions that prompt a yes-or-no answer. They don't engage someone as much in creating accountability because they don't require actual consideration to answer.

Comfortable: As a component of the Four C's approach for accountability conversations, beginning the conversation modeling the comfortable tone, body language, and mindset you want your employee to maintain throughout the conversation. For many leaders, looking at these development opportunities as conversations instead of confrontations, in addition to establishing a curious, caring and careful stance, helps create a more conversational and comfortable approach.

Competent: Being seen with the ability to meet expectations in any given moment. The second most important human need in the workplace to influence engagement and accountability. Often, the most triggering of the Hierarchy of Human Needs in the Workplace when threatened.

Confidence: Belief in one's ability to be competent (successfully meet expectations). Confidence significantly influences an employee's engagement and actual success. Confidence is a created perception, one that leaders can almost completely construct, and it's as easy to build up as it is to tear down.

Contribution: The action (effort) toward benefiting something or someone bigger than oneself in a valuable or meaningful way. To be fulfilled, employees must know how their work contributes (the resulting effect or impact), which is most often communicated or reinforced by his or her leader. The most important of the Hierarchy of Human Needs in the Workplace to influence engagement and accountability.

Contribution Context: Intentionally and proactively communicating why an ask, task, or project is meaningful. It highlights why the work an employee is doing qualifies as a meaningful contribution.

Contribution Conversations: Primarily used for longer-term goals. The contribution conversation approach leaves the employee reaching to contribute instead of the manager pulling for it. The employee will determine how they contribute, how their efforts can best be utilized, and ask for what they need to be successful.

Cortisol: A steroid hormone commonly called "the stress hormone." Cortisol curbs functions that would be nonessential in a fight-or-flight situation. It alters immune system responses and suppresses the digestive system, the reproductive system, and other growth processes to prioritize systems more beneficial to the threat.

Creature Brain: Slang term for the parts of the brain that manage our threat-response system, commonly known as "fight, freeze or flight." This part of the brain does not think rationally and operates mostly from associations that connect a perceived threat with a physical neurochemical response.

Cue: The sensory input, or what is noticed with the five senses, that becomes associated with expecting reward.

Culture Values and Action Steps (CVAS): Words or short phrases that describe how employees are "expected" to consistently act, interact, and prioritize; defined with actionable clarity. General descriptors and personalized action steps are added.

Curious: As a component of the Four C's approach for accountability conversations, the stance of wondering, "What's in the way?" of an under-performing employee trying to get their needs to be seen as contributing, competent, and important. This also includes asking yourself, as a leader, "What's possible?" for their growth. Curiosity combines the Results Model questions with the Hierarchy of Human Needs.

Daily Standup Meeting: Inspired by Agile Project Management Methodology, a quick "standup" meeting held daily for a team, maximizing the accountability in more frequent revisiting. In Inspiring Accountability's format, this includes reporting: 1) "How did you contribute successfully yesterday?" 2) "What's in the way today?" 3) "What's possible today?"

Desired Result: A goal, objective or expectation clarified enough using the Accountability Anchor Conversion Checklist to be used to inspire accountability and be Revisited in the Results Model.

Dignity: The sense of inherent worth that comes from being human. A sense of dignity is exactly what is honored and protected when we feel that we are contributing, competent, and important.

Disengagement: Feeling negatively and hesitant about a task, resulting in less enthusiasm and effort during the task.

Dopamine: Neurochemical released with a feeling of "I did it!" When it comes to personal accomplishment, reaching a goal, or completing a task, dopamine rewards us for favorable behaviors and motivates us to repeat them.

Effort: The conscious and subconscious choice to apply an amount of capability through attention and action.

Employee Engagement: The percentage of *effort* toward the results and the *feeling* experienced during this effort.

Empowerment: Actual or perceived authority and external ability to take action to fulfill one's role and responsibilities. Except for one's perception of their own authority, empowerment is determined by factors outside of oneself.

Engaged (in work): How much are employees feeling seen as contributing meaningfully, competently, and importantly? And how much effort are they offering?

Engagement: The experience of feeling engaged, having interest, putting in effort, taking action, and feeling good doing it.

Engagement and Experience Indicators: Synonym for neurochemicals.

Engagement and Experience Loop: Feeling confident and optimistic about engaging in a task, on a project, or with a person, resulting in positive feelings and effort during the action or interaction that solidify a pattern of engagement.

Engaging Leadership Language: Language tools that leaders can use to inspire accountability and get better results in conversations with employees, primarily facilitating engagement, receptiveness, and resourcefulness.

Engaging Questions: Asking a question that requires thought, attention, and a participatory response. These "open-ended" questions usually start with *what* or *how*, and require the brain to formulate a unique answer and thoughtful response. Alternative to "Inviting Questions."

Excuses: Self-protection in an attempt to justify why we didn't meet a Desired Result. Excuses are golden opportunities to unearth and address what's in the way so leaders can explore what's possible.

Expectations: Predictions about what will happen or be true whenever we experience familiar sensory input.

Explanation Meaning: Creating meaning to rationalize what's happening. Explanation meaning answers, "Why is this happening? What is it about me, another person, group, situation, or environment that is making this happen?"

Four C's: Key components of one's leadership approach that establish a positive and productive mindset for approaching historically uncomfortable accountability conversations. The Four C's are to be caring, curious, careful, and comfortable.

Guilt: A feeling of responsibility or remorse for some offense, crime, wrong, whether real or imagined.

Hierarchy of Human Needs in the Workplace: Inspiring Accountability's modern version of Maslow's hierarchy tailored to address employees' needs in the workplace, giving leaders clear guidance on what to address when engagement and accountability are low.

Human Brain: Slang term for the parts of the brain that manage rational thought and resourcefulness; primarily the prefrontal cortex.

Important: A perception of being personally and professionally valued. The third most important human need in the workplace to influence engagement and accountability.

Impossible Expectation Threshold: When what's expected feels more impossible than inspiring or trying to focus on too many behavioral changes at once. Once the threshold is crossed, employees respond as hopeless and worried about disappointing their leader, not inspired.

Inattentional Blindness: What we choose to pay attention to can make us consciously blind to even the most obvious of conflicting evidence. Contributes to how difficult it is for our conscious brain to notice or care about exceptions to our beliefs. Also called perceptual blindness.

Indignant: Feeling or showing anger or annoyance to prove we are worthy. This often looks like getting angry or resentful, grasping to prove one's self, acting out, disconnecting, or shutting down completely.

Innovation and Efficiency Meetings: Regular team meetings held every one to three months to unearth what's in the way of success and to brainstorm what's possible to improve innovation and efficiency.

Inspiring Accountability: A modern leadership methodology including proactive and responsive accountability strategies that inspire employees to be engaged in their work, receptive to feedback and improvement, and resourceful toward results.

Inviting Questions: Asking a question that only invites the brain to passively respond, producing a simple answer like yes or no. These "closed-ended" questions often start with *is, are, can,* or *do.* These may *imply* a more thorough response is needed but don't actually require it by the nature of the question. Use Engaging Questions instead.

Leadership Principles and Action Steps (LPAS): Leadership values that define what it means to be a leader at a given company, highlighted with actionable clarity. General descriptors and personalized action steps are added.

Meaning: The explanation we create to make sense of a new experience, which usually determines our response (how we feel) before, during, or after the experience. Meaning is how we make sense of any given moment. The details of what's happening may be the same, but the meaning we make creates different feelings and, therefore, a completely different experience.

Micromanaging: When a manager's behavior causes the employee to sense a distrust of his or her competence. The better alternative is to check in with the intention to see if the employee needs any support to stay on track to meet the result, supporting competence instead of doubting it.

Natural Consequences: Issues that naturally occur when a Desired Result is not met. Natural consequences simply exist and don't require criticism, judgment, or punishment to empower an employee to start fixing them. Natural consequences offer opportunities for the leader to empower an employee to correct a situation, whereas punishment doesn't actually relieve or compensate. Natural consequences support dignity whereas punishment degrades dignity.

Needs: See Hierarchy of Human Needs in the Workplace.

Needs Impact Meaning: Usually *subconscious.* Needs impact meanings answer the questions, "How does this fulfill or threaten my needs?" or "What does this mean for me?"

Neurochemicals (Engagement and Experiences Indicators):
Chemicals our brains release in response to sensory information,
which affect our nervous system, health, and sense of well-being
in a variety of different ways. These include dopamine, serotonin,
oxytocin, adrenaline, and cortisol. They create our feelings and
internal experiences as well as reward and incentivize effort and
behavior. They let us know if we are feeling engaged (or not). In
the workplace, when neurochemicals feel good, engagement and
resourcefulness increase. When neurochemicals feel bad, engagement and resourcefulness decrease.

Norepinephrine: A hormone released with adrenaline during the
fight-freeze-flight response to help the physical responses and sensory systems become more responsive, shifting blood flow to areas
like the skin and muscles.

Open-Ended Questions: Questions that require the employee to
think and respond with a unique answer. In addition to requiring
engagement and accountability, you get a real response instead of
a rhetorical one. Used in Engaging Questions.

Ownership: A false and unuseful synonym for accountability,
usually because empowerment is not equal to the ownership
demanded. Look for more specific words and phrases to accurately describe the behavior sought in employees.

Oxytocin: Neurochemical released when experiencing a feeling of
"We did it!" Creates feelings of connection and trust. Oxytocin is
also the feeling of friendship, love, and connection. Workplace
environments fostering oxytocin are marked by effective, collaborative, and celebratory teams.

Perceived Capability: Expressing genuine belief in another's abilities in a way that raises their own perception of what's possible.
Can provide advance "You can do it" serotonin reward.

Perception Language: Questions or statements that allow multiple
perceptions of an event or interaction; a linguistic tool part of
Engaging Leadership Language.

Perceptual Blindness: See Inattentional Blindness.

Perks: Appreciation celebrations offered regularly (expected). Important to why employees cite it's positive to work at a company. Perks are nice but offer only a small serotonin boost.

Possibility Ceiling: The limit on what one believes is possible, especially in relation to an employee's potential, abilities, and competence. Each employee has their own possibility ceiling, and a leader's beliefs of what's possible for the employee can expand or contract that.

Possibility Thinking: When the brain is re-trained to think more about what's possible than what's in the way; built into the Results Model.

Prefrontal Cortex: The most newly-developed segment of our brain responsible for executive function, generalized as an origin of rational thought compared to the creature brain's reactive impulsivity.

Proactive Accountability: How to best ensure the result is met the first time, preventing a need for responsive accountability.

Proactive Accountability Measure (PAM): Any proactive tools and methods that make it easier for an employee to meet expectations.

Receptive/ness: One's willingness to thoughtfully listen to feedback, participate in improvement, and be accountable for their contributions.

Resourceful/ness: One's interest and ability to contribute to creating solutions. In an engagement context, one's availability to access the rational, problem-solving prefrontal cortex part for our brain (in an un-triggered state).

Responsive Accountability: Responding productively if the result is not met to better get the result in the future. "Productively" includes maintaining employee engagement, receptiveness, and resourcefulness.

Results Conversations: The Results Conversation is dedicated time in one-on-one meetings to conversationally present a new Desired Result or Revisit an active one, using the Results List as to guide the conversation. May also be applied to team meetings when useful.

Results List: A list of active Desired Results, having been qualified through the Accountability Anchor Conversion Checklist, that employees are actively working toward. Employees use this list as a base agenda they maintain and bring to one-on-one Results Conversations or team meetings.

Reticular Activating System (RAS): Acts like a bouncer between our conscious and subconscious, deeming what is important enough to bring from our subconscious into our conscious awareness.

Retribution: Punishment inflicted on someone as vengeance for a wrong or criminal act. An unproductive traditional accountability strategy.

Revisiting: The act of using the Results Model format to follow up on a previously introduced Desired Result. A leader specifically helps the employee continuously improve by Revisiting the impact of their contribution toward a result, calibrating how well expectations were met, and adjusting what's needed to better get the results. Accountability always requires revisiting.

Reward: A neurochemical response that feels positive, usually from dopamine, serotonin, or oxytocin. Rewards are usually received as recognition, celebration, and fulfillment, and satisfy our need to be seen as contributing, competent, and important.

Self-Protection Effort Withholding: When we subconsciously limit giving our best effort to protect ourselves from our best not being good enough.

Self-Protection Mode: Becoming defensive and putting one's own needs over the company's when under perceived threat. Primarily activated by a fear of being fired or seen as a poor contributor, incompetent, or unimportant.

Sensory Input: What we consciously or subconsciously notice with our five senses. The brain evaluates this information for meaning, establishes beliefs, and looks to make associations based on similar input. This process and the patterns that result create an Engagement and Experience Loop. Senses include what we see, hear, smell, feel (physically or emotionally), and taste.

Serotonin: Neurochemical released with an acknowledgment of "You did it!" or equivalent. Creates feelings of significance when recognized for having done a good job or completing something successfully.

Shame: A painful feeling of humiliation or distress caused by the consciousness of wrong or foolish behavior. A loss of respect or esteem; a person, action or situation that brings a loss of respect or honor. As a verb, (of a person, action or situation) make (someone) feel ashamed.

Success Criteria: How the employee and leader will know the employee met expectations and/or achieved the Desired Result. Answers the question, "How will we know when you are successful?" The actionable clarity required to create success criteria also indicates the completion moment that will release rewarding dopamine and serotonin. Without actionably clear success criteria, an employee may not experience positive neurochemicals. Includes ACES.

Threat-Response System: The physiological process the creature brain uses to protect and defend against threat, although disproportionately out-of-date for workplace threats. Includes the fight-freeze-flight response, feeling triggered, and the effects of adrenaline, norepinephrine, and cortisol. Diminishes the very receptiveness and resourcefulness we need most in these moments.

Traditional Accountability: (Of a person, organization, or institution) required or expected to justify one's actions or decisions. *Synonyms*: responsible, liable, answerable; to find blame.

Trigger and Disengagement Loop: Feeling negatively and hesitant about a task, project, or person, resulting in less enthusiasm and effort during the action or interaction. Activated when under threat or negatively associated, solidifying a pattern of disengagement. The inverse of the Engagement and Experience Loop.

Triggering: When something perceived as threatening jolts one into a tense, self-protective, and unresourceful state. Often caused by a neurological response that releases adrenaline and cortisol.

Known as the fight-freeze-flight response, and, more often than not, includes freezing and fawning in the workplace. Usually triggering threats arise from the neglected or damaged needs to be seen as contributing, competent, or important (see *Hierarchy of Needs in the Workplace*). Also referred to as "being triggered" or in a "triggered state."

Trigger Trench: Slang to describe the brain learning to trigger the same neurons each time in response to similar experiences, strengthening and solidifying the connection with every repetition. Usually results in an exaggerated response to smaller evidences of the trigger, seen easily in minor pet peeves that produce disproportionate frustration.

Values: Words or phrases that describe how employees are expected to consistently act, interact, and prioritize within a company. Values without effective accountability structure are only invitations. Values can be excellent accountability anchors only when defined with clear action steps.

About the Author

Elaina Noell is the founder and principal of Inspiring Accountability in the Workplace. Her management strategy consulting firm utilizes neuroscience to empower leaders to design company cultures that increase employee engagement, productivity, and accountability.

In 2015, after holding tenure as a VP of Marketing at a busy financial institution just north of San Francisco, Noell left the marketing world to backpack South America and finish her first book, *Happiness is Overrated — Live the Inspired Life Instead.*

Continuing her study of human dynamics and happiness, Noell became a certified Transformational Neuro-Linguistic Programming coach at the esteemed NLP Marin, and now helps individuals and organizations update old patterns to carve new pathways toward success.

Her approach focuses on working with natural human brain proclivities to positively inspire sustainable results instead of trying to enforce ideals that lead to defensiveness, frustration, and disengagement.

Noell combines her coaching experience and skillset to bring powerful, transformative, and actionable content to workplaces committed to authentic excellence. She helps leaders and employees contribute in ways that maximize personal and professional fulfillment.

Based in California, Noell offers Inspiring Accountability culture design, employee engagement consulting, leadership development trainings, and one-on-one leadership coaching. Her approachable style and wit leave clients of all levels feeling empowered, hopeful, and ready to take action.

Learn more about Elaina and her work at

www.inspiringaccountability.com

and www.elainanoell.com.

Follow at:

Instagram: @inspiringaccountabilityatwork, @elainanoell

Made in the USA
Monee, IL
06 June 2021